J. Patton Anderson, Confederate General

J. Patton Anderson, Confederate General

A Biography

JAMES W. RAAB

McFarland & Company, Inc., Publishers
Jefferson, North Carolina, and London

ALSO BY JAMES W. RAAB

W.W. Loring, CSA — Florida's Forgotten General
(Sunflower University Press, 1996)

A Dual Biography:
Lloyd Tilghman and Francis Asburn Shoup:
Two Forgotten Confederate Generals
(Southern Heritage Press, 2001)

Photographs on pages 176 and 177 from *Generals at Rest: The Grave Sites of the 425 Official Confederate Generals,* 1997. All rights reserved. No part may be reproduced in any form without permission in writing from the publisher, White Mane Publishing Co., Inc., P.O. Box 708, Shippensburg, PA 17257 (or) email: marketing@whitemane.com.

LIBRARY OF CONGRESS CATALOGUING-IN-PUBLICATION DATA

Raab, James W.
    J. Patton Anderson, Confederate general : a biography
/ James W. Raab.
        p.   cm.
    Includes bibliographical references and index.

    ISBN 0-7864-1766-8 (softcover : 50# alkaline paper)

    1. Anderson, James Patton, 1822–1873.   2. Generals —
Confederate States of America — Biography.   3. Confederate States
of America. Army — Biography.   4. Southwest, Old — History —
Civil War, 1861–1865 — Campaigns.   5. United States — History —
Civil War, 1861–1865 — Campaigns.   6. Florida — History —
Civil War, 1861–1865–Campaigns.   7. Anderson, James Patton,
1822–1873 — Correspondence.   8. Anderson, Etta, d. 1917 —
Correspondence.   9. Mexican War, 1846–1848 — Biography.
10. United States marshals — Washington (State) — Biography.
I. Title.
E467.1.A53R33   2004
973.7'42'092 — dc22   2004006358

British Library cataloguing data are available

Cover: Confederate flags ©2004 Pictures Now; General J. Patton Anderson

Manufactured in the United States of America

McFarland & Company, Inc., Publishers
    Box 611, Jefferson, North Carolina 28640
    www.mcfarlandpub.com

Contents

Preface

Throughout the past one hundred years it has been perfectly natural for individuals interested in the American Civil War and in the Confederacy to read biographies of such leaders as Robert E. Lee, "Stonewall" Jackson, Nathan B. Forrest or President Jefferson Davis. On the other hand, hundreds of meritorious general officers have not received appropriate recognition. Why have these patriots of the same common cause for southern independence not sparked the same level of interest? Candidly, with over four hundred Confederate generals to examine, it becomes obvious the generals outnumbered the journalists.

Consider the state of Florida. Referred to as "the tadpole of the seceding states" by the Federals in 1861, it nevertheless provided its share of enlistments, volunteers and generals who sacrificed their economic well-being in support of the new Confederate States of America. One such patriot was J. Patton Anderson, who was among the region's war leaders. Anderson experienced a difficult childhood in Kentucky, although he was well-schooled. As an adult he volunteered for service in the Mexican War. In time he returned to Mississippi where he practiced law, and became a political ally of Jefferson Davis.

Davis later appointed Anderson as U.S. Marshal of Washington Territory. After two years in the wilderness with his bride, Etta, he returned to the states and abandoned the national political scene. He went to Florida to become overseer of the Casa Bianca plantation, becoming a states' rights activist and voting at Montgomery, Alabama, for secession. The war soon came to his home state of Florida, and he and others rushed to defend Pensacola Harbor. Contacts Anderson made here, especially with Braxton Bragg, led to his gaining a leading role in the Army of Tennessee. He commanded a division at Shiloh and Farmington, and was part of the Confederate invasion of Kentucky in 1862, which culminated in the battles of Perryville and Stones River. He was at Chickamauga and

1

Missionary Ridge; his narrative of the battles provides fresh perspective about the conduct of military operations under General Bragg. Promoted to major general, Anderson was ordered to command the Florida District, helping to form the Florida Cow Cavalry. With severe reverses in the battles for Atlanta, Anderson was called back to field command and was wounded severely at the battle of Jonesboro, Georgia. Despite the advice of physicians he returned to field duty for the Carolina cam-

Major General J. Patton Anderson, CSA

paign, which ended in defeat at Bentonville, North Carolina. At war's end, J. Patton Anderson had sacrificed everything for the cause; refusing to accept the results of the conflict, he would not take the oath of allegiance, openly proclaiming, "Any fate but submission."

The foundation of this book is an assortment of affectionate letters written between Anderson and his wife revealing what it was like to be alive at this time and what it took to keep their family intact against overpowering obstacles. The letters also bring to light previously neglected facets of Florida's contribution to the war effort. Access to these letters came about through the cooperation of the Putnam County Library System, Mary E. Murphy, archivist, Palatka, Florida. The letters came from a variety of sources: the papers of Etta A. Anderson (wife), Southern Historical Society, Richmond, Virginia; *Autobiography of Patton*

Anderson, from the collection of Margaret B. Anderson (daughter), Florida State Library; Margaret B. Anderson Uhler (granddaughter), Civil War Letters of Major General James Patton Anderson, the Florida Historical Society; and materials about Washington Territory, the Washington State Historical Society and Washington State Archives & Records Management Division.

I also acknowledge Larry Rayburn's *Wherever the Fight Is Thickest— General James Patton Anderson*, the James Patton Anderson papers, Special Collections, Robert Manning Strozier Library, plus the many source materials as outlined in the notes.

I am indebted to Beth Mansbridge, Mansbridge Editing and Transcription, who was generous with her time and expertise in editing the manuscript; and Jean Light Willis, artist, who provided the fine maps of Anderson's battles.

James W. Raab
St. Augustine, Florida
March 2004

I

Scholastic and Impressionable Years

James Patton Anderson was born into a military family on February 16, 1822, at Winchester, Tennessee. His father, William P. Anderson, was from Virginia, and during the second term of George Washington's administration he had received a commission of lieutenant in the United States Army and in the War of 1812 he was a colonel in the Twenty-fourth U.S. Infantry. After the war he became surveyor-general for the District of Tennessee where he met and married Margaret L. Adair, fifth daughter of Major General John Adair, who fought with Andrew Jackson at the battle of New Orleans in 1814.

Patton, one of seven children, spent his childhood on the family farm until his father's untimely death in 1831. Soon thereafter his mother took the family to the home of her father, John Adair, in Mercer County, Kentucky. The burden of supporting the family resulted in two of the brothers being placed with relatives, and Patton, at age ten, was sent to his mother's youngest sister, Mrs. Charles Bufford in Scott County, Kentucky, where he lived for a year, attending a rural school. Returning home, Patton spent the next year being tutored at home, and then was sent to another sister of his mother's in Frankfort, Kentucky, who was married to Judge Thomas B. Monroe. While there he became a pupil at Judge Monroe's Montrose Law School for a year.

His mother married Dr. J. N. Bybee of Harrodsburg, Kentucky, in 1835. Patton returned home and attended school at Harrodsburg. At age fourteen he was sent to Jefferson College (one of the predecessor institutions of Washington & Jefferson College) at Canonsburg, Pennsylvania.

At age fifteen his education was again interrupted when financial problems at home compelled Patton to be withdrawn from school. Returning home he worked with his stepfather, performing a variety of duties including driving the doctor's horse and buggy while the doctor made his medical rounds in the countryside. In this capacity Patton learned a little about the medical vocation, which contributed later to the mistaken belief that he was a doctor.[1] At age sixteen, in 1838, he was sent to Three Forks on the Kentucky River, in Estill County, where his stepfather had established a sawmill and open-surface coal mine. In the fall the adventuresome Dr. Bybee decided to move the family to northern Mississippi. This area was a new frontier, as the Indians had been removed west of the Mississippi River. Patton and his stepfather rode 450 miles on horseback from Harrodsburg, Kentucky, to Hernando in DeSoto County, Mississippi, which is south of Memphis, Tennessee. During the winter they constructed rough-hewn logs into cabins and cleared some land in anticipation of the arrival of the rest of the family. At this time Dr. Bybee's financial situation improved enough to allow Patton to resume his studies at Jefferson College. He returned to Canonsburg, Pennsylvania, and after graduating in 1840, returned home to Hernando.

Having studied law at Montrose Law School, he began to read law in the office of Buckner & Delafield, and at the young age of twenty-one was admitted to the bar by Judge Howry in 1843.[2] Without a question, Anderson's early years, when he was moved from one home to another, instilled a great deal of self-confidence. In the fall of 1843, having no money with which to support himself, and the local bar being crowded with older lawyers, Anderson accepted the position of deputy sheriff of DeSoto County, offered to him by his brother-in-law, Col. James H. Murray. At the same time he became active in the county's militia regiment, eventually becoming a colonel. He was deputy sheriff until 1846, when prospects seemed favorable to commence the practice of law. He formed a partnership with R. B. Mayes.[3] Anderson, like many other enterprising Americans living on the frontier, would find himself moving to new opportunities seeking to advance his career and sustain himself. His law career would be short.

Manifest Destiny began to play out in Mexico as the United States' proclamation of war on May 13 saw legions of American volunteers form into companies and divisions for the invasion of Mexico. At the beginning of the Mexican War, the only sizable American army in the field was a so-called army of occupation on the northern bank of the Rio Grande. President James K. Polk thought that if the army advanced into Mexico and occupied a part of the country, the Mexican government would make peace on American terms. The army crossed the Rio Grande and defeated the Mexicans in several engagements. To the Americans' surprise, the Mexicans were not disheartened by their reverses and gave no indication that they were going to quit the war.[4]

President Polk then called on the ranking general in the army, Winfield Scott, known as "Old Fuss and Feathers" for his devotion to military regulations, to devise a plan of victory. He proposed uniting this army with additional forces from other theaters. Their rendezvous would be Tampico, Mexico. From there the navy would transport the army to the port of Vera-cruz, and the army could move west on the national highway to Mexico City. Scott believed that the Mexicans would fight for their capital and that the defeat of their army and the occupation of the city would end the war. He commanded what is by modern standards a very small army; it never numbered more than 14,000 men and sometimes sank as low as 9,000.

In February, Scott arrived in Tampico to take command as army bands played and guns boomed salutes.[5]

While American forces invaded Mexico, Polk continued to call for more reinforcements. A third requisition was made in 1847 for a battalion of five companies of riflemen, under which Gov. A. G. Brown of Mississippi issued his personal call on July 29, 1847. Various reasons were assigned for the apathy of the response to the governor's call; he had to make a second, urgent appeal in October to organize a battalion of Mississippi riflemen. In answer to the governor's call, Anderson organized a company of volunteers from the regiment of Mississippi militia in DeSoto County. He was elected captain. There is little information in records or newspapers regarding this battalion.[6]

Captain Anderson's command, his recruits and volunteers hurriedly transferred to Camp McClung at Vicksburg. After the rendezvous, five companies embarked upon steamboats headed to New Orleans for equipment and organization. Receiving tents, arms, clothing and orientation, they were put aboard ship on January 2, 1848, and sailed to the Mexican coast at Tampico.[7] Meanwhile, after the storming of the Castle of Chapultepec in September by the American army, Mexico City surrendered later and hostilities ceased as an armistice brought the war to an end. A new Mexican government took office and concluded the peace with the Treaty of Guadalupe Hidalgo on February 2, 1848, with the cession to the United States of more than half of Mexico's territory, and an

American boundary which would run from the Gulf of Mexico up the Rio Grande to the new Mexican border and continue west to reach the Pacific Ocean near San Diego. The new military arrivals would have no opportunity for glory, being confined to the role of keeping the peace as occupation troops. They remained stationed at Tampico, northeast of Mexico City on the Gulf of Mexico. This period of command served as a good military school apprenticeship for Anderson. On February 22 he was elected lieutenant colonel to command the Second Battalion Mississippi Rifles, in which he served through the Mexican stay.

While these negotiations were being decided, the officers from various commands formed the Aztec Club, a society that congregated in the mansion of Senor Boca Negra, the former Mexican minister to the United States. Organized on October 13, 1847, its initial roster included names destined for greater distinction in the coming Civil War: Beauregard, Hardee, Hooker, Grant, Lee, Johnston, Magruder, McClellan, Twiggs, Wilcox, Ewell, Pemberton and Franklin Pierce, who succeeded to the presidency upon the death of Zachary Taylor in 1850.[8] These West Point graduates, as they assembled to rehash their recent triumphs in the "Halls of Montezuma," undoubtedly discussed the sectional differences and grievances of the North and South. A byproduct of the Mexican War was a competent office corps which split its allegiance as the nation drifted toward settling the infernal slavery question. Patton Anderson was not a member of this organization of elite officers as he was not a West Point graduate. Unfortunately, commonplace with Mexican service were diseases such as smallpox, malaria and "Montezuma's revenge" (diarrhea). Colonel Anderson was stricken with malaria while on duty there and his health was impaired for the rest of his life.

With a treaty in the summer of 1848, occupation forces returned to the United States and were feted as heroes. Anderson's battalion mustered out at Vicksburg on July 1, 1848. *The Vicksburg Sentinel* reported: "By general subscription of our citizens a collation [light meal] was given on Thursday last to the battalion from this state, just returned from its station at Tampico. An address was delivered by Mr. Horace Miller and Lt. Col. Anderson replied on behalf of his command."[9] Anderson traveled to his home in Hernando, arriving on July 4. He resumed his practice of law and soon became active and involved in Mississippi politics, resulting in his election as one of the members of the Mississippi Legislature from DeSoto County in 1849. He was seated in 1850.

At this point there was great concern by the free states that the newly acquired territories would adopt slavery. Two years earlier, Great Britain's claim to Oregon and Washington Territory was settled by peaceful compromise giving the United States the Pacific Northwest to the 49th parallel. With this agreement and the new Mexican treaty, the borders of the continental United States were established and Americans and others could pour unrestrained from the East into the new land of the West.

One of the issues of the day was the proposed Wilmot Proviso that would outlaw slavery in any territory acquired as a result of the Mexican War. This brought the issue of slavery extension to the forefront as the Congress began debating the admission of California as a free state, plus other measures that were eventually consolidated into the omnibus Compromise of 1850.

These were America's years of Manifest Destiny, the doctrine that the United States had the right and duty to expand throughout the North American continent. Up to now California had seen a Mexican frontier colony thinly populated with a few coastal settlements where trading ships picked up cargoes, and with a dotted interior of cattle ranches and wheat farms. This changed on March 15, 1848, with the explosive news that gold had been found at Sutter's Fort in California, beginning the California gold rush of 1849.

The hope of finding gold went back into antiquity. Searchers lusted and killed for gold, and their greed helped speed the exploration and settlement of the world. No other metal could equal the rare, beautiful gold which could be worked by hand and for ages was the measurement and storage of wealth. It was the only way a poor man could become a rich man — discover and mine gold.

Within the next three years these Forty-Niners numbered over 100,000 would-be miners who invaded, poached, and unlawfully infringed on property rights in the name of gold. They came by land and sea from all over the world to gain their due. With men from all sections of the United States, the question of slavery traveled along in their souls. Would slavery be permitted to expand into the new territories?

Jefferson Davis, a veteran of the Mexican War, had been elected to the U.S. Senate from Mississippi in 1848. As a plantation owner, he quickly emerged as a strong champion of southern rights and slavery, arguing that Congress had no right to discriminate between different types of property in the territories, and denying that a territory composed of "first comers" had the right to exclude slavery.[10] Representing the opposite viewpoint was Mississippi's other senator, Henry A. Foote, who saw the admission of California as a free state and the other acts of the Compromise of 1850 as honorable and constitutional.

The political system in Mississippi was rocked with heated debates by former states' rights Gov. J. A. Quitman and Senator Foote, who undertook a statewide canvass to influence the selection of delegates to an upcoming state convention scheduled for November, to decide whether to accept the Compromise of 1850.[11] Representative Anderson eagerly entered the political fray and became an ally and supporter of Jefferson Davis. "I took the same view of the questions with Senator Jefferson Davis and States' Rights Gov. Quitman, and voted for a resolution in the Mississippi House requesting Foote to resign his seat inasmuch as he did not reflect the will of the people of the state in voting for the Compromise Bill."[12] The resolution failed to pass and Senator Foote remained seated.

The September election for delegates to the state convention resulted in a Unionist triumph (Foote) over the States' Righter (Quitman) by a margin of 28,402 to 21,242. Realizing his chances of gubernatorial re-election were nil, Quitman quit and was replaced by candidate Jefferson Davis on the ballot. Davis rallied to his side a number of young aspiring politicians, including Patton Anderson and Thomas C. Hindman. Despite full-scale debates of the issues, Davis lost his bid for governor and the whole States' Rights Democratic Party was left in the minority, including Anderson who lost his seat in the state legislature. The Compromise Bill of 1850 resulted in a tradeoff, allowing California to be admitted as a free state in exchange for the passage of a more vigorous fugitive slave law. "I believe," said Anderson, "that great injustice and wrong was done the South in the passage of the bill."[13]

The Union Democrats' and Whigs' victory was short lived as events in Congress and the growth of abolitionism in the North saw more Mississippians embrace southern rights.[14] Davis was not out of politics very long before he was called upon by the new president, Franklin Pierce, to serve as secretary of war in the new administration.[15] Anderson returned home and resumed the practice of law. "I succeeded as well as could be hoped; my health still bad from fever and ague from the Mexican War. Jefferson Davis, in answer to a letter of mine, advised me to proceed to Washington city where he would use his influence to procure me a commission in the new rifle regiments then about to be raised by Congress for frontier defense. I accepted Mr. Davis's proposal and traveled to Washington in early 1853 where I learned that the bill to raise a rifle regiment had failed. My health at this time was so bad from the effects of malaria that friends advised me to stay in the cooler temperature."[16] By coincidence, Anderson's uncle, John Adair, who had moved to Astoria, Oregon Territory, in 1848 as customs house officer,[17] was visiting Washington at the same time. Calling on Anderson, he implored him to move to Oregon Territory and join his two younger brothers, who had moved to Astoria in 1850. By favorable chance, a bill to organize the Territory of Washington was signed into law on March 3, 1853, the last day President Millard Fillmore was in office. Through the instrumentality of his uncle and Jefferson Davis, Anderson was appointed United States Marshal for the new Territory of Washington. He was now part of the new administration of President Franklin Pierce. "I accepted the offer and set about making preparations for the journey."[18]

II

The Marriage, and Honeymoon in Washington Territory

Anderson had several options available to reach the Washington Territory. He could ride a prairie schooner over the Oregon Trail, a two-thousand mile trip via the Continental Divide and the South Pass. This would entail months of hardship, crossing the difficult mountain ranges winding through a maze of shortcuts and bypasses, experiencing prairie storms, rain, mud, Indians, snakes, wild animals, and ever depending on a freight wagon for provisions. It was the only satisfactory route for a poor man.

However, if a person possessed money and stamina, he could ignore the overland route by taking passage on a sailing ship from New York, Boston or New Orleans. Yankee ship owners and others had opened up these lanes of commerce many years earlier. This route was a six-month trip and upwards of thirteen thousand miles of sea voyage around Cape Horn. On the other hand one could cut the sailing time in half by taking a shortcut across the Isthmus of Panama, risking yellow fever. Pressed for time, Anderson decided on the latter route to get to the Washington Territory.

During the spring and summer of 1853, Anderson admitted that he was on the horns of a dilemma with this decision. "First, the want of money to make the trip, and second, I was engaged to be married to my cousin, eighteen-year-old Henrietta Buford Adair. I doubted the policy of taking her into such a wild and new country with no other help or dependence for a support than my own exertions. I returned to Memphis, Tennessee, where she was, consulted with her and we agreed to try our fortunes on this unknown sea."[1]

The Anderson family was an old Virginia family, closely related, with many intermarriages having taken place between them and the Pattons and Prestons of that state.[2] Etta was born in Tompkinsville, Kentucky, in June 1834. "My husband and I were first cousins (but had never seen each other until a short time before we became engaged), both being grandchildren of Gov. John Adair of Kentucky, and niece and nephew respectively of Mrs. Ellen White, who lived on a plantation in Florida. When we were married I had recently returned from quite a lengthy stay in Europe with Aunt Ellen where I had enjoyed with her all the luxuries and social advantages that riches and prestige can give, so the contrast was all the greater to begin our married life among the wilds of the sparsely inhabited new Territory of Washington."[3] Etta's father gave them $800, and by borrowing, Anderson raised about the same amount from among his Mississippi friends for the trip. The couple was married in Memphis, Tennessee, on April 30, 1853.

Thirty-one-year-old Anderson's enthusiastic acceptance of the adventurous life ahead, as well as his vigorous philosophy, are both apparent in the lines he composed to his bride of the day of their marriage.

> *The wise and active conquer dangers*
> *By daring to attempt them: sloth and folly,*
> *Shiver and shrink at sights of toil and hazard,*
> *And make the impossibility they fear.*[4]

Etta was still two months short of turning nineteen years old: "We were both young and looked upon it as a great adventure, and never for one moment regretted the very happy years spent there."[5] An hour after the wedding ceremony, the Andersons were on their way aboard a Mississippi River steamer bound for New Orleans and then the Pacific coast. They embarked at New Orleans on the 7th of May on board a steamer bound for Greytown in Nicaragua.[6] Unfortunately for the newlyweds, the first day at sea Etta was taken very ill with fever. "For several days her life seemed to be suspended by a thread. These were the most anxious days of my life. Happily, she was better by the time we reached Greytown. Taking a small river steamer there we commenced the ascent of the San Juan River. After several days of toil we reached Virgin Bay, only to learn that the steamer from San Francisco, on which we had expected to reach that city on her return trip, had sprung a leak and was compelled to go down the coast to Panama for repairs, and that she would probably not return for a month. This was a great disappointment to the eight hundred passengers at Virgin Bay, who were eager to reach the gold fields of California, but to me it was a matter for rejoicing, since a few weeks' rest in Nicaragua would probably restore my wife to health before undertaking another long sea voyage. We remained at Virgin Bay nearly a month.

"My wife recovered, and we embarked at San Juan del Sud the first week in June, and reached San Francisco in fourteen days, where we had to stay near a fortnight in wait for the steamer which was to the Columbia River. At the expiration of this time we set sail in the steamer, *Columbia*, bound for Astoria, Oregon. Among the passengers were my Uncle John Adair and his oldest daughter; Capt. George B. McClellan, U.S.A.; Maj. Larned, U.S.A.; and several other officers of the army, besides two companies of infantry.

"After passing the bar at the mouth of [the] Columbia, a reckoning was taken between my wife and myself of the state of finances. It was ascertained that the sum total on hand was exactly one dollar. (Paper money would not pass on the coast.) It would not pay for landing our trunks at Astoria, which place was then in sight and was our destination. I threw the dollar into the raging Columbia and began to whistle to keep my courage up. Just then an officer came on deck whom I had not seen at the table or elsewhere during the voyage.

"He inquired if Col. Anderson was in the crowd. I replied and introduced myself to him. He made himself known as Lieut. Rufus Saxton, U.S.A., and said he had left New York on the steamer that came out a fortnight after I had left New Orleans, and that he had an official communication for me from the Secretary of the Interior, at the same time handing me a paper in a large official envelope. Taking it in my hand I began to deposit it in my coat pocket without breaking the seal, when Saxton requested I would open it and see whether he had brought it and contents safely to hand. On opening it I found it contained instructions for me as United States Marshal to proceed at once to take a census of the inhabitants of the new Territory of Washington, and also a Treasury draft for a thousand dollars, to defray my expenses in the work. This was a piece of good fortune in the nick-of-time, for in two minutes more the steamer dropped anchor off the city of Astoria, Oregon, and soon we disembarked."[7]

Astoria was a modest little village of a few dozen long houses on a gentle slope toward the Columbia River. John J. Astor had established a fur post here in 1811. Homesteaders began settling in the 1840s. For the time being, the Andersons stayed at their Uncle John Adair's house, at the same time being reunited with Anderson's brother, Butler.

The Oregon Territory was created after the settlement of 1846 of a boundary dispute between the United States and Great Britain, and was becoming the destination for the pioneers going westward on the Oregon Trail. It included all of Oregon, Washington and Idaho with parts of Wyoming and Montana. The population as of the 1850 census recorded 13,204 inhabitants. (See note 8 for more census information.) The newly married couple would now have to separate; Etta remained in the house of her uncle as Anderson set out for Puget Sound to commence taking the 1853 census. Within a few days he reached Olympia, on the southern point of Puget Sound on the Fourth of July. On his trip north, Anderson realized how vast the country was, with endless wilderness and limitless boundaries, with small pockets of pioneers.

WASHINGTON TERRITORY — Anderson's assignment would take him to the territory north of the Columbia River and west of the Cascade Range. At Olympia, a Mr. Urban E. Hicks was given instructions by the county commissioners to accompany Anderson on his trip. Hicks's memory of this adventure is typical of what Anderson experienced on many occasions: "Anderson came to Olympia and desired to go down the Chehalis River to Grays Harbor, and from there, along the sea beach to Shoalwater Bay and the mouth of the Columbia River. Together they went to the north bank of the Chehalis, and there engaged two Indians with a small bark canoe, just big enough to hold four persons with blankets, fry pan, tin pot, cups and a few small articles, small sack of flour, a few pounds of bacon, a few raw potatoes, a package of ground coffee and a little salt. With this outfit we launched our frail barque on the shallow rapids of the winding stream, each with paddle and pole as propelling power.

"Downstream it was a wilderness of dense undergrowth lining the sides of the stream until we reached the present town site of Montesano. Here we found two individuals living in shanties. We found no more white settlers until we passed the small island at the upper end of the harbor, when we came upon a log cabin with a small out-building occupied by Dr. Roundtree and family. He would not listen to our going further that day and prevailed on us to stop overnight. That night two very hungry dogs got at our sack of provisions and ate up every morsel, even the raw potatoes.

"In the morning we started again on our trip minus all our supplies, which the doctor could not replenish from his scant larder. On arriving

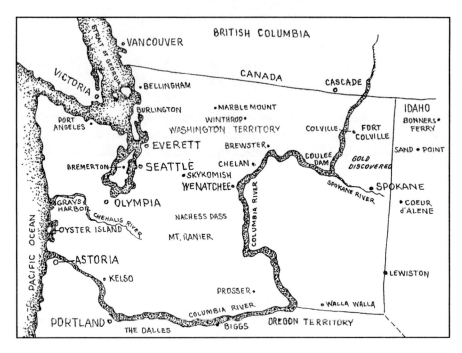

Washington Territory as part of Oregon Territory, 1853. Land Area: 66,512 square miles. Dimensions: North-South 230 miles, East-West 340 miles.

at Peterson's Point our Indians buried the canoe in the sand to prevent it being stolen, and we proceeded on foot along a wide beach, one of the most beautiful on any shore, fifteen miles to Shoalwater. On the way we came across a large party of Quileute Indians[9] gathering the Indian tobacco weed, kinninapick, which grew in great abundance on the sand ridges near the beach. We purchased a small quantity of very dirty rice and a piece of sturgeon, which the Indians caught in the surf. We reached the north shore of Shoalwater just at dark, foot sore and weary with our long walk over the hard beaten sands, where we set a fire and proceeded to cook the last morsel of our purchase from the Indians. The bay opposite was six miles wide, and the settlement all on the opposite side.

"Morning came and we watched the numerous canoes and small sailing craft going and coming from the oyster grounds on the other side. Despite our signals from the shore, no one seemed to notice us. Night came on and we laid down with a distressing emptiness of stomach. Sunday morning came and finally a small sloop came heading for us. When they discovered we were white men, the men aboard came ashore and assisted us on board with all speed and took us to the other side, where every luxury the settlement possessed was freely bestowed upon us. About twenty-five white persons were residents of Shoalwater Bay and vicinity at that time, most of them engaged in gathering the native oyster for the San Francisco market. The whites employed two to three hundred Indians, mostly from the Chinook tribe near the mouth of the Columbia, to gather the oysters and liberally paid them in whiskey and tobacco. Oyster Beach was thickly populated with a roaring, rollicking crowd of drunken men and squaws, everything apparently being held in common among whites and Indians.

"After feasting on oysters stewed, oysters fried, raw, roasted, fricasseed, broiled, baked, on the half-shell, whole shell and all, with copious draughts of salt-water whiskey, we took an enumeration of the inhabitants. Here Col. Anderson left me to proceed to the Columbia River while I had to make the return trip along with my two Indians. Arriving at Peterson's Point where we had buried our canoe, it was quickly dug up. While the Indians were digging, I gathered a small quantity of the beautiful blue-black sand which lay in shining ridges on top of the white sand on the point, the rain and early morning sun making it sparkle and glitter in beautiful colors. I had no thought of gold being found among it then, but learned afterward that considerable quantities of fine placer gold was washed from this sand.

signed
Urban E. Hicks"[10]

For the next leg of his trip, Anderson employed Chinook River Indians as watermen and guides as he traversed the treacherous Columbia River with its rapid, deep, cold currents and waterfalls. He explored its tributaries for seven hundred miles, taking the census. For two months Anderson was separated from Etta; he was engaged in census taking, frequently walking as much as twenty miles a day, carrying his blanket, provisions and papers on his back. He found mostly the wives of the settlers and their children alone in their cabins as the breadwinners of the family — the husband and father — and the older boys were compelled to seek work, and it was generally found in the logging camps, lumber mills or in loading the waiting ships with lumber. This kept them from home most of the time. Neighbors were few, and none of them sufficiently near at hand to render assistance in case of need.[11]

A significant incident occurred while Anderson was taking the census near The Dalles on the Columbia River. A U.S. army paymaster by the name of Captain Ulysses S. Grant, recently posted to the West Coast after the Mexican conflict, was suffering from mania (delirium tremens) from liquor, and had gotten away from his soldiers as they were camping on the bank of the river. The soldiers awoke Anderson and told him of Grant's condition and that he had left camp. Anderson awoke his Indian guides, made them understand the situation and put them on the trail. They tracked and found Grant by the pieces of his outside woolen shirt left on the bushes; he was crouched down under some bushes, ready to plunge into the river. The banks were solid rock hundreds of feet high and the water so cold that no one could live in it a moment without severe cramps. Anderson was big, strong and active. He climbed carefully until he was between Grant and the river, gave one spring against Grant's chest, forced him back to the ground and caught hold of the bushes to secure him and take him into camp. One false step and both would have gone down to their certain death.[12]

Anderson canvassed the counties of Pierce, Island, Jefferson, King, Thurston, Pacific, Lewis, and Clark, and reported a total population for the Territory of Washington of 3,965 inhabitants, of which 1,682 were qualified to vote.[13] Finally returning home to Etta, the balance of the year was mundane. Anderson's report to the Department of the Interior for the first six months in the territory, ending December 31, 1853: "During this time I held the office of marshal I had no duties to perform, and consequently received no fees, nor paid out any money."[14]

With the completion of the 1853 census, the Andersons paddled a canoe up the Cowlitz River to Olympia, where the capital of the territory was to be established. Isaac I. Stevens of Massachusetts had been appointed governor; Edward Lander of Indiana, chief justice; and J. S. Clendenin of Louisiana, United States district attorney. The Andersons were the first to arrive in the new capital.

Olympia is located on the southernmost point of Puget Sound, which had been named for Peter Puget, a member of the British Vancouver Expedition that visited the site in 1792. The U.S. Exploring Expedition under Lieutenant Charles Wilkes came to the site in 1841, and the first American settlers were Levi Lathrop Smith and Edmund and Clara Sylvester, who claimed the town site in 1846 and platted it in 1850.[15] It boasted the first customs house on Puget Sound in 1851, plus the only newspaper in the area, the weekly *Columbian*. The town developed around the waterfront and quickly became a hub of maritime commerce with Victoria, British Columbia, and San Francisco. The state government was housed in a series of temporary buildings including the courthouse. Upon arrival, the Andersons rented a home from Sylvester in December which they purchased in May 1854, with additional land purchases in July 1858 and June 1859. Marshal Anderson began practicing law in the territory as well as returning to politics, securing the nomination of the Democratic Party of the territory as delegate to the Thirty-fourth Congress in Washington city, meeting in December of 1856.[16]

As titular marshal of the territory he had plenty of time to canvass the territory as much as possible with speaking engagements. His recognition as the census enumerator clearly helped him to defeat Judge William Strong, the Whig candidate, and Joseph Cushman, the Free-Soil Party candidate. Elected on July 9, 1855, Anderson became the first person to hold the position of territorial delegate to the U.S. Congress. He resigned as U.S. marshal, and George W. Corless received the new appointment.[17]

Gold Discovered near Fort Colville

The report of gold discoveries near Fort Colville on the upper Columbia River reached Puget Sound. The mere mention of gold in these days acted like a fever, as men sought possession of this bright yellow metal as a mark of wealth. Several persons in Puget Sound began preparations for a trip into that region, and Anderson, not desiring to start for Washington city before October, decided to make the trip, wanting to learn about the extent of the new mining region and the nature of the gold deposits so he would be able to furnish Congress a description of the resources.

Fort Colville was three hundred miles to the northeast of Olympia and located in the wilderness. Leaving Etta at home, he started out in early June with seven other men, including an agent from Wells Fargo. On horseback with a train of pack animals to carry provisions, they began following a route that lay over the Cascade Mountains. "We passed through what was then called the Nachess Pass, across the Yakima River and Valley, striking the Columbia at the Priest Rapids, where we crossed it and took the Grand Coulee to the mouth of the Spokane River, then

WASHINGTON TERRITORY.

James Patton Anderson: Property transactions in Thurston County and miscellaneous recording

Source: Thurston County Property Records – Grantee Index 1854 to 1889

Date of filing	Grantee	Grantor	Transaction	Location	Am't	Description of property
Dec 9, 1853	Anderson, J. Patton	Edmund Sylvester	agrmt for deed	Deeds Vol 1 p41	$50	Lot 4 Blk 11 & Lot 5 Bk 10 Plat of Olympia
May 24, 1854	Anderson, J. Patton	John M. Swan	QCD	Deeds Vol 1 p108	$500	S2 of Lot 1 Blk 23 Plat of Olympia
July 28, 1858	Anderson, J. Patton	Edmund Sylvester	agrmt for deed	Deeds Vol 3 p84	$250	180x250 ft (see record) Plat of Olympia
[note: *Union and Columbus streets*]						
June 21, 1859	Anderson, J. Patton	Edmund Sylvester and Clara Sylvester, his wife	warranty deed	Deeds Vol 3 p358	$500	Block 80 Plat of Olympia

Source: Thurston County Property Records – Grantor Index 1854 to 1889

Date of filing	Grantor	Grantee	Transaction	Location	Am't	Description of property
May 24, 1858	Anderson, J. Patton	J.C. Cochran	deed	Vol 3 p53	$400	S2 of Lot 1 Blk 23 Plat of Olympia
March 25, 1861 August 1, 1861	Anderson, J. Patton " "	Bulter P. Anderson " "	power of atty	Vol 4 p2	n/a $300	*[authorize to sell or otherwise dispose of real estate in Olympia, Steilacoom & Seattle]*
April 3, 1867	Anderson, J.P. by atty	Henry Winson	warranty deed	Vol 5 p235	$300	Block 80 Plat of Olympia
April 26, 1872	Anderson, J. Patton and Etta B. Anderson	Francis Henry	deed	Vol 8 p424	$200	Lot 4 Blk 11 & Lot 5 Blk 10 Plat of Olympia

up the left bank of Clark's Fork, where gold was reported to have been found. The news had been true, as gold was being found in the beds of the stream. Placer mining took place at the scene as the men panned the gold by hand, washing and sifting out all the lighter material until only the glistering gold nuggets were left."[18] Anderson and others were being rewarded for their trip and efforts. But not for long. Few men waited for information to be brought back to Puget Sound. "By the middle of July all the trails leading towards the northeast were filled with hopeful gold hunters. I had not been at the mines a week till Angus McDonald of Fort Colville sent an express to inform me that the Indians along the route we had taken were becoming alarmed that their country would be overrun with whites in the search of gold."[19] The Anderson party, familiar with the massacre of missionary Marcus Whitman and thirteen other whites near present-day Walla Walla in 1847, and more recently the Rogue River Wars resulting from Indian anger at being driven from their lands, decided it was time to leave. "We were unarmed except for two guns and one or two pistols. Our provisions were being exhausted, and the appointed time for my return had arrived, so the miners concluded to return to Olympia. Fearful of the most hostile tribe led by the Chief Owhi, we decided to detour to the east in returning, crossing the Spokane River about forty miles above its mouth, passed by the old Whitman Methodist mission, crossed the Snake River about ten or twenty miles above its mouth, took down the Palouse to Walla Walla, then across the Umatilla near the mission and Billy McKey's, crossing the Des Shutes at its mouth, and then down The Dalles, the Cascades, Fort Vancouver, and up the Cowlitz back to Olympia, which we reached safely the first of October."[20]

The gold-hunting safari had taken three months. It was no ordinary field trip. Although the Andersons never revealed what wealth they may have acquired from it, they did have gold in their possession when they returned east. The time had come for them to leave Washington Territory. Their tenure had been successful, having acquired a home, furnishings, land investments, and the prestige of being a territorial representative to the Thirty-fourth U.S. Congress. They traveled by steamer to San Francisco, then to Panama, to New York City, and finally arrived in Washington city a few days before the meeting of the Congress.[21]

III

Florida Plantation Years

During the 1855 Christmas holidays the Andersons traveled out to Florida at the invitation of Mrs. Ellen Adair White Beatty, their rich aunt. During Florida's early years as an American territory, Aunt Ellen became one of the most fascinating figures. A keen mind and sparkling personality, together with a Madonna-like beauty, combined to make her the idol of intellectual and fashionable circles in Europe as well as in America.[1]

Born Eleanor Katherine Adair on June 5, 1801, near Harrodsburg, Kentucky, she was one of eleven children of General John Adair, veteran of the Revolution and the War of 1812 and eighth governor of Kentucky. Ellen married Joseph M. White of Franklin, Kentucky, a lawyer twenty years her senior. When Florida was purchased by the United States from Spain, President James Monroe appointed White one of the thirteen members of the Legislative Council of the newly created Territory of Florida. The Whites lived in Pensacola where Colonel White practiced law and became adjutant general of militia. He became an expert in international law, particularly as it applied to the transfer of Spanish deeds to American titles. Since his election as territorial representative to Congress necessitated having a permanent residence in the territory, White purchased 3,000 acres of land and constructed a palatial plantation home called Casa Bianca in Jefferson County.[2] Florida territory was sparsely

Florida seal

settled and built mainly on hope. It was sufficiently dependent upon out-side capital for development. Small plantations and farms became a fron-tier institution, much as in neighboring states, exemplified by settlers from older southern slave states and from abroad creating new slaveholding societies based upon the slave labor system. Without the abundant cheap slave labor, the process of carving new land from the wilderness would not have been achieved by the planter class.

Colonel White's career took the couple several times to Europe where they were received in the most eminent circles, including an audience with the pope in Rome,[3] and with Princess Caroline, Napoleon's sister.[4] Extravagant praise followed Ellen wherever she went. Colonel White died in 1839 after fighting a duel with a Mr. Bellamy, and Ellen was left with a sizable fortune in cash, land and slaves.[5] She continued her high soci-ety activities for five years, then married Dr. Theophilus Beatty, a mem-ber of the English nobility. While in the territory they divided their social activities between New Orleans and Casa Bianca, the latter becoming notable for its hospitality and charm. The territory continued to pros-per as planters infiltrated the land and developed plantations juxtaposed along small side farms with squatters who owned no slaves, and who mostly led lives that were only slightly above the Indians and Negroes. In 1845 the territory became the state of Florida. Two years later Dr. Beatty died and left Ellen alone and still childless. She now turned her affections to her niece Etta, daughter of her brother, Dr. William Adair. She sent the twelve-year-old girl to private school, took her on trips, and soon began to think of her as her own daughter.

Ellen took the young lady, at age fourteen, to Europe, giving her the advantage of schooling in Paris and then later in New York City. The closeness of this relationship continued until 1853 when Etta met her cousin, J. Patton Anderson, and married him. Naturally, Etta sacrificed everything when she moved to Washington Territory with her husband.

After an absence of almost four years, Ellen was more than anxious to see the couple; hence the Christmas invitation to come to Florida. It meant another long trip for the Andersons, traveling by rail and steamboat. They arrived safely at Casa Bianca Plantation in time for the Christmas holidays. The reunion found Ellen overjoyed and excessively sentimen-tal with her "adopted" Etta, while at the same time she lavished praise on Anderson for his accomplishments.

Ellen had not lost her touch; but the years without a husband diminished her fortune substantially because her talents did not include managing her finances and the vast plantation. Within a fortnight Ellen's Christmas invitation blossomed into a business proposal. She offered the Andersons the opportunity to come live with her at Casa Bianca and oversee the plantation operation for her, using the excuse that her health had become frail and she needed assistance. This was a generous offer to sway the Anderson's to stay on, and also a timely one, since Etta was expecting her first child.

Florida White. Because there were two "Whites" in the United States Congress at the time, Ellen became known as "Florida White" to distinguish her from the other Mrs. White, Mrs. Barton White, whose husband was a representative from New York. (from *Adair's Adair History and Genealogy*)

An Empire in Itself

Casa Bianca covered three thousand acres with only seven hundred acres under cultivation with cotton and thus the opportunity to double or triple the output. And better yet, Ellen A. Beatty owned 121 slaves to get the job done.[6] Anderson knew some of the Florida story. These were the flush years over the whole South. Cotton was bringing high prices, the banks seemed prosperous and people were extravagant because they had money. Paper note promises were abundant and speculation was wild in cotton futures. Good land was cheap, "to grow more cotton, to buy more Negroes to make more cotton grow," and so on in a vicious circle of rule for the planter.[7] Land in middle Florida bordering the Apalachicola and Suwannee rivers was extremely fertile and desirable for growing cotton. The heavily settled areas around Tallahassee represented the heart of the state's plantation belt. This was Florida's cotton belt and contained most of the state's 5,152 slave owners.[8] Casa Bianca was part of the planters' aristocracy, owning more than one hundred slaves and one thousand acres, alongside other plantations with titles such as Welaunee, Duice Domum, Lyndhurst, Rosewood and Wirtland.

Casa Bianca plantation house was a three-storied wooden mansion, a visible symbol of Ellen's wealth as a Florida planter. In the grand tradition of plantation palaces, large, wide porches surrounded the structure on two levels. Rocking chairs were plentiful and they were placed in favorite spots for surviving the sweltering Florida summers. A wide entrance hall led into the parlor, library, and one or more sitting rooms, plus the dining room and kitchen. In these rooms, "Florida" White displayed her wealth with European furnishings, rugs, paintings and imported artwork. On the upper floors, family members and guests enjoyed comfortable

Casa Bianca Plantation House

bedrooms. The uppermost floors were reserved for children's quarters or storage.

Surrounding the main house were small cabins built not far from the main building for the house servants: the field hands' cabins were farther away from the big house, as was the plantation's chapel. Florida pine and other hardwoods played a predominant part in the construction of Casa Bianca.

Florida plantations were not overly refined in comparison to the majestic plantations established over the last hundred and fifty years in cotton estates north of them. Isolated in the wilderness of Florida, they sought to enjoy their family while tended to by the Negroes, enjoyed politics, gambling, horse racing, plus long hours and plenty of work. Although retaining many of the characteristics of the frontier, it was a new agricultural region and increasing in population. Casa Bianca's economic system seemed simple to learn since it was based chiefly upon the growing of cotton and the exporting of it.

The Andersons were agreeably at the crossroads in their career. Considering their cosmopolitan attitude plus Etta's feelings toward her widowed and aging aunt, the couple surveyed the opportunity. "Yes," they would enter into a contract with her to oversee the running of Casa Bianca Plantation.

Anderson traveled back to Washington city alone for the sessions of Congress, and for the balance of his term he traveled back to Florida during the vacation periods. The Andersons' first son was born on July 14, 1856, at Casa Bianca Plantation, and christened William Preston Anderson. Subsequently, a second child was born, named Theophilus Beatty Anderson, in July 1858.[9]

"My term in Congress

Administrators Sale.
WILL BE SOLD,
AT PUBLIC AUCTION,

ON the 3d Monday of Septembea next, at 9 o'clock, in the forenoon, at the Auction Store of Henry Michelett, in the City of Pensacola,

A Negro Woman & Child,

The property of Henry Shepherd, Esq deceased. Terms made known at the time and place of sale.

Clark Jackson,
Ad'mr.

Advertisement of slave auction (from *The Floridian*, Pensacola, September 13, 1823)

Public Auction cut

expired March 4, 1857, the same day that James Buchanan was inaugurated president for four years. He appointed me Governor and Superintendent of Indian Affairs of the Washington Territory, but I did not accept. I declined the position tendered by President Buchanan, believing firmly that the days of the Union were already numbered; and not wishing to be absent from the land of my birth when her hour of trial came, I resigned the position and hastened back to Florida."[10]

Colonel Anderson, the new overseer, was tall, shapely, erect of carriage, handsome, chivalric in bearing, warm-hearted and genial in manner. In every respect he was the accomplished and loveable gentleman.[11]

Illustrative of his honesty and at the same time an indication he had a sense of humor is an advertisement he placed in the newspaper in his former hometown of Herando, Mississippi. When Anderson left Mississippi

Old way of picking cotton

to enter upon his term of office as territorial marshal, he borrowed money for the trip and for his honeymoon, amounts largely in excess of his ability to repay at the time. While in Washington Territory he made certain investments (possibly mining gold) which enabled him to meet his outstanding debts when he returned to the South. Once settled in Florida he inserted an advertisement in the Herando newspaper in Mississippi:

YOUR REDEEMER LIVETH
All creditors of J. Patton Anderson will, on presenting claims to the
undersigned, be paid in full on principal and interest of their demands.
(signed) J. Patton Anderson[12]

There is no record or mention of his paying any claims; most likely the personal loans were a purse to him and his new bride.

Becoming overseer of Casa Bianca naturally had its rewards in prestige, position and promise for the Anderson family; at the same time they became partners and players in regard to the issue of the day — slavery

Unique cotton harvester

in the United States. The United States outlawed the importation of slaves in 1808, but Florida, a Spanish possession and not a member of the original colonies, continued importing and smuggling slaves into the southern states until 1821, when Spain ceded Florida to the United States. It was known as the Florida Territory until 1845, when it entered the Union as the twenty-seventh state.

The enslavement of Africans in what became the United States first coincided with the colonial years from 1650 to 1790. At that time colonial courts made clear that Africans served their owners for life and the slave status would be inherited by their children. There was no sectional debate over this arrangement. After the American Revolution which began in 1776, the northern states came to see slavery as contradictory to the ideals of the revolution and began to preach and institute programs of gradual emancipation because there were fewer slaves in these states.

Circumstances in the southern states were quite different, as states such as Virginia and South Carolina had half of their population in African slaves. Therefore the southern states were determined to retain slavery after the revolution, beginning the division of "free states" from the "slave states."[13]

Faced with a surplus of slave families who were becoming too expensive to house, clothe and feed, the owners in the upper South, in states such as Virginia and Maryland, began trading and selling off their excess labor to the plantations in the lower South, many times splitting up first- and second-generation families. Accompanying this imbalance of Africans in the southern states was the Industrial Revolution in the northern states.

In 1793, Eli Whitney invented the cotton gin, which separated the cotton from the seeds. Prior to the invention of the gin, only long-staple cotton, which has long, soft strands, could be grown for profit. Its soft fibers allowed easy removal of its seeds. But this strain of cotton grew in America only along the coast and Sea Islands of South Carolina and Georgia. In contrast, short-staple cotton could grow in almost any non-mountainous region of the South below Virginia. Before the invention of the cotton gin, it took a slave many hours to deseed a single pound of lint of short-staple cotton. With the gin, as many as one hundred pounds of cotton could be deseeded per hour.

The revolution was that short-staple cotton could be grown almost anywhere in the lower South, resulting in an increased demand for slaves to plant and pick cotton. Rapidly, the plantation system was expanded over the virgin lands of the territories and southern states, creating the Antebellum South (i.e., the South prior to the Civil War). Coupled with the Industrial Revolution in the North and insatiable demand worldwide for cotton, the plantation owners welcomed new states such as Florida into their cotton kingdom, and lusted to expand their tentacles of profit into other states and territories. The Andersons became willing players and learned the simple economics of King Cotton.

Anderson had already expressed his opinion about the Compromise of 1850, believing it was unfair that the southern states could not expand slavery into the new territories. Theoretically, like the other plantation owners, he felt they had an alienable claim and right to leave the present loosely knit Union of the United States if they deemed it prudent.

These arguments were reinforced in 1857, not by additional aboli-tionist demands, but from events on Wall Street in New York City. The Crimean War of 1854 caused speculative issues of stocks and bonds being traded on the stock exchange. Concurrently there were immense invest-ments of capital in Western land speculation and especially in new West-ern railroads. A series of untimely events — the end of the Crimean War; a prediction that some railroads had expanded too quickly; a rumor that a major insurance company was set to collapse; and signs of an economic slowdown — triggered a sudden money panic as anxious depositors rushed to withdraw their funds from the banks. When a number of large banks suspended payment of specie, the depositors feared the worst, and an eco-nomic slowdown began in the northern states which lasted almost a year. Some northern cotton mills adjusted their production according to the local market as they saw the demand for their fabric decline, forcing mills to lay off workers.

Despite assurances by the press, the fact of the matter was that the new Florida planter class was largely a debtor society, and unlike the more established slave states to the north of them, they had no great accumu-lation of cash or credit to sustain themselves in slow economic times. There is no doubt that the Panic of 1857 had a rippling effect on Florida merchants, banks and plantations; moreover, it brought up the subject of secession.

Surprisingly, there was only a slight domino effect in the South. Although a few southern banks failed, the price of cotton rose well higher, due to increased worldwide demand. Now southern newspapers jeered the prostrate North, crying, "Why does the South allow itself to be tattered and torn by the dissensions and death struggles of New York's money changers? The wealth of the South is permanent and real, that of the North fugitive and fictitious. Southern newspapers took up the chant: Cotton is King. The panic of 1857 provided Southern anti–Union politicians a strong arrow for their quiver."[14]

The Andersons had hardly settled in when Ellen asked to borrow $20,000 from them. Why not from her New York bank? Probably she was already leveraged to the maximum. Ellen's fortunes had diminished even further because of her extravagant habits. As a show of good faith she offered her slaves as collateral for the loan.[15] She even told Etta she was going to leave her entire estate to her. Ellen Beatty was clearly a woman of many contradictions, as the Andersons were finding out. There are no records of the operation of Casa Bianca under the Andersons, although the capers of Ellen continued.

In 1859 the unpredictable Aunt Ellen, without consulting the Andersons, sold some of the slaves who were the Andersons' collateral on the $20,000 loan granted earlier. The slaves were Ellen's property and she could do with them whatever she pleased: "Patton became appalled at the cruelty of breaking up slave families, many being second and third generations. He attempted to keep mothers from being separated from their children and managed to buy back the house-servants and others."[16]

Years before the Andersons moved to Florida, a rudimentary plank of secession between the North and South was laid by the Protestant churches. The conflict centered around slavery, and the debates smoldered for decades. The southern churches protested against the actions of the northern religious bodies in trying to settle the slavery question politically. The response of the northern churches resulted in gradual alienation and separation of the southern members so that ultimately the Presbyterian, Episcopal, Baptist, Methodist and Lutheran churches divided into northern and southern denominations. The Roman Catholic Church did not divide.

Plantation owners viewed African rituals as a combination of witchcraft and superstition and denied the right of the slaves to practice the religion of their ancestors. Instead, the owners believed that Christianizing their slaves would make them more passive and would be uplifting from their barbarous past. "Of course, the Christianity taught to slaves by their masters was different from that which the owners practiced themselves. Omitted were the implicit and explicit messages in the New Testament about individual freedom and responsibility. Instead, some owners used the Bible selectively."[17]

Ellen had a chapel built at Casa Bianca where she could superintend the Sunday school when she was at home. She prayed and sang with the Negroes, and explained the Bible she read to them. It was for the interest of the master that the slave should be allowed a religious sentiment, as it was part of the planter's paternalistic role that help promote slave control. Christianity down on the plantation used Sunday school lessons to preach that obedience was the highway to heaven. The Ten Commandments were fine, but a faithful and dutiful Christian slave would become the freedman of his heavenly master. Recorded elsewhere was one black lady who mumbled, "Day never tale us nothing about Jesus."[18] There is no telling what Ellen was preaching. When Anderson became overseer he employed a Mr. Clisby to teach the Negroes the Bible. He was paid a regular salary besides his board.[19] From what information they understood, the Negroes evolved their own form of Christianity, which was a religion of hope and liberation.

Excerpts from the Jefferson County Tax Book in 1860 listed the owners of thirty or more slaves and the acreage. Casa Bianca was not one of the large plantations although it had the potential to become one. Florida's census showed 61,700 slaves.

Name	Acres	Slaves
J. G. Anderson Estate	2,300	135
*J. P. Anderson	400	54
William Bailey, Sr.	3,700	180
Wm. J. Bailey and Father	2,140	93
Wm. I. Bailey (Lynnhurst)	6,257	95
Zakariah Bailey Estate	1,000	42
Douglas Beaty	1,133	30
B. W. Bellamy	2,840	130
Guardian E. Bellamy	1,400	70
Guardian William Bellamy	1,680	64
Behethland Bird	1,820	42

Regardless of her actions at Casa Bianca, Ellen "Florida White" Beatty continued to travel outside of Florida. On her latest trip and social excursion outside of the state, she heard and recognized there was a conflict coming between the North and South. Besides Ellen's findings there were other signs. Bankers began to reduce and call in many of their loans, trade began dropping off and business failure increased. Trade at southern ports fell to a low point, credit was being reduced to southerners and uneasiness about the future prevailed. Worst of all, banks began refusing to redeem their own outstanding bank notes (paper currency) for coin, but instead hoarded their gold assets.[20] The election of Abraham Lincoln in November 1860 pretty well brought down the curtain on the antebellum plantation regime.

Succumbing to the fears of the day, Ellen and the Andersons decided to sell Casa Bianca to Robert W. Williams, a prominent lawyer and landholder in Tallahassee, for the sum of $18,000. The terms of agreement stipulated that Anderson and his family could continue to live on the property with the assistance of an overseer, a Mr. A. G. A. Godwin.[21] Aunt Ellen deposited her share from the sale of the plantation in a New York bank for safekeeping,[22] not realizing that once hostilities began, she could not withdraw any funds. Her assets were locked up in a New York bank for the next four and a half years. No longer able to travel because of wartime restrictions, she was forced to live with the Andersons for the entire war. She also sold her household slaves to them.

A third son, James Patton, Jr. was born October 2, 1860.

IV

Confederate Florida

Politically the nation had entered a period of sectional emotionalism. Could the Union endure half slave and half free? The effect of *Uncle Tom's Cabin* on thousands of people who before had cared nothing about slavery, and the raid of John Brown into Virginia, helped to create a crisis more powerful than all the speeches of abolitionist leaders and incendiary literature scattered among the slaves.

Florida, like other southern states, was controlled by men who had their political origins deep in the philosophy of states' rights and who were enraged by the instigative proceeding taking place in the abolitionist North.[1] The October elections in Florida saw the Democrats win as John Milton, a planter from Jefferson County, was elected governor. With the election of Abraham Lincoln in November, all hope or relief through congressional legislation or constitutional amendments was exhausted. The "Black" Republican Party was resolute in to granting nothing that would satisfy the South.[2] A second American Revolution was becoming a reality as Southern States became determined to separate themselves from the Northern States. The War Between the States was about to begin.

After South Carolina seceded from the Union on December 20, 1860, Florida's governor, Madison S. Perry, still in office, recommended the General Assembly take immediate steps to meet the crisis facing the state, and called a convention to be held at Tallahassee on January 3. The convention's task was to take into consideration the dangers of the position of the State of Florida in the Federal Union, and to amend the constitution of the state. Patton Anderson's political background and experience, as well as his proslavery and secessionist views, established him sufficiently to be elected as one of three delegates from Jefferson County. Sixty-nine delegates convened in Tallahassee and supposedly reflected the views of their constituents. On January 7, 1861, a resolution was adopted, affirming the right of a state to withdraw from the Union, arguing "that the consideration for which Florida gave her assent to become a member of the Federal Union has wholly failed, that she is not permitted enjoyment of equal rights in the Union, and the compact is therefore willfully and materially broken."[3] Anderson was appointed a member of the committee that drafted and recommended that the assembled delegates adopt an ordinance of secession from the Union, declaring Florida a sovereign and independent state.[4] The vote came on January 10, sixty-four to five in support of secession. The adoption meant the planters and politicians had won a single victory for immediate secession, for the resolution declared the rights of the convention to act for the people of Florida; there would be no popular vote taken for approval of the question of secession.[5]

The news of secession spread like wildfire across the state. People celebrated their new independence in towns and villages with parades, cannon salutes and fire-eating oratory against the abolitionist North. Local vigilance committees quickly formed to enforce a strict watch on the movement of Unionists in the state or for slave unrest. This radicalism soon found its way to the pulpit with complete ecclesiastical support from the churches. The only negative word came from ex-governor Richard Call, who denounced the secession as "treason against our Constitutional government and it was an event which was to open the gates of hell."[6]

The Seizure of Federal Property

While the convention was in session, Governor Perry deemed it prudent to seize forts, ordnance depots, arsenals, and post offices belonging to the Federal government. He ordered the state militia to be mobilized. On returning to Casa Bianca, Anderson learned of the call to arms issued to the militia in Leon and Jefferson counties. As captain of the Jefferson Rifles, he assumed command of both companies and marched them to the Federal Arsenal at Chattahoochee, which had been seized earlier by the Quincy Guards. A substantial amount of ammunition, small arms and artillery pieces were seized here and elsewhere in the state. The volunteers remained at the arsenal awaiting further orders from Tallahassee.[7]

At Pensacola on January 12 the first act of southern aggression occurred when seven companies of Alabama and Florida volunteers surrounded the U.S. Navy Yard and forced Commander James Armstrong to surrender it. It was a prize capture, as the yard included a million dollar dry dock, workshops, warehouses, barracks, a Marine hospital, 175 cannon, 12,000 projectiles and ordnance stores.[8] Next, the three forts at Pensacola should be seized. U.S. Lieutenant Adam J. Slemmer, learning that Alabamans had taken possession of Fort Morgan,[9] one of the key guardians of Mobile Bay, transferred his Federal forces from Fort Barrancas on the mainland to more easily defended Fort Pickens on Santa Rosa Island, which controlled Pensacola Bay, the largest deepwater port on the Gulf of Mexico. The southerners now held both Forts Barrancas and McRee, the largest naval station in the South, and the rail lines connected to it.

The circumstances at Pensacola mirrored a similar situation at Fort Sumter, South Carolina; they were the only Federal military possessions left under Federal control in the seceded states. If war were to come, it would begin at one or the other of these two forts; as long as the forts were not reinforced or resupplied, southern militia would not attack them. Still in office, a non-aggressive President Buchanan realized his administration faced the acid test to maintain peace. To surrender either fort would initiate an armed conflict that he opposed. Buchanan proposed

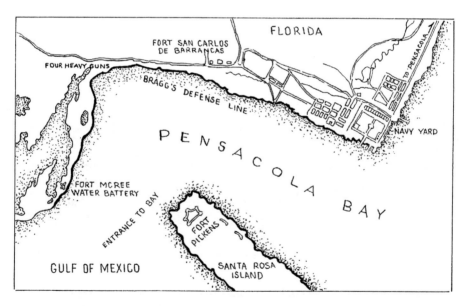

Pensacola Bay. Fort Pickens is on the western extremity of Santa Rosa Island, which is about forty miles in length. About a mile and a half on the mainland was the Confederate arch of defense running from Fort McRee along the shoreline to the captured navy yard.

a truce to the secessionists, which was successful. On January 18 telegrams were sent from a powerful group of southern senators: "We think no assault should be made. The possession of the fort is not worth one drop of blood to us. Measures pending unite us in the opinion. Bloodshed may be fatal to our cause. Signed by Senators Mallory, Yulee, Slidell, Benjamin, Iverson, Hemphill, Wigfall, Clay, Fitzpatrick, and Davis." With the Fort Pickens Truce at hand, Governor Perry disbanded the volunteer militia, but not before the legislature provided for the reorganization of the militia and appropriated $100,000 for military purposes.[10]

Almost as soon as the United States made the decision to forestall the secession by force, it adopted the policy of a naval blockade of the new Confederacy. There were hundreds of inlets and bays all along the thirty-five hundred miles from the Potomac River down the Atlantic seaboard and then west along the Gulf Coast to the mouth of the Rio Grande River in Texas. The small Union navy could blockade only the main ports which had either railroad or river connections with the interior, such as Pensacola and Charleston.

1861—The Confederate States—1865

By the end of January, Florida, Mississippi, Alabama, Georgia, Louisiana and South Carolina adopted similar ordinances of secession. These states decided to meet at Montgomery, Alabama, on February 4, 1861, to adopt a provisional constitution and form their own government. Patton Anderson, Jackson Morton and James Powers were the three Florida delegates.

Traveling to Montgomery, Anderson participated in the proceedings, and on February 8 the delegates adopted a provisional constitution. It was similar to the present U.S. Constitution except for its recognition of states' rights and the legality of slavery. Anderson reported: "All the principal measures of that body, passed or proposed during its first session and while I was a member, met my support. I was appointed to the Committee of Military Affairs and favored the raising of troops. I proposed to have the cooks, nurses, teamsters and pioneers of our army to consist of slaves."[11] The following day Anderson's old political ally, Jefferson Davis of Mississippi, was elected president, and Alexander H. Stephens of Georgia, vice president.[12] With the adjournment of the convention, Anderson and the other Florida patriots returned home, flush with secession fever. How would Etta react to all of this? he wondered.

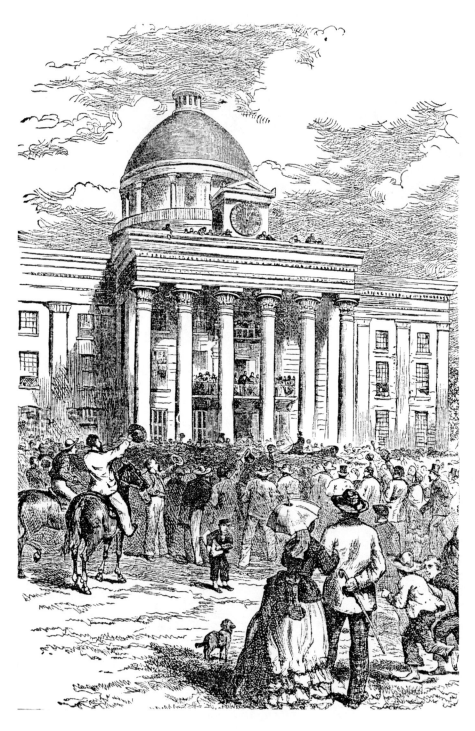

Inauguration of Jefferson Davis

In the interim that followed this split in the Union, both sides began marking time. A Washington Peace Conference (February 4 to 27) did not contain enough spirit of compromise on either side and satisfied no one, as it was rejected by the U.S. Congress and Senate. As war fever rose so did the rage of the Florida newspapers. "John Darby of Baldwin published a notice offering a $400 reward to the first company or regiment who gets or takes possession of Fort Pickens at Pensacola. The editor of Jacksonville's *Southern Confederacy* was just as belligerent, urging, in no uncertain terms, an end to the talk about Fort Sumter and the beginning of hostilities. Carolinians ... talk no more! Take Fort Sumter at once! Take it, if it should cost the lives of 100,000 men."[13]

The newly formed Confederate War Department directed a call for 100,000 volunteers for not more than twelve months' service, with the state of Florida being levied for five thousand men. The state with a scattered rural population of only 140,000 inhabitants, almost half of whom were Negroes, Indians, squatters and others, would have to make sacrifices among its white youth to meet this quota. The villages, towns, merchants and planters began outfitting companies by buying clothing, shoes, collecting rifles and recruiting among the population those who wanted to join in the fight but had no money to do so.[14]

The period of watchful waiting came to an end on March 4 with the inauguration of Abraham Lincoln as sixteenth president of the United States. Lincoln's opinion on the secession of the southern states was that their act was legally nothing and needed no repealing. Unlike the fence-sitter Buchanan, Lincoln ordered the small garrisons at Fort Pickens,

MONTHLY ARMY, 1861		
Rank	*Confederate*	*Union*
Private	$ 11.00	$ 13.00
Corporal	13.00	13.00
Sergeant	17.00	17.00
1st Sergeant	20.00	20.00
QM Sergeant	21.00	21.00
Sgt. Major	21.00	21.00
2nd Lieutenant	80.00	105.50
1st Lieutenant	90.00	105.50
Captain	130.00	115.50
Major	150.00	169.00
Lt. Colonel	170.00	181.00
Colonel	195.00	212.00
Brig. General	301.00	315.00
Maj. General	301.00	457.00
Lt. General	301.00	758.00 *
General	301.00	

* Added in 1864

Florida, and Fort Sumter, South Carolina, to be reinforced and supplied immediately, creating a secession crisis. During February, the United States slowly built up a formidable naval force outside Pensacola Bay. Up to this time the state authorities had permitted coal and water to be transported from the navy yard to the ships outside the harbor. With the present state of affairs, the mainland grew more warlike as all communications with the federal garrison on Santa Rosa Island were prohibited in an attempt to stop water traffic across the bay to the fort. There would be no more trading with the enemy, as martial law was declared by the Confederates. President Davis came from Montgomery and inspected the Confederate position, but with no evidence of a plan of attack on Fort Pickens.[15] Recognizing the existing danger, Governor Perry put out a call for militia troops for immediate service at Pensacola. Ten volunteer companies from middle and west Florida were hastily assembled and ordered to rendezvous at the Chattahoochee Arsenal to be organized into a regiment to be mustered in the Confederate service as the 1st Florida Infantry. Captain J. Patton Anderson was elected colonel and the regiment ordered to Pensacola. Filled with unrest and secession fever, Anderson's 1st Florida, nicknamed The Magnolia Regiment, marched through to Pensacola, arriving on the 11th and 12th of April. They reported to Braxton Bragg, who on March 8 had been appointed brigadier general and assigned to the city.

Bragg was born on March 22, 1817, at Warrenton, North Carolina. He received his early education there and entered West Point in 1833. He was fifth among fifty graduates in the class of 1837, and entered the U.S. Army as a second lieutenant. Bragg experienced combat against the Seminole Indians in Florida for several years before he joined Zachary Taylor's forces in Texas in 1845.

On the out break of war with Mexico, he was ordered to Corpus Christi and distinguished himself in the defense of Fort Brown, Texas. His gallantry in several engagements near Monterey, Mexico, earned him a brevet of major. His fame came at Buena Vista on February 23, 1847, where he managed his artillery in such a way as to fill the gaping holes in the American infantry lines and finally repulse the numerically superior Mexican force. In his report of the latter battle, General Taylor spoke of the skillful handling by Bragg of his artillery and gave him the proud distinction and credit of saving the day on the field. "A little more grape, Captain Bragg" became the slogan of the war.[16] "The victory largely won by Bragg helped make General Taylor and, to a lesser extent, Mississippi Colonel Jefferson Davis national heroes. In return, the young captain received a brevet lieutenant colonelcy from Taylor, and inaugurated a longtime bond with Davis."[17]

"Braxton married a wealthy woman from Louisiana, Eliza Brooks Ellis in 1849. Bragg resigned in 1856 because he was unable to have his way regarding the use of horse artillery in the army or duty stations. He moved to Thibodaux, Louisiana, to become a sugar planter. Realizing the need for trained engineers in Louisiana, he worked to establish the State Military School in 1860, now Louisiana State University."[18]

"With secession looming, Louisiana Governor Thomas O. Moore appointed Bragg to the state

General Braxton Bragg, CSA

military board to organize a 5,000-man army. On January 11, 1861, Bragg captured the Baton Rouge Arsenal at the head of 500 volunteers. Following the secession of Louisiana and its creation of an army, Bragg became its commander with the rank of major general on February 6; on March 8 he was commissioned a brigadier general in the Confederate Army to rank from that date, and assigned to command a portion of the Gulf Coast which included Mobile, Alabama, and Pensacola, Florida."[19]

"Of the eight men who reached the rank of full general in the Confederate Army, Braxton Bragg was the most controversial. His battery in the Mexican War, of which his battery of 'flying artillery' revolutionized in many respects the battlefield use of the arm, earned him a prewar reputation for strict discipline as well as a literal adherence to regulations."[20] Described as being "naturally disputatious" by others, he had difficulties in almost every relationship with either a superior or subordinate officer. His discontent was caused partly by his commitment to professionalism, and partly by his own personality. Many found Braxton Bragg, at age 46, quarrelsome, irritable, cantankerous and with a sour disposition. Yet he was eminently qualified in all respects for this command, as he brought his usual high standards of drill, discipline and efficiency to the predicament at Fort Pickens.

Bragg proceeded to construct a defensive cordon of batteries in an arch a mile and a half long extending from Fort McRee along the shoreline of the gulf to the captured navy yard, lacing the area with an armament of fifty light artillery pieces aimed at the Yankees encamped on Santa Rosa Island and Fort Pickens.

April 12, 1861— The beginning of hostilities. During the early hours, Captain Israel Vogdes, aboard the U.S. Navy sloop-of-war *Brooklyn*, anchored in Pensacola Bay, acted on orders he received from a special messenger sent by U.S. Secretary of the Navy Gideon Wells. He began to unload his artillery company for duty at Fort Pickens, breaking the truce. General Bragg, with 3,000 untrained recruits at hand, took no action to counter Vogdes's movement of men and supplies because he had been ordered not to do so. Elsewhere on this same date the Confederate forces at Charleston, South Carolina, with the same circumstances— began firing on Fort Sumter in Charleston Harbor, heralding the beginning of the war between the North and South. Although the two events day and dated one another, the relief of Fort Pickens at Pensacola, Florida, would only become a footnote to Civil War history.

Several months later, Richard H. "Fighting Dick" Anderson, after commanding his regiment at the bombardment of Fort Sumter, was transferred to General Bragg's command at Pensacola.

In the months that followed, the Federal position on Santa Rosa Island and Fort Pickens strengthened to over 2,000 bluecoats with an armament of twelve batteries and fifty-seven artillery pieces.

A VIVID "GLIMPSE OF THE CONFEDERATE ARMY"—1861
This spirited photograph by Edwards of New Orleans suggests more than volumnes of history could tell of the enthusiam, the hope, with which the young Confederate volunteers, with their queerly variegated equipment, sprang to the defense of their land in '61. Around this locality in Florida some of the very earliest operations centered. Fort McRee and the adjacent batteries had passed into Confederate hands on January 12, 1861, when Lieutenant Adam J. Slemmer withdrew with his eighty-two men to Fort Pickens in Pensacola Harbor. The lack of conventional military uniformity shown above must not be thought exceptional. (Florida State Archives)

The Army of Pensacola

Recruits from Florida, Alabama and Georgia supplemented General Bragg's militia force to over 5,000 infantry and artillery. He spent the hot summer training and equipping his army as the stalemate kept up. Bragg realized that as long as Federal forces held Fort Pickens, the Confederates would not be able to use Pensacola Harbor effectively.

On September 2, a bold Federal raiding party burned the dry dock anchored near the Confederate navy yard. Twelve days later a larger Union force made another assault; this time the bluecoats boarded and burned a Rebel schooner, *Judah*, being outfitted as a privateer to run the Union blockade. In retaliation General Bragg ordered an amphibious assault against the enemy on Santa Rosa Island. General R. H. Anderson from South Carolina, who had joined Bragg in August, organized the landing party.

Anderson ordered his selected detachments of troops to assemble at the naval shipyard on the evening of October 8. There, they embarked aboard the wood-burning steamer *Time* for the short ride to Pensacola. While en route, the troops were divided into three battalions. Anderson placed Colonel James R. Chalmers of the 9th Mississippi Regiment in command of the 350-strong first battalion. The second battalion, numbering 400 soldiers, was placed under the command of Colonel J. Patton Anderson of the 1st Regiment of Florida Volunteers. Colonel John K. Jackson, 5th Regiment Georgia Volunteers, assumed command of the 260-man third battalion. An independent company of 53 men under Lieutenant James H. Hallonquist, lightly armed with pistols and knives, was equipped for spiking cannons and burning enemy structures. In addition, a detail of medical officers and support personnel accompanied the expedition.

Upon arrival at Pensacola at 10 P.M., General Anderson transferred a portion of his force to the steamer *Ewing* and several barges so that the troops could be landed more quickly on Santa Rosa Island. A third steamer, *Neaffie*, was requisitioned to assist with the barges. Shortly after midnight on October 9, the flotilla departed for Santa Rosa Island. The harbor crossing was swift and uneventful, and the troops landed at about 2 A.M. on a secluded beach roughly four miles east of Fort Pickens.

Once ashore, the battalions mustered around their respective commanders, and Anderson set his plan in motion. He directed Chalmers to advance westward along the northern shore of the island. Patton Anderson's battalion was to cross the narrow strip of the island and turn westward

WHERE THE BLOCKADERS CAME TOO LATE

Many of these soldiers pictured here were soon fighting miles away from where we see them now; a great many were drafted from New Orleans, from Mobile, Savannah, and Charleston; Florida and Georgia furnished their full quota to the Confederate army. This photograph was taken by Edwards, of New Orleans, who, like his confrère Lytle, succeeded in picturing many of the stirring scenes and opening tableaux of the war, they afterward took advantage of their art and used their cameras as batteries at the command of the Confederate secret service, photographing ships and troops and guns of the Federal forces, and sending them to the commanding generals of their departments. Over the chase of the gun is Pensacola harbor. (Florida State Archives) along its southern gulf shore. Jackson was instructed to follow in the rear of Chalmers's battalion.[21]

Quietly, without the drummer's beat, the Confederate "butternuts" advanced in the pitch-black night over sand dunes and through cactus in a fatiguing three-mile march until they came upon Colonel Billy Wilson's 6th New York Zouaves cantonment which was east of Fort Pickens.[22] It was not long before the Rebels' movement was discovered by the Union picket who volleyed a shot into the darkness, alerting his comrades sleeping in tents. With the element of surprise gone, General Anderson ordered a direct assault upon the Zouaves encampment.

The New Yorkers, unaccustomed to the brightness of the sand dunes and the hot Florida sun, had covered their site with pine branches for shade, which had dried, making the site a veritable kindling pile.[23] Entering the camp, the butternuts applied the torch to the dried branches; the flames quickly engulfed the entire camp and the panic-stricken Zouaves broke and ran for protection from the batteries at the rear of Fort Pickens.

Wilson did his best to rally his frightened men but was unable to check their flight. Elated at their easy triumph, the Rebels stopped to plunder the evacuated camp. In doing so, however, they lost the precious momentum they needed to complete their victory.

It was not long before the battalions of Chalmers and Patton Anderson joined in the pillage of Camp Brown. The camp was thoroughly looted, and a great deal of property was stolen or destroyed. By 4 A.M., Hallonquist's men had spiked a number of cannons and set the camp ablaze. Following the seizure General Anderson attempted to reorganize his scattered forces in the darkness. "He quickly realized, however, that his plan of attacking the Federal batteries near the fort was impractical. Dawn was near, and the Federals were alert and ready. In the morning light his steamers would be easy targets for the Union gunboats in the bay. There simply was not enough time to mount a successful assault. Anderson therefore abandoned his original plan and issued a full and orderly retreat back to the barges."[24]

Union Captain Israel Vogdes, with two companies from the fort, was sent along the beach of the north shore in an attempt to flank the raiders in their retrograde. In the darkness, Vogdes overran the Rebels and was cut off from the fort. In this predicament there was musketry from both sides as the Confederates scrambled aboard their barges and flats to begin the crossing back to Pensacola. General Anderson was shot in the elbow and replaced by Patton Anderson, who took command of the brigade.[25] This was Florida's first land battle. The Confederate losses were 18 dead, 39 wounded, with 30 others missing or prisoners of war. The Federals' losses were 14 dead, 29 wounded and 24 prisoners, including Captain Vogdes.[26]

The encounter on Santa Rosa Island had no strategic value for either side. It gave the Confederate troops confidence in the cause and in General Bragg, while at the same time they were brought to realize the cost of the skirmish in dead and wounded patriots. Thereafter the opposing forces settled down to the mundane routine of drill, parade and the strengthening of their defenses. In the interim, General Richard Anderson recovered from his wounds and was assigned to a brigade in Lee's army in Virginia. There were great artillery exchanges between both sides in November and December. During a two-day bombardment the Federals expended 5,000 rounds of ammunition and the Confederates countered with 1,000 shot and shell.

With the beginning of military activity in 1861, Colonel Anderson's interest and time for overseeing the Casa Bianca Plantation operation became impracticable. Etta could not handle the day-to-day operation, so it was decided she should move to Monticello and stay with her sister and brother-in-law in Anderson's absence. Financially they were in good shape, since they did not spend any of the money from the sale of the plantation. Anderson turned over the newly printed Confederate bills to Etta for safekeeping.[27] His destiny was changing course from plantation owner and overseer to a patriot officer for the cause.

V

Shiloh and Farmington

During the nine months of service at Pensacola, Patton Anderson won the favor of General Bragg, who urged the Confederate War Department to promote him to brigadier general. Secretary of War Judah P. Benjamin wrote Bragg: "The President and myself have a very high opinion of the merits and soldiery qualities of Colonel Anderson."[1] On February 10, 1862, Anderson received his commission as brigadier general.[2] Along with the good news, Lieutenant Richard Turnbull, an officer under Anderson, presented him a Kentucky-foaled gray horse named Yancy. At the outset when Anderson was mounted on his war horse, he looked the personification of the conquering hero.[3]

Early in February, Fort Henry and Fort Donelson on the Cumberland and Tennessee rivers were forced to surrender to Grant's overwhelming force, resulting in over 14,000 Confederate prisoners and the first major Confederate defeat in the West. The Federals continued up the Tennessee River planning to destroy the Confederate railroad centers at Jackson, Humbolt and Corinth. Forced to establish a new line of defense, General P. G. T. Beauregard was sent to the west and placed second in command of Confederate forces west of the Tennessee River, establishing his headquarters at Jackson, Tennessee. He was joined there by General Bragg, who then ordered Anderson to report to him at Jackson. As the Federals invaded Dixie, it necessitated the withdrawal of Bragg's Army of Pensacola, virtually dooming the city.[4]

Anderson, Etta, the children and the children's nurse, Alice, journeyed to Jackson. It was a common practice with generals on both sides of the conflict to have their family with them in the field at certain times. During the short visit the Andersons lived in Army tents and enjoyed the services of Alice the maid, plus two Negro boys who were Anderson's personal servants.[5] It was a short visit because elements of the Army were rapidly being shifted east to Corinth, Mississippi. Etta and the children returned home to Florida.

As the Confederates abandoned Tennessee, General Albert Sidney Johnston moved his small army at Nashville and concentrated it with other scattered western Confederate forces at Corinth to head off Grant's invasion of Dixie. Corinth, located in the northeast corner of Mississippi, was the control center for the Memphis and Charleston railroads that connected the Mississippi River and Gulf of Mexico with Virginia and the Carolinas. The buildup of Confederate forces was swift. Joining Johnston's forces was General Bragg's army of Pensacola with over 8,000 men; General Daniel Ruggles from New Orleans with 5,000 infantry; and later General L. Polk's Army of Mississippi and Tennessee; plus General William J. Hardee and General John C. Breckinridge's corps. Total strength was 40,000 men. When Anderson arrived he was assigned to command a brigade of infantry in General Ruggles's division.[6] "This mob," as General Bragg referred to the assemblage, would have only two weeks to be formed into a cohesive fighting army.[7]

Federal troops were being transported south on the Tennessee River during March to a staging area at Shiloh in preparation for seizing Corinth. They came in divisions: J. A. McClernand; C. F. Smith; Lew Wallace; S. A. Hurlbut; and W. T. Sherman, under the command of General Ulysses S. Grant. In addition, Don Carlos Buell was ordered to march his Army of the Ohio to join Grant at a place called Pittsburg Landing. Buell was delayed because of flooding on the Duck River.

Until then Anderson's career in the military service of the Florida militia had been satisfactory. His tour of duty at Tampico, Mexico, with Mississippi volunteers, although without battlefield action, undoubtedly was valuable in developing leadership qualities and respect from the enlistees. In Confederate service for nine months at Pensacola under the command of West Pointers Bragg and R. Anderson, he sharpened his military skill and stature aided by *Hardee's Tactics*, a textbook on battlefield tactics. With the invading force on Santa Rosa Island in October, Anderson received his baptism of fire and the skirmish with the bluecoats toughened his vital processes. His apprenticeship had come to an end as he traveled east to Corinth to participate in his first major battle.

How would his psyche hold up during a pouring rainstorm, riding atop Yancy on a muddy road in some godforsaken place, keeping time with a makeshift band sputtering out a patriotic tune while headed to the arena of death where over 100,000 men wearing the blue and gray assembled to kill for their cause? The epic would be noisy, louder than anything he had ever heard. Screaming their lungs out to relieve their fear, the crowds of soldiers would charge in upright positions, firing tens of thousands of minie balls at one another. Who had time to aim? Artillery cannonballs the size of baseballs would be sent high and low, trimming trees and the limbs of the boys by the thousands. And it would all be over so quickly! Then ... the cries of the dismembered and wounded, pools of blood everywhere, and piles of corpses with their individual stench of death. Was this a place for a general on a horse? Yes, if you were a patriot general such as Patton Anderson.

There would be a lot of new generals for Anderson to meet and work with. At Corinth the second in command was P. G. T. Beauregard. Born in Louisiana, Pierre Gustave Toutant Beauregard was the son of a wealthy sugarcane planter. After the usual formal schooling, Beauregard was graduated second in the 1838 class at West Point where he had become a great admirer of Napoleon and was nicknamed "The Little Napoleon." Posted to the U.S. artillery, he was a staff officer with General Winfield Scott in the Mexican War where Beauregard won two brevets and was wounded at both Churubusco and Chapultepec. At the outset of the Civil War he resigned his captaincy in the engineers and offered his services to the South. He was placed in charge of the South Carolina troops in Charleston, South Carolina, where he won the battle for Charleston Harbor and was hailed throughout the South. Later he was ordered to Virginia where he commanded the forces opposite Washington and created the Confederate Army of the Potomac. As one of the heroes at the first battle of Bull Run, Beauregard was named a full general. Regardless of his military successes he was in conflict with President Davis and was sent West as Albert Sidney Johnston's second-in-command.[8]

Anderson would report to General Daniel Ruggles at Corinth. Fifty-one-year-old Ruggles was a West Pointer (1833) from Massachusetts. Marriage into a Virginia family linked him with the South. He too served in the Seminole and Mexican wars. In the early months of the Civil War he commanded along the Rappahannock River and was named a brigadier general and ordered to New Orleans and then sent to Corinth.

The question of whether the Confederates should wait for the Federal forces or advance upon them had to be decided. General Francis A. Shoup of the artillery reported, "Our generals understood this but there was a question on the military capacity of Commander Sidney Johnston. Johnston's loss of all that region from Bowling Green, Kentucky, to the

Mississippi line had set the Southern newspapers howling to such an extent that Johnston wanted to resign his command; his movements were open to serious criticism. We patched up a curious expedient. They got General Bragg appointed chief of staff, with plenary powers. Bragg accepted upon condition that he should retain immediate command of his own corps. A plan of operation was worked out by General Beauregard, and we were to attack and surprise the enemy at once."

April 3 — Thursday morning the Confederate forces were in readiness to begin a forced march from Corinth toward Pittsburg Landing, twenty miles away. Narrow country roads were ill suited for the movement of 40,000 men, horses and caissons. Rain fell Friday, making it slow going for all over the rutted, muddy roads. Marching all day on the Monterey Road, Anderson's tired Confederates reached their assigned position on the Savannah Road. The rain stopped and the evening air turned cool. A late officers' meeting was called at the commander's tent near the Mickey farmhouse. Here they learned from General Bragg of the next day's attack on the Federal forces encamped about Shiloh Meeting House. Hardee's corps would form the first line of attack, followed by Bragg's corps. Ruggles's division would constitute the left of Bragg's line, touching on Owl Creek. Anderson's brigade would be used as division reserve, positioned several hundred yards behind Ruggles's line.[10] Heavy rain spoiled the Rebel advance on Saturday.

Anderson took his brigade off the Savannah Road and moved through the woods toward Owl

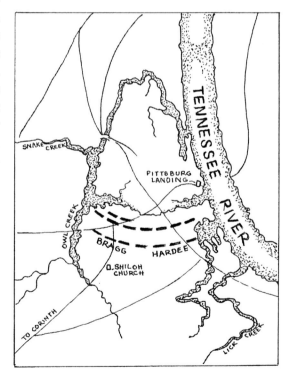

Shiloh — Pittsburg Landing

Creek, bivouacking 270 yards behind Ruggles. Early on Sunday, April 6, skirmishing by the Confederates surprised the bluecoats at breakfast, encamped near the small Methodist log church named Shiloh, a Hebrew word meaning "place of peace." The scattered Confederate forces were slow to fall in line because of the rough terrain and dense underbrush. Finally, long lines of Confederates, screaming the menacing "Rebel yell" appeared when Hardee's first wave of 10,000 men came running against the Union right followed by Bragg who had deployed his forces 1,000 yards to the rear. Among Bragg's forces was Ruggles's division containing Anderson's brigade.

Although the avowed battle plan was to strike the Union left flank, a haphazard, make-yourself-useful policy was being used by the command. Many of the battles in Tennessee and Kentucky can be likened to Indian warfare, a hide-and-seek in the dense forest. Bragg, when asked which way the fighting front was, indicated that the best way to find it was to follow the sound of the cannons.[11] General Hardee's attack was stalled by the resistant Federals as they came awake to the situation. Anderson's infantry came up by 8:30 A.M.

Anderson slowly moved his men forward over the rough terrain toward the enemy positions. He closed to within 300 yards of Hardee's line but halted until the proper interval could be regained. Fierce rifle

1st Florida at Shiloh

fire reverberated through the woods as Bragg ordered the advance to resume. Despite Anderson's efforts and those of the other commanders, the southern movements were uneven and uncoordinated. Rough ground separated the men, and there were wide gaps between the brigades. Anderson led his force against the first Union camp without support, and was forced to halt his men temporarily when he realized this dilemma. When two other brigades appeared, he swept forward again. A swamp lay between Anderson and the Union force; surrounding the swamp were dense thickets which made it difficult to maintain formation. Ignoring these obstacles, Anderson pushed into the swamp with Russell's brigade supporting his right. In the deep, nearly impassable swamp, many men lost their way and Anderson's command emerged badly scattered. Before order could be restored, a Union battery opened fire and Anderson was driven back. Reforming his men, Anderson renewed his advance, now with reinforcements on his right. The Federals slowly moved back as Anderson and his men pushed through the enemy camp.

Anderson continued to assault the Union right. Troops to his right wavered as if they might fall back, but realizing the danger, Anderson began waving his hat so his troops would easily see him as he rode across the front line. "This gesture seemed well understood," he said, "and the command 'Forward' which it implied was most gallantly executed." The Confederates surged ahead, and Anderson's force overwhelmed a battery. He then wheeled his brigade to the right, and captured another portion of the Union line in flank.

Anderson withdrew from the front around noon as the fire around him slackened and the Union right retreated toward Pittsburg Landing. He wanted to rest his men and replenish his ammunition, but as he was withdrawing he received orders from Bragg to "go wherever the fight is thickest." Anderson accordingly marched his force to the right, where Union soldiers held out against a succession of Confederate assaults in what became known as the Hornets' Nest.[12]

The entrenched division of Union General W. H. L. Wallace, which was posted along a ridge under cover of heavy thicket and supported by heavy artillery, had throughout the early afternoon unflinchingly held its ground, repelling with great slaughter every Confederate infantry attack made upon it; these frontal attacks appeared almost suicidal. This Federal salient became known as the Hornets' Nest because the concentrated fire of minie balls made a sound like thousands of buzzing bees.

At approximately 3:00 P.M., the 3rd Kentucky, late of Trabue's brigade, advanced with Anderson's brigade east along the Pittsburg Road "to the point where the firing seemed heaviest," Duncan Field. They took up a position in the center of the field with Stewart's brigade on their right and Cleburne's brigade on their left. From there they participated in the final assaults against the collapsing Hornets' Nest.

At 4:00 P.M. the 3rd Kentucky, temporarily under Anderson's command, mounted the Confederates' final unsupported assault of the day against the Hornets' Nest. Ordered to make it through the thickets at the south end of Duncan Field and the open field beyond as quickly as they could, the 3rd Kentucky rushed past the mangled piles of wounded and dead from previous assaults. They were met with a blinding hail of musketry followed by deadly pinpoint blasts of canister and deadly accurate howitzer blasts that decimated their ranks.

Anderson's brigade, in some disorder now, had to fight its way back to Confederate lines. Anderson, shouting encouragement to the troops as he rode among them, rallied the Kentuckians as they withdrew to the

Sons of Confederate Veterans have constructed an authentic replica of the Shiloh log church as it stood in April 1862.

safety of Ruggles's massed artillery positioned in the woods at the east end of Duncan Field.

General Ruggles ordered all Confederate field guns that could be collected from the left and right to be assembled as rapidly as possible. On the left was Captain S. P. Bankhead and to the right was Major F. A. Shoup, who for some time had been massing and collecting artillery pieces. A total of sixty-two guns was assembled, mostly of the six-pounder and twelve-pounder howitzer type. With a range of about 500 yards across an open field, both artillery groups began firing around 4:30 P.M. It thundered as round after round roared and went sailing into the Hornets' Nest. The howitzers quickly neutralized the Hornets' Nest, inflicting great casualties on the Unionists. General Wallace was mortally wounded,[13] and General B. Prentiss surrendered his 2,200 survivors of the division.

Altering their position somewhat, Anderson, with the command "Forward," again led his brigade and the exhausted 3rd Kentucky across Duncan Field to the vicinity of a log cabin and a few bales of cotton, dislodging the enemy near the road on the extreme left side of the field. Here the 3rd Kentucky, still a part of Anderson's makeshift brigade, saw the Federal colors lowered and a white flag of surrender raised over the sunken road where they had fought so gallantly.

After the Federal surrender, the 3rd Kentucky, with the rest of the Confederate forces fresh from their victory at the Hornets' Nest, pursued the fleeing Federals toward the banks of the Tennessee River and Grant's last desperate line of defense. There they came under the fire of the Union gunboats *Tyler* and *Lexington*. During the waning moments of daylight they rejoined the rest of Trabue's brigade, falling back farther to the destroyed Union camps of the 6th Iowa and 46th Ohio near the Owl Creek Bridge on the Purdy Road. There they stayed the night in a driving rainstorm, recounting the deeds of the day, while feasting on the vast quantities of foods abandoned by the previous occupants of the camps.[14]

SECOND ARMY CORPS.

Major General BRAXTON BRAGG

Second Brigade

Brigadier General PATTON ANDERSON

1st Florida Battalion:

Major Thaddeus A. McDonell

Captain W. G. Poole

(SECOND ARMY CORPS.)
Captain W. Capers Bird
17th Louisiana, Lieut. Colonel Charles Jones
20th Louisiana, Colonel August Reichard
9th Texas, Colonel Wright A. Stanley
Confederate Guards Response Battalion,
Major Franklin H. Clack
Washington (La.) Artillery, 5th Company,
Captain W. Irving Hodgson

Anderson made bivouac near Bragg's headquarters and spent most of the rainy night rounding up stragglers and reorganizing his brigade. He ate with his men and slept under an apple tree with his saddle for a pillow and a blanket over his head. During the night, thousands of Union reinforcements arrived and Grant decided to attack in the morning. Soon after dawn, Anderson and the other brigadiers moved their commands to the front to meet the Federal counterattack. The Confederates stubbornly contested their hard-won ground, and the Union advance was cautious. As the Confederate right weakened, Anderson was sent to strengthen it. There he observed that Federal artillery was playing havoc with the exposed Southern infantry. He wanted to charge the battery and silence it but could get no support from nearby troops. Angrily, he withdrew his own men over a small hill to protect them somewhat from the destructive fire. While thus sheltered, he rallied scattered fragments from other commands to meet the impending Union advance. When the Federals cleared the crest of the hill over which he had withdrawn, Anderson's men inflicted heavy casualties, and the Union advance was temporarily checked. As the afternoon wore on, the Federals continued to push the weary southerners back. The tide of battle turned against the Confederates, and Anderson noted that "large numbers of stragglers could now be seen in all directions making their way to the rear." The men were exhausted, disorganized and nearly out of ammunition. About 3:30 P.M. Beauregard ordered a withdrawal. Anderson's men joined the march down the muddy roads to Corinth. The route was crowded by long lines of wagons filled with wounded soldiers and as the army marched, a torrential downpour added to the misery of the men.[16]

The two-day battle at Shiloh Church or Pittsburg Landing became a bloodbath for the inexperienced soldiers and officers who were making

---

Organization of the Confederate Army at the battle of Pittsburg Landing, or Shiloh, Tenn., April 6–7, 1862.

ARMY OF THE MISSISSIPPI.

General ALBERT SIDNEY JOHNSTON.*
General G. T. BEAUREGARD.

FIRST ARMY CORPS.

Maj. Gen. LEONIDAS POLK.

FIRST DIVISION.

Brig. Gen. CHARLES CLARK.†
Brig. Gen. ALEXANDER P. STEWART.

SECOND ARMY CORPS.

Maj. Gen. BRAXTON BRAGG.

ESCORT.

Alabama Cavalry, Capt. Robert W. Smith.

FIRST DIVISION.

Brig. Gen. DANIEL RUGGLES.

First Brigade.

Col. RANDALL L. GIBSON.

1st Arkansas, Col. James F. Fagan.
4th Louisiana:
    Col. Henry W. Allen.*
    Lieut. Col. Samuel E. Hunter.
13th Louisiana:
    Maj. Anatole P. Avegno.‡
    Capt. Stephen O'Leary.*
    Capt. Edgar M. Dubroca.
19th Louisiana:
    Col. Benjamin L. Hodge.
    Lieut. Col. James M. Hollings-
    worth.

Second Brigade.

Brig. Gen. PATTON ANDERSON.

1st Florida Battalion:
    Maj. Thaddeus A. McDonell.*
    Capt. W. G. Poole.
    Capt. W. Capers Bird.
17th Louisiana, Lieut.Col.Charles.Jones.*
20th Louisiana, Col. August Reichard.
9th Texas, Col. Wright A. Stanley.
Confederate Guards Response Battalion,
    Maj. Franklin H. Clack.
Washington(La.)Artillery,5th Company,
    Capt. W. Irving Hodgson.

Third Brigade.

Col. PRESTON POND, Jr.

16th Louisiana, Maj. Daniel Gober.
18th Louisiana:
    Col. Alfred Mouton.*
    Lieut. Col. Alfred Roman.
Crescent (La.) Regiment, Col. Marshall J. Smith.
Orleans Guard Battalion, Maj. Leon Querouze.*
38th Tennessee, Col. Robert F. Looney.
Alabama Battery, Capt. William H. Ketchum.

---

* Wounded.	† Killed.	‡ Mortally wounded.

OR Series I, LII
Part I, p. 27

[15]See note for complete roster of Army of the Mississippi

their maiden fight. At the end of the second day, a large number of brigades on both sides had melted away. Commanding General Albert S. Johnston, while leading a Confederate force on the battlefield, received a gunshot wound in the lower leg; not realizing it was lethal he continued riding and bled to death.

The ranks were decimated. The Federals had 1,754 killed, 8,408 wounded and 2,885 missing out of 62,682 effectives; the Confederates lost 1,723 killed, 8,012 wounded and 959 missing out of 40,335 effectives.[17] This armageddon was a precursor of the next three years for Anderson and the other patriots who fought for the cause. Yet the survivors of such carnage seldom lost heart. The southern scornful eye of contempt for death was displayed in a poem of the soldiers:

> "We went to church last Sunday week, didn't we?
> Yes, to Shiloh Church
> Well, I'm not going anymore. I don't like the
> Sermons they preach."

A cynical General U. S. Grant would later write: "Shiloh was a high price to pay for a country church and a steamboat dock."[18]

This was Anderson's first big battle. Of his performance at Shiloh, Bragg wrote: "General Patton Anderson was among the foremost where the fighting was hardest, and never failed to overcome what resistance was opposed to him. With a brigade composed almost entirely of raw troops, his personal gallantry and soldierly bearing supplied the place of instruction and discipline."[19]

After the stalemate at Shiloh, President Davis called for more Confederate reinforcements to confront the accumulation of Union forces before them who were threatening the heartland of Dixie. Corinth became a rallying point for a greater Confederate army. General E. Van Dorn came across Mississippi with his Army of the West; General E. Kirby Smith sent all forces he could spare from East Tennessee; and General J. C. Pemberton sent a considerable number of men from the Carolinas. The aggregate number increased to over 50,000 effective grayclads ready to fight for the cause. The Federals, with the arrival of General J. Pope's forces at Pittsburg Landing now numbered 110,000 Unionmen now under the command of General W. H. Halleck. General Beauregard ordered the Confederates to prepare a semi-oval fortified line, covering Corinth to the northeast; and in front of this, up to where the Mobile & Ohio Railroad crossed the Tennessee line. The works stretched for three miles.

Anderson's Mississippi legislature colleague, General T. C. Hindman, was appointed a major general to command General Ruggles's division as the latter assumed administrative duties. This change lasted but a few days, as Hindman was transferred to Arkansas as commander of the Trans-Mississippi Department, leaving the open division command to devolve upon Anderson since he was senior brigadier.

The cautious General Halleck began moving his assemblage of bluecoats from Pittsburg Landing, entrenching as they moved ever so slowly. The distance from Pittsburg Landing to Corinth was approximately twenty miles, which the Confederate forces had marched in two days. However, the Union forces under Halleck moved at a snail's pace, taking almost the month of May to get to the defenses placed around Corinth. One cause of the delay was the poor road. Another cause was the Confederate engineers, who had ingenious and deadly ploys for the unsuspecting Yankees.

The farmhouses the blue devils loved to loot were often booby-trapped. They had to beware of bread left on the table, as it may has been poisoned. Barrels half full of cornmeal or potatoes in the outer buildings may have had strings and levers attached which exploded a torpedo if moved. The engineers planted live shells with fuses attached in the roads leading to town, and in houses, buried them in the parapets, cisterns, etc. If time permitted on a retreat, "Large uncultivated fields which stretched on both sides of the road, along which and in the field were small heaps of fresh earth at intervals. These heaps were also in the middle of the road. The heaps of earth were thought to be planted torpedoes by the Confederates. It would take the Union artillery men hours to turn these over to be sure they did not have a live shell."[20] Stopping and starting a large army takes time.

Even though the Corinth position was strong, Beauregard pondered whether the permanent fortification was of much value as 100,000 bluecoats crept forward. He knew of Halleck's advance but did not have enough cavalry to bother the crawling mass of men, horses, wagons, artillery pieces and sutlers.

The cunning Beauregard was also on the alert for a chance to strike a blow at any fraction of Halleck's forces that got itself separated from the main army. "Early in May he thought he had this chance. One of Halleck's generals, John Pope who just had a major success at New Madrid and Island #10 and the advance on Memphis, had joined Halleck and was advancing at a faster rate than his commander, pushing his troops forward toward Farmington, about four miles east of Corinth, where a swampy area divided him from the nearest Federal force. Beauregard quickly formed a plan to trap Pope. While troops from Bragg's corps attacked Pope in front, General Earl Van Dorn was to get on his left flank. In a pre-attack proclamation to the troops, Beauregard emphasized that for the first time the Confederates were to meet the Federals in strength. 'Soldiers, can the result be doubtful?' he asked. 'Shall we not drive back into the Tennessee [River] the presumptuous mercenaries collected for our subjugation?' The attack in front was delivered in time by Anderson's forces but Van Dorn was unable to get into position and Pope retired to safety. Later in May, Pope advanced again to Farmington, and once again Beauregard tried to spring his trap. The outcome was the same disappointment as before. The attack in front was effective but Van Dorn, although he informed Beauregard that he felt like a wolf and was going to fight like one, could not get his men in place."[21]

There are fragmented accounts of this Rebel maneuver.

Anderson's division was at Shope's Hill, four and a half miles from Corinth, an outpost on the Monterey Road.[22] General Pope's advance forces approached the village of Farmington. On May 8, Van Dorn, with Anderson's brigade included, marched out of the Confederate works and formed a line north of the Memphis & Charleston Railroad. This movement resulted in severe fighting between the forward units of Pope's forces. Afterwards, Anderson reported of Colonel D. J. Brown's regiment, which was in its first field service: "A large portion of the

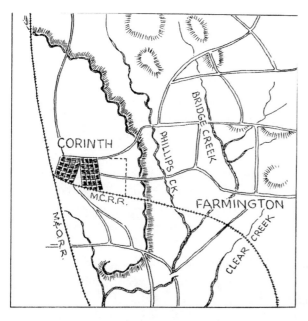

Farmington disappointment

Thirty-sixth Mississippi Regiment, although never having formed a line of battle or heard a hostile gun before, behaved with that gallantry and spirit which characterized the troops of that chivalrous State on every field. When advancing under fire their eagerness was such as to require restraint rather than urging forward."[23] Skirmishing continued on May 10 and 12. On the eighteenth, Van Dorn's division, again with Patton Anderson's forces, were ordered to the line of battle; on the 20th of May the grayclads drove the bluecoats off the Monterey and Purdy roads, with additional skirmishing at Widows Serratt's and Phillip's Creek.[24]

May 25 — On Sunday, General Beauregard called a council of his generals to discuss the situation and decide on the army's strategy. An offensive was impossible, as Halleck's Union forces had closed in too tightly, and to remain in Corinth and try to withstand a siege or be flanked would be hazardous. Men, horses, wagons, equipment and ammunition were jammed together in their locations. Limited and poor drinking water, imperfect sanitation and swarms of flies made the situation worse, resulting in disease and death spreading quickly through the encamped army. Upwards of 20,000 men were on the sick list.[25] It was agreed to abandon Corinth and move the army to Tupelo, Mississippi, where there was good water and a defensive line could be fronted by the Tupelo Swamp.[26] Commencing the night of May 29, General Beauregard, with great skill and efficiency, pulled his Confederate army out of besieged Corinth. The immense Federal army under Halleck sat a few miles outside the town to the north, oblivious to the strategy going on so short a distance away.[27] That evening the Confederate bands sounded retreat, tattoo and taps. The old trick of Quaker guns, made of wood and stuffed patties of straw for gunners, was employed along the lines. The next morning advances made by Federal forces and their cannonading had no response of any kind. The Confederates had skedaddled. After more than a month's posturing by both sides, the important rail and road center at Corinth was given up to Halleck's forces without a shot.

VI

Invasion of Tennessee and Kentucky, the Great Railroad Move, and the Battles of Perryville and Stones River

Anderson recalled: "I commanded a division in the retreat from Corinth till we reached Clear Creek, near Baldwyn, where I was taken ill with fever, and Major General Sam Jones was assigned the division. I rejoined some weeks later at Tupelo, and was given command of a brigade in Sam Jones's division."[1] General Beauregard, reaching Tupelo on the 9th of June, turned his command over to General Bragg and returned to Mobile. Bragg began reorganization by assigning General William J. Hardee as commander of the Army of Mississippi.

The departure of Beauregard and assignment of Hardee would further Anderson's military proficiency. His first instructor was Braxton Bragg, followed by P. G. T. Beauregard, and now Hardee, a premier general in the western theater. This Georgian graduated in 1838 from West Point. Soon thereafter he was directed to proceed to France for a year's study at the Royal Cavalry School at Saumur. The school, founded by Louis XV in 1768, was located in the town of Saumur, seventy-five miles southwest of Paris. Accompanied by Washington Irving Newton and Captain Lloyd J. Beall (later the only commandant of the Confederate Marine Corps), "the officers were to complete the course of instruction offered at Saumur in one year and, upon their return, were to introduce French practices into the American service, thereby modeling the cavalry service after that of France. The year spent at Saumur had a significant impact on Hardee, as it broadened his military perspective and it showed him the weaknesses inherent in a rough, semi-trained, semi-disciplined citizen army, such as the United States possessed."[2]

Hardee served in the Seminole Indian War, and in the Mexican conflict he won two brevets and was wounded at La Rosia, Mexico. He was a member of the Aztec Club that was formed at that time. Thereafter he was a tactics instructor. He published a cavalry tactics manual (*Cavalry Tactics*), which became the standard textbook for the services and was widely used by both sides during the Civil War. Joining the Confederacy, his assignments to date included: colonel of cavalry; brigadier general, commanding the Upper District of Arkansas; major general, commanding the Central Army of Kentucky; and now the commander of the Army of the Mississippi. In the recent action he was wounded at Shiloh and led his corps during the defense of Corinth.[3]

While Bragg's forces encamped at Tupelo, the huge Union army began to be broken up in June. Some forces were assigned to Grant and Sherman, who began to move toward central Mississippi; others were sent to the army of Don Carlos Buell, who began moving south and east along the Memphis & Chattanooga Railroad, toward eastern Tennessee and possibly Chattanooga. The possible loss of Chattanooga by the Confederates would be calamitous, as it would cut the Confederacy in half by severing the line of communication and supply between Richmond and Atlanta. Only the small force of General E. Kirby Smith in east Tennessee, which lacked sufficient manpower, might curtail Buell's activities.

For General Bragg to move to Chattanooga and join with Smith's army, he would have to move his 30,000 men, horses and artillery from Tupelo across northern Alabama to Chattanooga, a distance of over four hundred miles by land. That would be a formidable undertaking since he did not control the railroad and would be in the presence of General Buell's Federal cavalry.

The innovative General Bragg devised a dramatic alternate plan for a swift movement east to Chattanooga. Returning General Van Dorn's independent command to Vicksburg, and leaving General Sterling Price to guard Grant's movements, Bragg on the 21st of July began sending the horse-drawn elements of his army, i.e., the artillery, cavalry, engineers, supply trains — east across Alabama under the protection of Forrest's and Morgan's cavalry. Their presence helped to slow Buell's advance. General Bragg next instructed General Hardee to move the 30,000 men and officers by railroad to Chattanooga with all possible haste. Energetic Hardee, always exacting in the performance of his duties, appointed a military superintendent of railroad, who alerted all railroad lines that the army would need every passengercar, boxcar, and flatcar that could be pressed into service.

The plan was to move the army from Tupelo to Mobile, Alabama, across the bay by steamboat, then north to Chattanooga, a distance of 776 miles via six different railroads.[4] Relying on the capabilities of the iron horse, a division was sent on a trial run of the route. They made the trip to Chattanooga in six days! Thus would begin one of the largest and longest Confederate troop movements of the war by rail. Based on the amount of rolling stock available, a plan was worked out to dispatch one division every two days, starting on July 23.[5] On boarding, each soldier was supplied seven days' cooked rations, with additional supplies available at the many railroad stations along the way. Troopers arriving at Mobile were ferried across the bay by steamboats and up the Tensas River to the rail yards of the New Alabama & Florida Railroad that carried the cheering and singing forces to Montgomery. From there the Montgomery & West Point Railroad transported the troops to Opelika, Alabama, thence to Atlanta, Georgia, where they boarded cars on the Western & Atlantic Railroad for the last leg of the 700-mile trip to Chattanooga.

The flow of troops was well organized. Anderson and his brigade, plus Yancy, boarded at Tupelo on July 25, riding along with General Hardee for the seven-day rail trip.[6] The leading units of the army began entering Chattanooga on July 27. Within ten days Bragg's four divisions had arrived, completing the feat and reshaping the war in the West because of the potentialities of the railroad. Bragg's command acquired a new name, the Army of Tennessee.[7] The army was divided into two wings, totaling about 28,000 men; General Polk's wing consisted of the divisions of Cheatham and Jones Withers, while General Hardee's wing contained Simon Buckner and Patton Anderson's divisions.[9] Patton had been returned to his old division as General Sam Jones was assigned to Chattanooga.

On the move, Hardee picked up Company B, 3rd Florida Infantry Regiment stationed at Mobile. General Hardee was married to a St. Augustine lady and welcomed his friends, who immediately broke out their flag: white lettering on a blue background herald, "ANY FATE BUT SUBMISSION." It was a gift from the ladies of St. Augustine, Florida.

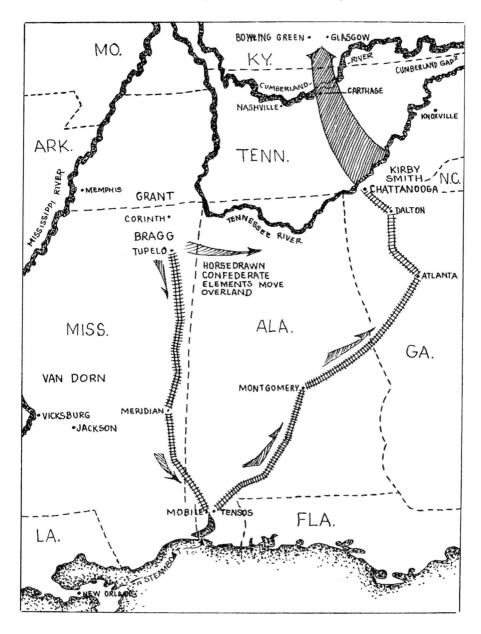

Movements of Bragg's army from Tupelo, Mississippi, to Chattanooga, Tennessee.[8]

The Invasion of Kentucky

August 1862 — Generals Bragg and E. Kirby Smith arranged a conference where they concurred that while Bragg waited for the balance of his cavalry to arrive overland, Smith's forces would wait until a combined movement of the two armies could join in the invasion of Kentucky. Scarcely a week after the meeting, General Smith decided not to cooperate with Bragg; instead he moved his forces out and, by bypassing the Federals at Cumberland Gap, invaded Kentucky first, securing Richmond and Lexington, and then capturing the state capital of Frankfort on September 3.

General Bragg's army delayed moving out until the artillery and wagons came in to Chattanooga. On August 16 elements of his command began crossing the Tennessee River, and on August 28 both his wings started over Walden's Ridge, bypassing the Federal forces at Murfreesboro and Nashville. They moved along the Sequatchie Valley to Pikesville and from there the Rebels made a night march over a large arm of the Cumberland Mountains to Sparta, Tennessee.[10] At Sparta, Anderson had a chance to write to Etta.

> *Sparta Tennessee*
> *September 7th, 1862*
>
> *Dear Et,*
> *Today being Sunday and the men and animals tired from the toilsome march across the mountains — we rest. But will proceed tomorrow in the work of redeeming Tenn. and Ky. Thus far everything has worked well. Kirby Smith's and Lee's success with our advance movement has caused Buell to "change his base." I believe he will back into Ohio or Indiana.*
> *I am quite well — suffered some with my ear for two or three days after I left you but for the last forty-eight hours have not felt it at all. Indeed my general health has improved. We have had no rain yet, consequently the dust is very suffocating on the march; but have reached a region of cornfields, clover patches — running water, all of which rejoices the heart of both men and beast.*
> *I believe all of our Monticello boys are well. I saw D. Williams yesterday; he has stood the march finely. I write in great haste at Colonel Beard's board in the open air and have no time to elaborate.*
> *Kiss the dear boys, Willie, The & Pat. Much love to Aunt. I wish you were here in this region somewhere. We meet no Union people this side of the mountains.*
>
> *Your Patton*[11]

After the layover at Sparta, the Army of Tennessee turned northwest toward Carthage. Once across the mountains they brushed by McMinnville, threatening it with Hardee's wing, which at times moved in an extended formation, with Buckner's and Anderson's divisions sometimes ten miles apart.[12] The army crossed the Cumberland River on September 9 and 10 at Carthage with Hardee's wing, while Polk's wing crossed the river farther east, all the time advancing without tents and with a limited food supply. Days of marching, climbing and road cutting over mountains supposed to be impassable brought the mighty Army of Tennessee to Carthage. On September 14 Bragg's entire army, footsore and tired, rested at Glasgow, Kentucky. The invasion was real and Federal General Buell knew it. On Monday, September 15, the bold Kirby Smith's forces appeared before Covington, Kentucky, on the Ohio River, across the river from Cincinnati, Ohio, but retired rapidly.[13]

Even though General Bragg's field army met with initial gains in capturing Munfordville on September 17 and occupying Bardstown on September 21, the Confederate forces were scattered over north-central Kentucky. General Buell, having received reinforcements from the midwestern states, began his advance upon the dispersed Rebels from

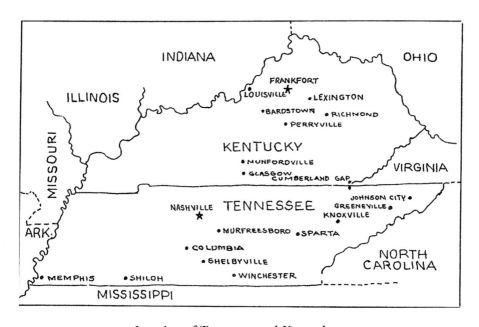

Invasion of Tennessee and Kentucky

Louisville with 60,000 troops marching in four columns. The main body of General Buell's force marched so as to converge towards General Polk's army, which was in the vicinity of Bardstown. In addition, as a feint to draw attention away from his primary target, General Buell sent two divisions east advancing toward General Kirby Smith at Frankfort.

In response to this latter move, Bragg ordered Polk to march his force to Frankfort, Kentucky, in support of Kirby Smith's position and hit Buell's flank. However, General Polk's cavalry informed him differently, i.e., two-thirds of Buell's army was actually marching toward Perryville, southeast of Bardstown. When Polk's cavalry confirmed this movement, the general decided to disregard Bragg's order. He called a council of war with his generals to discuss the situation. When Anderson heard of Polk's plan to disobey Bragg's orders, he objected.

Anderson later explained that failure to comply with Bragg's orders could be disastrous since it could upset his friend's strategy.[14] Nevertheless General Polk convinced Anderson to go along with the majority view, and ordered an immediate movement toward Perryville. Anderson's division camped at Salt River between Perryville and Harrodsburg, Kentucky.[15]

October 7, 1862 — General Hardee placed his 16,000 Confederates in a concave line facing west between Perryville and Doctor's Creek. Most of the line was covered by Hardee's wing as it gave them command over all the ground suitable for fighting.

General Simon Buckner's division protected the extreme right of the battle line; two brigades of Anderson's division, Dan Adams and Sam Powell, were placed across the Springfield Road, while General B. F. Cheatham's division guarded the left. Later in the afternoon General P. Smith's brigade of Cheatham's division was added to Anderson's division.[16]

General Buell did split his army. Two divisions went to Frankfort to battle Kirby Smith's forces, while he retained 37,000 Federals to advance on Perryville. Marching in the wilderness and forest without proper roads, it was difficult for Buell's forces to arrive at the same time at Perryville. Added to the long march were unusual autumn heat and the want of water by both men and beasts. After thirty-six hours the bluejackets became desperate for water. Upon learning there were shallow pools of water in the bed of Doctor's Creek, a tributary of the Chaplin River northwest of Perryville, they hardly could be restrained from reaching the area.[17]

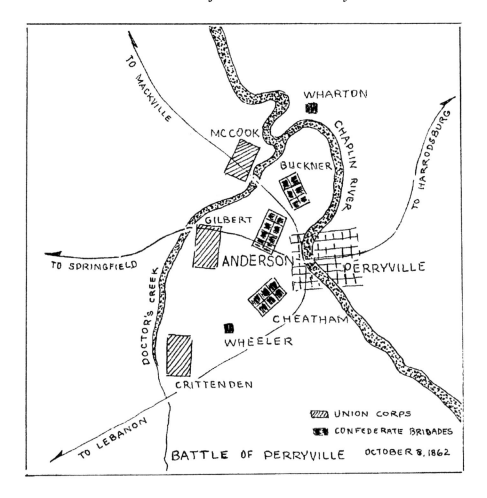

TO MACKVILLE

WHARTON

MCCOOK

CHAPLIN RIVER

TO HARRODSBURG

BUCKNER

GILBERT

TO SPRINGFIELD

DOCTOR'S CREEK

ANDERSON

PERRYVILLE

CHEATHAM

WHEELER

CRITTENDEN

TO LEBANON

UNION CORPS

CONFEDERATE BRIGADES

OCTOBER 8, 1862

BATTLE OF PERRYVILLE

Battle of Perryville[18]

Before daybreak the Union men began skirmishing as they tried to secure the water supply. Bragg, arriving on the scene, ordered his forces at Doctor's Creek to bring on a quick engagement by attacking the enemy. Anderson's brigades would be in the center of the advance, and by early afternoon his brigades were lined up, with elbows touching to the right, in order that their lines might be unbroken.[19] Advancing across Doctor's Creek in full force and ascending the bluffs on the west side, Anderson found the Federal forces positioned behind rail and stone fences. Phil Sheridan's division was in Anderson's front with L. H. Rousseau's division off to the right. Anderson's frontal assault became a desperate close-quarter fight as the graybacks advanced, leapfrogging from stone fence to rail fence to stone fence endeavoring to claim the bluff. Federal forces were on high ground but in haste had left unguarded a depressed area which exposed both Sheridan's and Rousseau's flanks. Anderson, with one brigade, kept Sheridan's men occupied to the front while General Bushrod Johnson's brigades kept the left flank threatened, thus preventing the two Union forces from assisting one another.

Companies of butternuts began pouring through the open space,[20] forcing the weary Lincoln men into panic and fleeing for their life. Replacements moving up from the rear found the badly cut-up corps which had retreated a mile. The Federals filled ranks, rallied and slowed the anxious Confederate assault with artillery and musketry fire. Although General Buell's headquarters was only two and a half miles away, he did not know until 4 P.M. of the battle that had reached its peak at 2:30 P.M. Two corps commanders likewise did not realize until late in the day that the Union army was under heavy attack. This was due to atmospheric phenomenon by which battle noise was not heard back of the lines (acoustic shadow). Consequently only nine Union brigades were engaged in the battle, while fifteen others were within supporting distance. Likewise, parts of Bragg's army were still in the Frankfort area. It was a disjointed engagement where parts of Buell's army battled portions of Bragg's army. Anderson had barely managed to hold his own against Sheridan's numbers and guns in the afternoon, while his compatriots had poured through the open gap. Now in the time still remaining at sunset, fighting flared up again and Anderson found himself heavily outnumbered by reserved divisions that had come up from the rear to Sheridan's support. Together with Sheridan's forces they counterattacked, forcing Anderson to retreat steadily toward Perryville. Aided by the lateness of the long day and darkness, Anderson secured the army's flank at Perryville. The battlefields were a ghastly scene of dead and wounded men. The Federals had 845 killed, 2,852 wounded and 515 missing. The Confederates had 510 killed, 2,635 wounded and 251 missing. The ferocity of the battle and the news of large bodies of Union forces approaching Perryville led General Bragg to call a council with his generals who, upon learning of General Buell's overwhelming forces, agreed with Bragg that Perryville should be abandoned and a junction formed with General E. Kirby Smith. By midnight the Confederate forces began pulling back their lines. There was no victory here for either general.

The Confederate army joined General Smith's forces at Harrodsburg on October 8. The lateness of the year, a three hundred-mile supply line from his home base and failure to secure any aid from Kentuckians or gain support for the cause brought about Bragg's decision to abandon General Smith and Kentucky. "Bragg succeeded in getting away with the largest amount of provisions ever obtained by an army. He brought out 15,000 horses and mules, 8,000 beeves, 50,000 barrels of pork, and 1,000,000 yards of Kentucky cloth. It was said Bragg's train of wagons was forty miles long."[21]

The Return to Tennessee

After the army had rested for a while, the tired foot soldiers with their long train of captured ordnance and other supplies began pulling back on Monday, October 13. The army would again have to traverse mountains, cross rivers and march three hundred miles, re-entering Tennessee on October 26. Anderson noted the route: "We returned from Kentucky through Cumberland Gap, Knoxville, Chattanooga, Bridgeport to Allisona in Franklin County where I visited for the first time in many years the grave of my father at Craggie Hope. From Allisona the army proceeded to Shelbyville where they halted for ten days, and then to Eagleville, where in December, my division was broken up and I was assigned to the command of a brigade in General J. M. Withers's division of General Polk's corps, the brigade formerly under the command of General Frank Gardner."[22]

Back in Tennessee General Bragg began preparing to make an advance on Nashville, which was occupied by two Union divisions and surrounded and contained by small Rebel forces which never made any effort to recapture the capital. In the East, President Lincoln apparently disagreed with General Buell, who blamed his commanders for the Union failures at Perryville, Lincoln discharged Buell and replaced him with General W. Rosecrans, who, determining to hold Nashville, ordered General G. H. Thomas to push towards the capital. By the middle of November General Thomas marched to the relief of the garrisoned capital, bringing with him reinforcements and much-needed provisions. Feisty Bragg, reacting to the Federals' move, began moving his corps north to join General J. C. Breckinridge at Murfreesboro, thirty miles southeast of Nashville.

President Davis on his western inspection tour reviewed General Bragg's army at Murfreesboro on December 13 and was favorably impressed. At the same time he dealt Bragg a serious blow by insisting on the transfer of General C. L. Stevenson's division of close to 10,000 men to reinforce General Pemberton at Vicksburg.[23] With the approach of the Christmas season it was obvious that the position at hand would prevent anyone from returning home. A clever observation was made that the Union and Confederacy had begun splitting into "eastern and western" theaters of war. "In the battle of Virginia, a Southerner really had some people to hate, some real humdingers. There you had Yankees and those foreigners from New York, babbling away in strange tongues — they weren't even Americans yet. And then you had those New Englanders who were so righteous and bloodless, all they wanted to do was to tell other people how to lead their lives. But in Tennessee it was mostly farm boys fighting farm boys now. On the Union side the young soldiers came mainly from small Midwestern farms, from homes and communities that were similar to those who fought on the other side. They were not firebrands of liberation. They weren't wading into the slaughter to free slaves and make democracy work. Any number of reasons — there had been some criminal insurrections, mischief by the Southerners, and they were coming to get them and to have some adventure, and to wear a uniform and shoes and shoot a gun. Here they looked alike, talked alike. They both knew about milking cows and slopping hogs. Any number of reasons, now misted over by time, made those farm boys from Indiana, Ohio, and Illinois slough through the Tennessee mud to disembowel the 'Secess.' And what infuriated the graybacks was that they were walking right over our own God-given property."[24]

December 26 — Rosecrans, "Old Rosy" to the men of the Army of the Cumberland, began moving his army in the direction of Murfreesboro, believing that if he could clear Bragg out of the town, he could secure his supply line and eliminate future threats from the Rebels until spring. Due to the rough terrain and muddy roads it took Rosecrans's corps four days to cover the thirty miles to Murfreesboro.

Bragg, hoping to destroy the enemy, used the days of Rosecrans's slow advance to plan the coming battle. With 38,000 seasoned veterans, he began deploying them along a four-mile front arching inward, about one and a half miles west and northwest of Murfreesboro, with his lines covering and blocking the Nashville Pike, plus covering the winding Stones River which passed behind his forces.[25]

December 27 — As the Union men approached, "Fighten Joe" Wheeler's cavalry contested the advance with skirmishing at Jefferson, LaVergne, Rock Spring and Nolensville.[26] Orders were issued to move at an early

THE BATTLE OF STONE'S RIVER.

CONFEDERATE FORCES.

	KILLED.		WOUNDED.		MISSING.		TOTAL.
	Officers.	Men.	Officers.	Men.	Officers.	Men.	
Third Brigade.							
Brig.-Gen. E. C. Walthall (Brig.-Gen. J. Patton Anderson commanding).							
45th Alabama, Col. James Gilchrist....	0	13	5	66	..	7	91
24th Miss., Lt.-Col. R. P. McKelvaine .	0	8	5	103	..	..	116
27th Miss., Lt.-Col. James L. Autry....	2	9	5	66	..	1	83
29th Miss., Col. W. F. Brantley and Lt.-Col. J. B. Morgan	4	30	14	188	..	..	236
30th Miss., Lt.-Col. J. J. Scales.......	6	57	10	136	..	..	209
39th North Carolina (temporarily attached on the field), Capt. A. W. Bell.	1	1	3	33	..	6	44
Barret's Mo. Batt'y, Capt. O. W. Barret.	0	..	..	4	..	..	4
Total	13	118	42	596	..	14	783
Fourth Brigade.							
Brig.-Gen. J. Patton Anderson (Col. A. M. Manigault commanding).							
24th Alabama........................	1	19	3	92	..	3	118
28th Alabama........................	1	16	11	77	..	11	116
34th Alabama........................	0	11	6	71	..	..	88
10th S. Carolina....................	0	16	6	85	..	2	109
19th S. Carolina, Col. A. J. Lythgoe ...	1	7	8	64		..	80
Waters's Battery, Capt. D. D. Waters..	0	1	..	5	..	..	6
Total	3	70	34	394	..	16	517

hour the next morning and form a line of battle. Leaving their canton-
ments on the outskirts of Murfreesboro the Confederate brigades marched
in the cold December rain, finally drawing up in line of battle at right
angles with the Nashville Pike. Cheatham and Withers's divisions were
on the front line with their right resting on Stones River. Westerly from
the river J. M. Withers's four brigades, J. R. Chalmers, A. M. Manigault,
J. Q. Loomis, and Patton Anderson were placed. The right was Breckinridge's division extending east from Murfreesboro to Readyville and the
left was Hardee's division of Cleburne and McCown, extending *twenty
miles* west to Eagleville. Anderson was placed in temporary command of
E. C. Walthall's brigade because of the general's sickness and because
Anderson had commanded these troops before in March.[27]

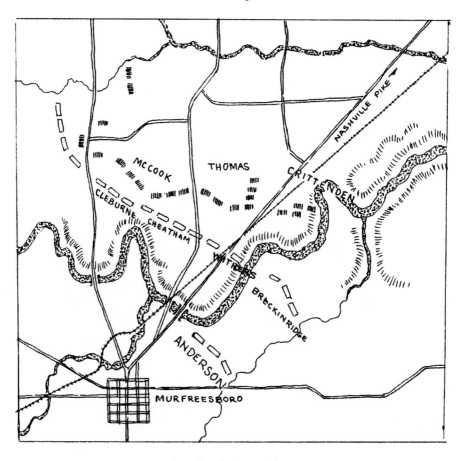

Battle of Stones River

December 29 — Rifle pits and earthworks were thrown up in the rain to protect the Confederate cannoneers and horses from the Yankee sharpshooters while the regiments in the cedar forest erected temporary breastworks of stone. Light skirmishing began this day, and on the thirtieth the skirmishers became more hotly engaged by the buildup of personnel on both sides. Then came a simultaneous movement of Union troops on several roads that convinced Bragg this was a general advance by Rosecrans's forces.

December 31, 1862 — The battle of Stones River. At 4 A.M. the roll of musketry and artillery from both sides greeted the last day of 1862, announcing that a storm of a battle was commencing as Bragg's forces struck at daylight. The butternuts were irresistible as they charged in close columns, heads down, with a front several ranks deep. This immense charge caught the Yankees cooking and eating breakfast with rifles stacked. The Union men attempted to fight but could not stop the fierce onrush of Confederate gray, forcing the Northerners to flee in panic. By 10:00 A.M. Bragg's army had shattered an entire corps of Rosecrans's army across a four-mile area, and by noon the Union right was doubled back at right angles. If only the last of "Old Rosy's right could be pushed aside, all would be well for Dixie."[28]

"This defiant, crucial and challenging Union position which had to be taken was a salient at the left center of Rosecrans's line, which was on a slight rise just east of the Nashville-Murfreesboro Pike. It contained a four-acre clump of trees called the Round Forest. Rosecrans realized its crucial importance and placed every available brigade he could spare at that point and backed them up with massive artillery on the high ground back of the Round Forest."[29]

Riding front, Anderson led his brigade forward with the rest of Withers's division. Opposite them were three Union batteries' strongly supported infantry. Anderson's orders were to take the batteries at every cost.[30] Crossing an old cotton field in the rain, his soldiers rushed forward with their accustomed yell, striking the Federals on the flank. Their ranks were greeted with grape and canister and were woefully torn apart in minutes. Time and again terrific fire checked Anderson's advances. Despite his losses from massed artillery, Anderson rallied his determined men as they raced toward the well-positioned corps of General G. Thomas.[31] Calling for and receiving reserves, Anderson rallied a second time to sweep over the second Federal line and drive the weary Union defenders through the cedar forest onto the Nashville Pike, despite his brigade's suffering a frightful slaughter. The Federal forces abandoned their ground, retreating westward, back on the main body of their troops, where their position was strongly protected by the cover of their artillery. Despite this, the objective of the charge — to dislodge the enemy from its position in the Round Forest — was not gained.[32] Even the color bearers were shot.

"The Thirty-fourth Illinois was the first regiment that felt the Rebel assault; it was immediately in front of the right regiment of [Matthew] Ector's brigade. The Confederates steadily advanced, and the Thirty-fourth not giving way, came to hand-to-hand fight in many instances. When the Tenth Texas dismounted cavalry of Ector's brigade came close to their line, the color-bearer of the Thirty-fourth waved his flag, urging his regiment to charge the enemy. The gallant men responded; they fought but a score of feet from the butternuts with all the might and fury of brave soldiers. Singularly enough it so happened that the flag of the Tenth Texas was immediately opposite that of the flag of the Thirty-fourth Illinois, and the color-bearer of the Texas regiment jumped forward, seized the flag of the Thirty-fourth, while the brave Illinoisian grasped that of the Texas regiment. Instantly a struggle ensued between the men, each filled with desperate valor to save his own, and take the enemy's flag. Suddenly shots fired by the color-guard of each regiment struck the opponent's color-bearer to the ground; quickly new men sprang forward to seize the treasured emblems, and again and again the men fell dead or wounded, till the last color-guard was disabled; at this moment the Illinois regiment was forced to retreat to avoid capture. No blush of shame need rest on the regiment whose flag was lost when so ably defended."[33]

By this time Anderson's men were almost out of ammunition and were permitted to retire from the field as other Confederate forces elsewhere appeared to have won the day from Rosecrans. Anderson reported: "The Mississippians behaved most gallantly as they have always done in this war. They took nine pieces of artillery but lost many of their best officers and men. The casualties for the brigade of killed and wounded on this last day of the year totaled 732."[34]

The last day of the year 1862 belonged to the Confederates. Toward day's end the Union troops were in full retreat. "The Confederate troops were too full of enthusiastic zeal, and our own troops too much discouraged, to keep up this unequal contest for a long time. All of R. W. Johnson's division fell back, fighting here and there, where fences or rocks permitted them to make a stand, until, more like a mob than organized troops, they reached the Meccas of the retreat — the Nashville Pike; while others ran like madmen through the timber. The Rebel cavalry, being ordered in pursuit of our extreme right, began to shell them and then charge. Our infantry was speedily overtaken by the Rebel cavalry. Officers too brave to run, or who tried to rally their men — though in vain — were ordered to deliver their swords; while hundreds of soldiers, bewildered, and not knowing in which direction to turn to reach our line, were taken prisoners and quickly sent to the enemy's rear."[35]

1863 — Second Day's Battle at Stones River

January 1, 1863 — The first day of the great fight at Stone's River decided nothing except that both commanders had failed to carry out their respective plans. The two armies remained on a par in strength despite being equally exhausted. If either was to be crushed, the work must be begun anew.

General Rosecrans formed a new battle line overnight; when General Bragg got up on New Year's Day and found the Union army still in position, it was a great disappointment, as he had imagined he had won the battle the previous day. This Union determination proved very disconcerting to Bragg.[36] No significant fighting occurred on New Year's Day, and Anderson was not engaged. Rosecrans's new line on rising ground west of the Nashville Pike and facing southwestward, was observed by the Confederates. Fresh Federal troops, 12,000 strong, had been added and on the crest of a knoll, Rosecrans was gathering his artillery in heavy masses. What was not obvious on that cold January 1 was that Rosecrans was preparing to resume the offensive and had sent General H. P. Van Cleve's division to seize the heights upon the east side of Stones River and plant batteries there, thus threatening the town of Murfreesboro. This movement was unopposed and apparently not discovered until the next morning, January 2, when the Federal batteries began to enfilade the whole of General Polk's front divisions and it became necessary for General Bragg either to storm the position or remove his army. By early afternoon, where the Nashville Pike crosses Stones River, a large mass of gray troops could be seen moving rapidly from the east side of the river toward the west, aiming their rifles at the smoke of the Federal artillery. It was General Breckinridge with 4,500 Confederates, entrusted with an attack on Van Cleve's elevated position. Advancing under galling fire with no time to mourn the fallen comrades they found, the bluecoats concealed themselves in sinkholes, hid behind rocks and in the thick forest.

"What a carnival of death followed! What a deafening noise all around! Cheers here; yells there. Suddenly the ground shook as if rocked by a fearful earthquake, and the fifty-eight cannons emptied their double-shotted contents on this living human mass in front of them; but a few seconds intervened, and again and again the fifty-eight cannons spread death into Breckinridge's men; while Negley's regiments quickly rose up when the enemy reached the opposite bank of the river, and from the crest of the hill poured forth a terrific fire. The enemy halted. The yells, the cheers, of the pursuing Rebels grew fainter and fainter, and at last ceased. Look at them! See how many throw up their arms; see how they fall over; and the large gaps in this mass of men where the shells and canister plough through it; look at the quivering bodies, at the streams of life's blood flowing from a thousand wounds! It was a scene that made the heart sick, and touched a spring of sympathy in the souls of all, though the men that were suffering and dying were enemies, and would gladly welcome us to bloody graves."[37] Breckinridge's men fell by the hundreds; under raking fire his lines faltered, then quit, leaving 1,700 men killed or wounded on the field.

About 4 P.M., Anderson received orders to cross Stones River and support Breckinridge's brigades; Anderson pushed his men forward and found Breckinridge's ranks disoriented and retreating as he reached the field. He threw forward a line of skirmishers to halt any Federal advance.[38] "I was sent to reinforce Breckinridge on the right, who had been roughly handled that afternoon by superior numbers. We reached the scene of conflict about sundown, and after the heaviest fighting was over, in time, however, to have several officers and men of our skirmish line severely wounded. By interposing a fresh line between the victorious enemy and Breckinridge's shattered columns, gave time for the latter to rally and resume a line they had held in the morning."[39]

"Breckinridge, leaving Anderson, rode back to his line to inspect the remnant of his brigades. He grew increasingly angry as he witnessed the results of Bragg's attack order. Tears broke from his eyes when he beheld the little remnant of his own brigade. Over 500 Kentuckians had been lost in the attack. Unable to contain his sorrow, Breckinridge exclaimed, 'My poor orphan brigade! They have cut it to pieces.' The general's unwitting sobriquet caught on. Thereafter the men in the command would always be known as the Orphan Brigade."[40]

Major E. T. Sykes, adjutant general of Anderson's brigade in the absence of General Walthall, quoted at length in the history of Walthall's brigade a sketch of Breckinridge's movement after the battle in the afternoon of January 2.[41] "That night General Anderson reported through me in writing to General Withers that he could find no line to support, that there were no Confederate forces, save his own picket line, in his immediate front."[42] Breckinridge and his troops had just made a glorious fight, and on being repulsed and in falling back they did not rally and form on the line designated, but formed further to the rear than ordered to, thereby leaving Anderson's brigade front and flanks uncovered and exposed to the enemy.[43] The Anderson report was forwarded to General Withers and then to General Bragg at corps headquarters in Murfreesboro. While Anderson and Sykes were sitting astride a log with the capes of their overcoats thrown over their heads as a protection from the cold and drenching rainfall, a courier rode up and delivered an order. It directed General Anderson or his assistant adjutant general to report to the army headquarters without delay. Owing to the precarious condition of affairs, Anderson did not deem it prudent to absent himself from the brigade, and directed Sykes to accompany the courier.

"Following the courier for several miles we finally drew up in front of one of the finest mansions in Murfreesboro, and on entering and making myself known, I was invited into a large drawing room, elegantly furnished, and where sat General Bragg, surrounded by his corps and division commanders. Besmeared with mud, and tired from exposure and loss of sleep, I felt decidedly out of place in this galaxy of generals. General Withers, rising and introducing me as Anderson's adjutant, invited me to be seated. After a few words responsive to the pertinent questions propounded to me on Anderson's report, I realized that General Bragg was satisfied and convinced of the accuracy of the statements obtained in said written communication."[44]

In addition to Anderson's report, other details of the battle were aired, such as that General Breckinridge ordered his infantry forward without any assurance from the cavalrymen themselves that they would cooperate. Also, the general misused his artillery by instructing it to move forward only after the infantry had taken the enemy position. Bragg also criticized the way the attack was delivered, also charging Breckinridge did not fight as well as he should have.[45] This affair gave rise to much bitter feeling between Generals Bragg and Breckinridge.

Anderson's forces remained on line of battle during the day; many, however, were sent to the rear on account of sickness caused by fatigue and exposure during the past six days and nights. It rained all day on the 3rd, and at times so violently that fires could not be kept up and blankets and clothing were wet, and the cooked rations were in a condition not at all inviting even to a half-famished soldier. "I received an order from General Withers to withdraw my command. At 1 o'clock in the morning of January 4, my command moved right in front, following the rear of [Gideon] Pillow's brigade until we reached the public square in Murfreesboro, where I rejoined Withers's division."[46]

Stones River was rising dangerously because of the rain, thus the pullback to Murfreesboro. Documents captured by Wheeler's cavalry told General Bragg that the Federals now numbered 70,000 and reinforcements were still coming. Bragg called in Polk and Hardee and they decided on a quick retreat. The Confederate troops retreated in a downpour. Fittingly. Heads bowed, homespun soaked, many ill, many more maimed, the Confederates departed Murfreesboro, leaving 2,000 patriots behind who were too badly wounded to move.[47] Patton's brigade of 1,800 had 119 killed, 584 wounded, and 63 missing.[48]

Bragg's official report stated that Patton Anderson's brigade encountered the enemy's troops close upon the Confederate artillery which had been left without support. "This noble brigade under its cool and gallant chief drove the enemy back, and saved all the guns not captured before its arrival." The general further stated: "Anderson deserves special mention, for coolness, judgement, and courage with which he interposed his brigade between our retreating forces and the enemy, largely superior to him, on Friday evening (January 2nd) and saved our artillery."[49] As it was, the battle seems less clearly a Federal victory than the battle of Shiloh. Offensively it was a drawn battle, as looked at from either side. General Anderson thought it was a victory.

General Anderson reports: "In endeavoring to give a simple statement of the part taken by the troops (Walthall's brigade) under my command in this great engagement, the capture of several batteries has been mentioned in passing. I have abstained from making a statement of the number or kind of pieces taken, for the simple reason that I did not stop to count them or examine their caliber. The 27th, 29th and 30th Mississippi, all participating (but the 30th suffering more severely than the others), captured a battery, of from four to six guns, near a log cabin in the edge of the cedars, on the right of the Wilkerson pike, and not far from a well used by the enemy in procuring their water on the night previous to the battle. This battery included a small iron rifled piece, somewhat detached from, and a short distance to the right of the other pieces, and lay in front of the 29th Mississippi, which took it. In the log cabin, and strongly supporting the battery, was a company of sharpshooters, all captured by the 27th Mississippi.

"Farther to the left was a battery, nearer the Wilkerson pike, from which the enemy was driven by the 24th Mississippi, supported by the 45th Alabama. Some 15 or 20 prisoners were here captured at the pieces.

"Another battery was posted still farther to the left, and nearer the Wilkerson pike, close by which the left of the 45th Alabama (my left regiment) passed simultaneously with the right of Colonel Manigault. This battery, however, was silenced a few minutes before we reached it—I think by one of our batteries playing from a direction where I supposed Colonel Manigault's left to be."[50]

Many officers were West Point trained, others such as Anderson were not. But it was amazing. In less than twelve months Confederate forces, first organized from local militia and volunteers, then trained and supplied, became small state armies which matured into the Army of Tennessee. The flexibility of the southern generals, such as Patton Anderson, to lead men with these ethnic and sectional backgrounds, was remarkable as they were assigned and reassigned from one division or brigade to another. The comfort of the familiar when faced with the enemy invoked a spirit of cooperation among them in winning and losing battles because they were all fighting for the same cause.

Case in point was Anderson commanding G. E. C. Walthall's brigade in Wither's division of Polk's corps at the battle of Murfreesboro. Anderson took over Walthall's Brigade of Mississippians because Walthall became ill. Likewise, General Jones M. Withers, former mayor of Mobile, Alabama, and who commanded at Shiloh and Perryville, was taken ill and took a thirty-day leave of absence to Mobile, leaving Anderson in charge of the division.

Despite these added duties, Anderson had time to write letters to Etta.

VII

Love Letters and Poetry

Winchester, Tennessee
January 8th, 1863

Dear Et,

  I telegraphed you from Shelbyville two days ago that I was well. It
was the first opportunity that I had after the battle of the 31st, Dec.
Again, I have had much to be thankful for. While so many were killed
and wounded, I escaped without a scratch. You will wonder why I am
here, after such a victory at Murfreesboro. Well, I do not know that I
can give any satisfactory reply to the inquiry. On Sunday night (the
3rd) after lying in the trenches in rain and mud for *nine days* and fighting more or less all the time with but little opportunity to cook and eat,
the men were in such an exhausted condition that it was thought best
by our Generals to fall back to where our baggage and provisions had
been previously sent, to wit, to this place. We arrived here last night
and will return to Shelbyville this evening or tomorrow. The troops are
now resting and cooking rations. I am commanding Walthall's Brigade
in Withers' Div., of Polk's Corps. It is composed of the 24th, 27th,
29th, 30th, and 27 Miss and 45 Alabama. All except the 39th you will
observe, are my old troops. When my Division was broken up, a portion assigned to Hardee and the rest to Polk, I fell to the latter. At the
same time Col. Walthall of Miss. was promoted to Brigadier and was
given to Miss. Regiments to command. I was assigned to a Brigade
composed of three Ala. And two S. Co. Regiments. The day before the
battle Genl. Walthall was taken quite sick. The Mississippians petitioned for me to command them in the fight. Their petition was
granted. So I commanded them in the fight and will continue to do so,
till Genl. Walthall's recovery. They behaved most gallantly as Mississippians have always done in this war. They took *nine* pieces of artillery
but lost many of their best officers and men. One Regiment alone (the
30th) had 62 men killed and 132 wounded on one acre of ground, just
in front of the enemy battery. This is, I believe, the heaviest loss of any
one Regt in any one fight of the war. The others lost many, but not so
many as the 30th. The total loss of killed and wounded in the Brigade
(none missing) was 732. About 216 more than any other Brigade in the

fight. The victory was a great one, though I am afraid its whole moral effects will be lost by our falling back. We took altogether about five thousand prisoners. 31 pieces of artillery and any number of colors, wagons, mules, horses, etc. I see by the papers that the Tennesseans did *all* the fighting!!! That they took the batteries etc. the very ones which the Mississippians charged. Well, they may have taken them, but it was after my Brigade had driven the enemy from his guns and were *pursuing him two hundred yards* in *advance* of the Tennessee troops!! Who will ever be able to write a *truthful* history of this war?

The Floridians were not in the main fight of the 31st. They are in Gen. McPreston's (of Ky) Brigade. They were in the fight of the evening of the 2nd Jany. when Breckinridge on the right attacked the enemy, left and was *repulsed* with heavy loss. My Brigade was ordered over to his support late in the evening, but not in time to prevent the *rout* which had begun *before* I got there. I formed a line between them and the enemy, which enabled our officers to rally their men while night put a stop to pursuit by the enemy. Of this however, you need not speak. The Floridians lost but a few. I cannot hear of any casualties among our acquaintances except St. John Bailey who was wounded; how severely I could not learn. My informant could only tell me that it was not a dangerous wound.[1]

I recd a letter from Aunt Ellen a day or two before the battle dated the 17th Dec. in while she said you were writing at that time. Yours has not yet been received. I wrote her a short note not to comply with Mr. Hogues requests, nor to make any acknowledgment of indebtedness to Cheever on account of the land etc. I fear my letter to her and yours to me had a *collision* somewhere between Murfreesboro and the places while everything there was being sent back here so rapidly. Perhaps they will turn up after a while.

I don't know when I can get home. The campaign here proposed to be an active one; Genl. Bragg is more unpopular with this army than ever since he fell back from a victorious field. The victory was a much more decisive one than that at Perryville, but I doubt if we reap any of its fruits beyond the artillery and other captured property which we brought away. But all of that and much more would not repay us for the loss of four or five thousand gallant men.

I do want to see you and the boys badly. Kiss them all a thousand times for me. Willie and The and Pat, bless their souls; and they must each kiss you for me also. Love to Aunt. I believe I wrote to you that Uncle Tome Monroe was dead. He died at Mr. Hardins about a month ago, so Genl. Breckinridge tells me. Love to Mol and her Gals. Remember me to all the servants especially Charles and Aunt Ann, Rebecca and Alice. The boys are all well and send howdys.

Tell Harry I saw Willie on the day of the fight. He had two horses killed

under him but was not hurt himself. I never saw him looking so
well.

Here's a thousand kisses from

Your
Patton[2]

Shelbyville, Tenn.
Jany 11th 1863

Dear Et,

I wrote you a few days ago from Winchester and remarked that I
expected to return soon to this place. A few hours after I wrote, I was
placed in command of Withers' Division in Polk's Corps, and ordered
to return to Shelbyville. Genl Withers has gone home sick on thirty
days leave of absence.

I have little to add to what I wrote before; am quite well, comfortable
fixed in a house, and the citizens appear anxious to do all they can to
contribute to our comforts. Genl. Cheatham is in command of the
Corps. I can give no further particulars of the battles near Murfreesboro, having been on the march and counter march ever since we
left there; and it has been raining nearly all the time. Today however,
the sun shines out brightly, looking more like spring than mid-
winter.

We do not expect another battle in this region this winter. We take
Duck River as a line of defense, and feel confident that Rosecrans, in
his badly shattered condition, will not, nay cannot advance upon us.
Indeed I think it more probably that they cannot advance upon us.
Indeed I think it more probably that our Cavalry under Morgan, For-
rest, Wheeler, and Wharton will so harass him, in his position about
Murfreesboro, that he will find it necessary to fall back to Nashville
before the 1st March.

In assigning me to the command of Withers' Division, Genl. Bragg
intimated that it was to be a permanent thing, though I do not desire it
or expect it really. I would prefer the Brigade of Mississippians, which I
had in the Murfreesboro fight to any Division in the Army. It is true, it
composes a part of the Division, but the other Brigades are not at all
like it. Their conduct on the field has reflected additional luster upon
the arms of their state, and has won for me the position now assigned
me. Alone and unassisted they took nine pieces of artillery and brought
them off the field. I do not calculate on a Major Generalship for the
reason that there are already as many as there are Divisions for them to
command. Love to Aunt Ellen, I wish I could spend a month at least
with you all, about this time. I think the *peace plot* thickens at the
North; God grant it may come speedily and honorably to us. Kiss

Willie and The and Pat for me. Remember me to the servants. A bushel of kisses for yourself from

Your

Patton

Several weeks later, Etta joined Anderson at Shelbyville, and shed additional light on the Breckinridge incident by inserting a note of her own in her husband's autobiography: "*I was up at the army when the Breckinridge incident was going on. You heard it everywhere by friends and enemies. All gave the brigade and General Anderson credit for all that Generals Bragg and Robertson claimed for them. There is no use talking— General Breckinridge was drunk at the battle and had his men cut all to pieces.*" General Bragg would not stand drinking in any of his officers. Mrs. Anderson's account of General Breckinridge's inebriation was taken from eyewitness reports.[3]

Controversy about the battle of Murfreesboro continued to swirl about the camp as others said that General Benjamin Cheatham was slow in moving forward to aid Cleburne. Braxton Bragg reported that Cheatham was so drunk on the field all the first day that a staff officer had to hold him on his horse.[4] An eyewitness in Company K of the 6th Tennessee Infantry Regiment told a friend that "at the beginning of the battle of Murfreesboro while his troops were standing in line waiting for orders to move, General Cheatham rode out in front and in attempting to wave his hat to make an appeal to his Tennesseans, rolled off his horse and fell to the ground as limp and helpless as a bag of meal — to the great humiliation and mortification of his troops. It was Christmas, John Barleycorn was general-in-chief. Our generals, and colonels, and captains, had kissed John a little too often. They couldn't tell our own men from the Yankees."[5]

— BOOZE IN BATTLE AND BIVOUAC —
Just before the battle, Mother,
I was drinking mountain dew.
When I saw the Rebels marching
To the rear I quickly flew.
(A parody of George F. Root's immortal
Just Before the Battle, Mother)

Discussing the subject of tipsification in the armed forces during the Civil War where excessive drinking was undoubtedly common, it is a fact that hard drinking was common on both sides. According to George W. Adams, author of *Doctors in Blue*, "Alcohol was the sovereign remedy of the Civil War, rivaled only by quinine. Bourbon and brandy was prescribed by the medical officers for everything imaginable, from bites of rattlesnakes, to combat malaria, as a substitute for brackish drinking water, as a stimulant after periods of unusual exposure to dampness or of excessive hardship, to counteract shock and as an appetizer for convalescents. Primarily it was used as a prophylactic against the fear of battle and death. Whiskey and beer were readily available in almost every town and hamlet and easily found its way into the army via the sutler's wagon. Generals Braxton Bragg and George B. McClellan, both noted as blue-nosers (non-drinkers) led the fight against the use of whiskey and its demoralizing effects. Bragg claimed that over half of the courts-martial cases in his army rose out of drunkenness and complained that his army had lost more valuable lives at the hands of whiskey sellers than by the ball of the enemy. When the war was over Bragg further wrote that 'whiskey was a great element in our disasters.'"[6] Patton Anderson was not one of the "boozy brigadiers."

On March 18 General Withers returned from Mobile and resumed command of his division. Anderson then took command of J. R. Chalmers's Brigade of Mississippians. "It contains many of my old Mississippi acquaintances and friends — and at their solicitation Chalmers made a parting request to General Withers that I should command them."[7] The army settled into winter quarters around Shelbyville and Wartrace and would remain there for six months. As Anderson noted: "General Bragg is more unpopular with this army than ever since he fell back from a victorious field," meaning Stones River and Perryville. While here, General Joe Johnston was sent out by Jefferson Davis to investigate and report upon the operations and discipline of the army. He found both satisfactory, and so reported.[8] Others disagreed.

"A soldier on Bragg's staff said Bragg seemed sick and despondent and was an old, worn-out man, unfit to continue to actively manage an army in the field. Bragg admitted that he had been suffering from a siege of boils [on the backside] that culminated in a general breakdown. He claimed he had recovered, but Hardee considered him too feeble either to examine and determine his line of battle or to take command in the field."[9] Bragg had little talent for field command but was an excellent organizer and disciplinarian. Higher-ranking officers also thought that the president should have appointed Bragg inspector general or chief-of-staff of the Confederate armies. "One of the great ironies of Confederate military history is that Jefferson Davis, who prided himself so on his knowledge of the capabilities of those former regular army officers who fought for the South, failed early in the war to assign Bragg to a position where his talents could be best used."[10] Even more cruel were the remarks by Senator James Orr of South Carolina: "The President's attachment for General Bragg could be likened to nothing else than the blind and gloating love of a mother for a deformed and misshapen offspring."[11]

"Referring to newspaper criticism of commanders in the field, which was contributing to Bragg's early retirement from active command, General Robert E. Lee remarked, 'We made a great mistake in the beginning of our struggle, and I fear, in spite of all we can do, it will prove to be a fatal mistake.' On being asked what mistake he referred to, the general replied: 'Why, sir, in the beginning, we appointed all our worst generals to command the armies, and all our best generals to edit the newspapers. As you know, I have planned some campaigns and quite a number of battles ... but, when I fought them through, I have discovered defects, and occasionally wondered I did not see some of the defects in advance. When the battle was over I found by reading a newspaper, that these best editor generals saw all the defects, plainly from the start. Unfortunately, they did not communicate their knowledge to me until it was too late.'"[12]

The same ostracism fell upon Union generals as well. *The Examiner* in England on March 15, 1862, could find little praise for the Union Army and General Grant after his splendid victory at Fort Donelson: "The success, it appears, was achieved without generalship, at a great sacrifice of life that generalship would have saved. Here again, one Northern regiment fired into another, of fellow combatants who ran for miles in panic; and the captured Rebel officers laugh at the stupidity of General Grant, who, they say, with a single field-piece, planted in a particular spot, could have prevented the escape of Generals Floyd and Pillow."[13]

During the extended encampment of the army around Winchester, there was a flow of letters between the Andersons. One time he wrote, "*I received a letter from you in five days after it was mailed from Florida.*" This was wartime Confederate mail service and not too bad.[14] As was the custom in this period of time, and if you could afford to do so before the summer heat, "make an exodus from Florida's miasmic climate, considered to be all right for men and mules, but hell on women and horses."

An outbreak of smallpox in Monticello prompted Anderson's concern: "*I do fear the fatiguing effects of any trip upon you and the children as well as the exposure to small-pox would be too much. Has the vaccination taken properly on three of the children? By all means do not let them stir from home till they have been vaccinated and it properly taken.*" When Etta was satisfied it was safe to travel, she made arrangements for herself and the boys to come up from Florida and join Anderson at Shelbyville. A quick reply from the general: "*The very thought of seeing you so soon makes me wild with delight. I have been so fortunate during this war, and have so much to be thankful for that I can hardly hope for this crowning act of good fortune, but I will hope. And here's a long, long kiss for Et from — Your Patton.*"[15]

Leaving Monticello, Etta and the children traveled by train and buggy to reach Shelbyville, much to Anderson's delight. They resumed their family life in a house! "*Our boys dressed in Confederate uniforms that had been cut down to their size, and their father instructed them in the manual of arms outside their tent.*"[16] During these months the Andersons became acquainted with other officers and their families and attended parties and reviews staged by the various encamped army cadre.

Two of their new acquaintances were Edward and Mary Walthall. Edward was born at Richmond, Virginia, on April 4, 1831. At a young age he was moved to Holly Springs, Mississippi, where he received his academic education, was admitted to the bar in 1852, and practiced law in Coffeeville. Walthall was twice married. His first wife died within a year after marriage, leaving no children. His second wife, to whom he was married in 1860, was Mary L. Jones of Mecklenburg County, Virginia. He entered the Confederate service in 1861 and was made a field officer. He fought at Mill Springs and then was made colonel of another regiment. He was at Corinth and in the Kentucky campaign. On the evening of December 27, 1862, Bragg assigned Anderson to the temporary command of Walthall's brigade because Walthall was ill and had returned to Virginia. Anderson commanded the brigade at Murfreesboro. Walthall sufficiently regained his health and returned to the army at Shelbyville on January 17, 1863, where he found awaiting him his commission as brigadier general.

There were common denominators between the two generals. Both were Mississippian, neither had attended West Point but were generals, and each had married young, attractive women. "Mary, from the day she made her first visit to 'My Edward' at Camp Autry, near Shelbyville in

February, was a constant and indispensable integral part of her husband's brigade, and shared with him his honors. She considered their camp her home, and each member of the brigade as a part of her household."[17] Of course the women had servants and their homes were well guarded, so they naturally were free to socialize, but the best thing was that they were with their true loves.

The spring passed without any major engagements, and the brigades rotated monthly with others in performing outpost duty on the principal roads leading from Nashville.

Each army remained in the same vicinity facing each other, their fronts about thirty miles apart, Rosecrans at Murfreesboro, Bragg at Shelbyville and Tullahoma. Things were not quiet as each general began to have his cavalry raid behind the other's lines in hopes of cutting one another's communications and supply lines. Railroad bridges, trestles and rails were destroyed; stations, cars and engines were demolished as the cavalry expeditions on each side became almost campaigns. "In warfare of this kind the Confederates had the advantage, as their cavalry was more numerous and better trained. With them Bragg had set his heart upon starving his antagonist (Rosecrans) into retreating."[18] These cavalry battles were very energetic and resulted in a steady loss of life as well as in disrupting food and forage supplies.

In this interval both Union and Confederate forces were parked facing each other for months; this naturally led to espionage and intelligence gathering by both sides. Under the guidance of General Ulysses S. Grant, a Union spy network in the western theater was established and put in action by his generals, including Rosecrans. Most of these spies were civilians who provided the generals with information on Confederate numbers, positions and terrain maps. One such operative within Bragg's lines was Pauline Cushman, a member of a traveling theater company, whose attractiveness gained her invitations to accompany Confederate officers within their lines. She soon became the darling of the troops. Her performance and fact gathering was successful until wiser heads became suspicious of her actions and a surprise search revealed secreted notes and papers — she was a Yankee spy. Taken to Bragg's headquarters, Cushman was quickly court-martialed and then sentenced by an insensitive Bragg who told her coldly, "You'll be hanged — that's all." The hanging was to be in ten days; however, the sentence was delayed because Cushman was in ill health, or so she claimed.

By May 1863, Generals Pemberton and Johnston, the hard-pressed defenders of Vicksburg, tried to get back their cavalrymen they had sent to General Bragg earlier in the year but were refused their due. A timid and cautious Rosecrans asked for, and received, more men so that by the beginning of June he had built up his army to 87,000 effectives. The tide of war in the East had surged back and forth for over a year in Virginia and Maryland and now found General Lee preparing to invade Pennsylvania. President Lincoln, in order to dissuade the Confederates from sending any forces to the aid of Johnston or Lee, ordered "Old Rosy" to move immediately on Bragg's army at Tullahoma and Shelbyville. The Andersons would be moving with the army.

As the siege of Vicksburg progressed towards its fatal close, and with the Mississippi River in possession of the Federals, Rosecrans was free to move toward Tullahoma without fear of exposing his flank and rear. Moving in full force on the 24th of June, Rosecrans commenced a series of feints with a view of creating the impression of a main advance on Bragg's center in the direction of Shelbyville while he would strike a rapid march to the right of Bragg's forces and move on Tullahoma. It did not take the experienced Bragg long to realize he was being flanked; he ordered a retreat via Sewanee and Jasper, crossing the Tennessee River below Chattanooga, Tennessee, a small frontier town of 5,000 inhabitants. The importance of Chattanooga was its strategic location in the mountains; it was the center of great railroad lines radiating in every direction to the Mississippi, the Ohio, the Atlantic Ocean and the Gulf of Mexico. By the first week of July Bragg occupied Chattanooga and established headquarters for the Army of Tennessee. In nine days "Old Rosy" had driven the Confederates from middle Tennessee without a battle.[19] He also picked up twenty-eight-year-old Pauline Cushman, who was forgotten by Bragg's officers. Her execution was never carried out and she lived to write a book, *Life of Pauline Cushman.*

In actuality, Bragg was in no condition to face Rosecrans. By this time the general knew of the tragic events going on in the other Confederate theaters of war. Vicksburg had surrendered, throwing the whole Mississippi Valley into chaos. Joe Johnston and his Army of Relief were trying to save Jackson, Mississippi. Because of Sherman's overwhelming numbers of bluejackets, Johnston was in retreat trying to preserve his dwindling defenders. In the East at Gettysburg, Pennsylvania, the army of General Lee had been defeated in a three-day battle, and it was now across the Potomac River facing the possibility of a move by the Federals on Richmond, Virginia. And so General Bragg sat in the middle of the country, pretty well convinced he would receive little help from any source.[20]

On this move Anderson and his brigade were ordered southwest twenty-eight miles to the town of Bridgeport, Alabama, for observation of the Union's movement. He was located in the vicinity of where the Nashville and Chattanooga Railroad crossed the Tennessee River.

July 30 — At Taylor's Store, Alabama, Anderson advised General Polk, "At a point about two miles south of this place on Sand Mountain a fine view of Stevenson, Alabama, and the surrounding country may be had. With a signal station at this point on Sand Mountain and another here, the commanding officer could be daily advised on the Union's movement at Stevenson. I would suggest that the Signal Corps supply such a station."[21] Such a signal tower was right on target.

With ten corps and in mountains that defy description, Rosecrans approached Chattanooga slowly. Once he left his home base he had to support himself by the railroad running from Louisville through Nashville to the front, a very long line for their supplies. In addition the Tennessee River was of no use, as it was not navigable for ships of war or supply. Although the most direct approach to Chattanooga was through Therman and over Walden's Ridge, "Old Rosy" chose an alternate route — through Bridgeport and Stevenson.[22] Beyond Anderson's reconnaissances, Rosecrans's corps made no demonstrations until late August when his forces began arriving and seemed to loom everywhere. Within the radius of *ten* miles there were 70,000 Federals and 43,000 Confederates awaiting the conflict.

This was the most difficult country in which any commander would ever attempt to do battle. A series of parallel mountain ranges, hard to climb and penetrable only through narrow defiles, was in everyone's way. Some mountains were 100 miles long, with bold crests nearly 3,000 feet above sea level, with steep palisades more than 1,400 feet over the swift and cold Tennessee River. From its summit, parts of seven states could be seen. The area bore a similar relation to that held by the mighty Alps of Switzerland. The forest of huge trees was so thick that you could hide an army in it. And that's what each commander did. There would be no marching to battle here; instead, Indian tactics would be used to immobilize the superior forces of the enemy by sudden acts of harassment. Cavalry would be of little help and artillery little better than a burden.

General Anderson informed Bragg that a large column of blue infantry was moving down Sweden's Cove toward Jasper. The Federals began crossing the Tennessee River by a pontoon bridge constructed a short distance above Bridgeport and Shellmound. Unlooked for in this epochal movement of both armies were dear Etta and Mary Walthall! When the Andersons had to abandon their home in Shelbyville, the general went with his brigade, and Etta and her mother had to make their own way. "On this retrograde, Etta, her mother, and General Walthall's wife came near to being cut off from the command as it moved towards Chattanooga. The party was intercepted and fell into the hands of the Yankees, and was detained at Bridgeport. As it resulted, they were most courteously treated by the officer in command, and as soon as practicable were sent forward to the Confederate lines under an escort furnished by their host, Brigadier General William H. Lytle, who was a well-known American writer, best remembered for his poetry, including *Antony and Cleopatra*."[23]

William H. Lytle was born in Cincinnati, Ohio, on November 2, 1826. His father had been a general and later a member of Congress. William was graduated from Cincinnati College, studied law, participated in the Mexican War, and became major general of the Ohio Militia. At Carnifax Ferry, Virginia, he commanded a brigade and was severely wounded; at Perryville, he was wounded and left on the field for dead. Nursed back to duty, he was exchanged and promoted to brigadier general. His mother was a literary lady, a writer, and she cast a romantic glow over his persona.[24]

Antony and Cleopatra

I AM dying, Egypt, dying.
    Ebbs the crimson life-tide fast,
And the dark Plutonian shadows
    Gather on the evening blast;
Let thine arms, O Queen, enfold me,
    Hush thy sobs and bow thine ear;
Listen to the great heart-secrets,
    Thou, and thou alone, must hear.

Though my scarr'd and veteran legions
    Bear their eagles high no more,
And my wreck'd and scatter'd galleys
    Strew dark Actium's fatal shore,
Though no glittering guards surround me,
    Prompt to do their master's will,

I must perish like a Roman,
    Die the great Triumvir still.

Let not Caesar's servile minions
    Mock the lion thus laid low;
'Twas no foeman's arm that fell'd him,
    'Twas his own that struck the blow;
His who, pillow'd on thy bosom,
    Turn'd aside from glory's ray,
His who, drunk with thy caresses,
    Madly threw a world away.

Should the base plebian rabble
    Dare assail my name at Rome,
Where my noble spouse, Octavia,
    Weeps within her widow'd home,
Seek her; say the gods bear witness —
    Altars, augurs, circling wings —
That her blood, with mine commingled,
    Yet shall mount the throne of kings.

As for thee, star-eyed Egyptian,
    Glorious sorceress of the Nile,
Light the path to Stygian horrors
    With the splendors of thy smile.
Give the Caesar crowns and arches,
    Let his brow the laurel twine;
I can scorn the Senate's triumphs,
    Triumphing in love like thine.

I am dying, Egypt, dying;
    Hark! the insulting foeman's cry.
They are coming! quick, my falchion,
    Let me front them ere I die.
Ah! no more amid the battle
    Shall my heart exulting swell;
Isis and Osiris guard thee!
    Cleopatra, Rome, farewell!

William Haines Lytle
1857[23]

VIII

Chickamauga and Missionary Ridge

By the end of August, Rosecrans crossed the Cumberland Mountains and descended into the valley of the Tennessee River, and on August 20 began shelling Chattanooga from across the river. The bombardment of the town was unexpected and surprised Bragg, who quickly ordered the town evacuated on September 6 and moved twenty-five miles south to Lafayette, Georgia. From this location he hoped to fall heavily upon the Federal columns as they debouched from the mountain passes in pursuit of the Rebels. Anderson's brigade was withdrawn from Bridgeport to Lafayette, where he joined Etta.[1] The family remained a few days in Lafayette, a coming war zone. Anderson took them for a ride and pointed out the two lines of battle and the Federal army now in Chattanooga. The next morning when firing began, Anderson realized that he was needed at headquarters. Etta's advanced pregnancy made her return to their home in Monticello imperative. Anderson bid his family goodbye, and they were evacuated to Marietta, Georgia, where Etta stayed with her cousin, Mr. H. Leroy, Esq., for a short time. She then returned to the home of Dr. Robert and Mollie Scott, her sister and brother-in-law in Monticello, Florida, who in Anderson's absence, managed his business affairs in Florida.[2] Etta's movement to and from Florida was safe at all times, as she was always accompanied by a staff officer or physician who was returning home or going to rejoin the army. Elizabeth Cromwell, their first daughter, was born.

After vacating Chattanooga, Bragg began receiving reinforcements from Mississippi and Virginia; the army spread throughout the Chattanooga Valley. As noted before, this is rugged country, divided into series of ridges and mountains, separated by creeks extending southward for miles like the fingers on a hand. This formidable country could only be penetrated through narrow, rough roads that cross the mountains through a series of gaps. General Bragg assessed this location in his usual monotone form: "Mountains hide your foe from you. They are full of gaps through which the enemy can pounce on you at any time. A mountain is like the wall of a house full of rat holes. The rat lies hidden at his hole, ready to pop out when no one is watching. Who can tell what lies behind that wall?"[3]

General Rosecrans, under the misapprehension that the Confederates were in full retreat toward Atlanta, ordered General Thomas to cross the mountains from west to east, through two rugged gaps in Lookout Mountain into McLemore's Cove and hit Bragg's west wing near Lafayette, Georgia. As Generals U. S. Negley and A. Baird led their divisions into McLemore's Cove, surrounded by sheer mountains, Bragg got his opportunity to cripple his foe; they had to be hit before they could

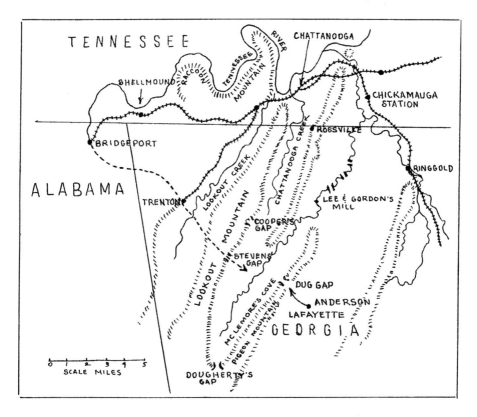

The Battle at Chickamauga: Anderson at McLemore's Cove

be reinforced or retire. Bragg directed Hindman's division to march south up the headwaters of Chickamauga Creek and bottle up and attack Negley's division of 6,000 bluecoats now sitting in a cul-de-sac. Hindman was to be supported by Cleburne's division, headed by newly arrived General D. H. Hill, who was holding the gap in Pigeon Mountain.

September 19–20, 1863. General Anderson had been with Withers's division but in August, Withers's health began to fail and he was replaced by Major General Thomas C. Hindman, under whom Anderson was now serving. "We had moved from Lafayette earlier and were on the west bank of the Chickamauga Creek. The brigade was made up of the 7th, 9th, 10th, 41st, 44th Mississippians plus the 9th Mississippi Battalion Sharpshooters. We took positions in line from two to three hundred yards in rear of General Deas's left and General Manigault's right, as the reserve brigade of Hindman's division."[4] "We bivouacked on the field that night, and received orders to take up and continue the attack as ordered to be made on the right at daylight of Sunday, the 20th. At 11 A.M. General Hindman sent for me and turned over to me the command of the division, Hindman having received a neck wound which disabled him from further service."[5]

General Anderson's handwritten report on his location on the battlefield at Chickamauga details his role in the battle at McLemore's Cove. "The attack on our right was not made however until between 10 and 11 o'clock. (General D. H. Hill was supposed to attack at daylight, and did not do it till about 11:00, losing four or five hours of daylight.) When it was promptly taken up by Generals Z. C. Deas and A. M. Manigault in my front, the whole division moved confidently on the enemy's first line. Deas swept everything before him, without halting or even checking up in his advance to and over the enemy's first line of breastworks. Manigault was checked and diverged to the left, unmasking my two left regiments. The whole brigade was moved steadily forward, gradually closing the space between it and Deas's line till the ascend of a range of wooded hills was reached, where the enemy by reason of his advantageous position for both infantry and artillery, had brought Deas momentarily to a standstill. Three pieces of his artillery strongly posted about two-thirds of the way up the hill, and supported by infantry, were causing Deas's left regiment to waver, when I ordered an advance. The command was most gallantly responded to, the artillery captured, the heights carried, and the enemy so badly routed as he was unable to make any real stand again upon that part of the field. I continued to pursuit however, for half a mile or more when finding my lines imperfect by reason of some being able to follow faster than others. I rode to those in advance and soon succeeded in halting them till the line could be perfected. Before the new alignment had been completed, a staff officer from General Hindman recalled me from further pursuit on account of a flank fire which had been opened by the enemy with artillery and small arms on my rear and left regiments, the 41st and 9th Mississippi." Anderson continued:

"After reforming, the command was marched back by General Hindman's order in the direction from which it had advanced, a distance of about a half or three quarters of a mile. Then changed direction to the right over an open field, towards a position where J. B. Kershaw was reported to be heavily pressed. My brigade reached the position about 3 P.M. in the afternoon, and was ordered to form a line on J. B. Kershaw's left to support him in an attack upon a wooded hill in his front where the enemy was strongly posted." Here Anderson's brigade joined with General Bushrod Johnston and J. B. Kershaw. "The attack was soon made by the whole line. It was stubbornly resisted from a very strong position just behind the crest of the hill. A portion of two of my regiments gained the crest of the hill and planted Colors there, but the position was a hard one, and some breaking took place to the left. The troops were rallied on the slope of the hill, lines reformed and all in readiness to resume the attack, when the enemy advanced his line immediately in my front down the hill with some impetuosity. The line was instantly ordered forward to meet the charge and the command quickly responded to. The enemy was met by a volley and charge which did much execution, his lines broke and his troops fled in some confusion, but as there was no corresponding forward movement by the brigades on my right — and left, and as the hill near the crest was very difficult to ascend, he had time either to reform or bring up a second line before me. We reached the top of the hill and another repulse was the consequence. Troops never rallied more promptly and without confusion or clamor. On taking position near the foot of the hill it was found necessary to distribute ammunition, and while this was being done, Colonel J. H. Kelly came up with his brigade and moved forward to the assault. Soon after two Florida regiments under Colonel J. J. Finley also moved forward to Colonel Kelly's support. It was now nearly nighttime and the importance of completing the day's work, thus far so handsomely accomplished by the left wing, was apparent to all.

Night at this time put an end to further pursuit. Every preparation was now made for a renewal of the conflict early the next morning.

"The light of the morning of the 21st disclosed the fact that the enemy had under cover of darkness hastily withdrawn towards Chattanooga, from a field in which he had been so severely but justly punished."

The balance of Anderson's report details what was captured, such as "Deas's brigade along the Chattanooga Road captured 3 pieces of artillery, killing many of the cannoneers at their guns, and taking prisoners; the 41st Mississippi captured a battery of 5 guns. Several stands of Colors were also taken. The captured prisoners were ordered to the rear without guards or escort. Nine ordnance wagons loaded with ammunition, plus their mules and horses were taken. He closes his long report with laurels to his troops in the skill and gallantry they displayed in the battle for McLemore's Cove. Lastly the grim toll of 80 men killed, 454 wounded and 24 missing. (signed) Patton Anderson."[6]

In the course of the day's battle, thirty-seven-year-old U.S. General Lytle, the gentlemanly, courtly and gallant Federal officer from Ohio who had befriended Etta and her party a few days earlier at Bridgeport, did not fare well.

Author John Bowers, in his book *Chickamauga and Chattanooga*, renders a profound description of General Lytle's death. "Lytle saw that his position was untenable; grayclad soldiers were overlapping both sides, rushing forth like a stream of water around a boulder. It was unthinkable that Lytle would do anything but hightail it for the rear like everyone else. It was all hopeless, lost. It was then that Lytle borrowed a gesture that might have come straight from the other side, the Cavalier South. He pulled on his riding gloves, turned to one of his staff and announced, 'If I must die, I will die a gentleman.' He ordered his brigade to stand — to die if necessary, 'with their harness on.'

"It was noontime and Lytle wore a dark overcoat without an insignia but with a gold cord around the crown of his hat to show his rank. He started his brigade on a counterattack against the horde and was quickly wounded — in the spine. He agonized in pain but stayed in the saddle. The Rebs might push them back, but he was going to be out in front of these men, leading them, as long as he could hold the reins. Then a fusillade hit him — three deadly shots simultaneously. He went down — smiling, it was later reported, to those of his staff who were gently easing him to the ground. They were trying to get him somewhere, anywhere, where the minie balls and shells weren't flying. Two hovering orderlies were shot dead trying to move him. The best the survivors could do was to lay Lytle beneath a large tree on a far knoll where his troops were making a final stand. They placed him down in the heart of the battle. Speechless, the life force ebbing away, he motioned weakly for his troops to leave the scene and save themselves. He moved his hand as long as he could, and then he died.

"Then came the Southerners. Learning who Lytle was — a brigadier general and a recognized poet — they stood guard over his body. A Major Douglas West secured Lytle's pistol, spurs, sword belt, scabbard, and memorandum book. He was a fan of *Antony and Cleopatra*. Brigadier General William Preston, who commanded the division on the Confederate left, passed by and saw the attention being paid a slain figure. 'What have you there?' he asked. 'General Lytle of Cincinnati,' the answer came. 'Ah,' said Preston, 'the son of my old friend Bob Lytle. I am sorry it is so.'

"Next a curious visitor came to pay homage. It was Confederate surgeon E. W. Thomasson, who had served with Lytle in the Mexican War, and he positively identified the body and had it taken to his private tent. There, in keeping with a nineteenth-century ritual, he snipped off a lock of Lytle's hair, which he sent to Lytle's sister. He also sent Lytle's wallet and a poem he had found in the general-poet's pocket. Thomasson dressed Lytle's wounded face with green leaves and placed a transparent silken net over it. Lytle lay in state. While the fighting went on, though, the Southerners showed no sentiment save to kill. They had swept romantic Lytle out of the way and expected no one else to be so foolhardy."[7]

Anderson, upon learning of Lytle's death and recalling the kindness extended to Etta, took it upon himself to secure the body. Many of his personal effects had been pilfered. With Bragg's approval Anderson exchanged Lytle's body for General D. W. Adams who had been wounded and captured. Under a flag of truce Lytle's body was sent to General Rosecrans at Chattanooga.[8]

While we remain focused on Patton Anderson, the battle of Chickamauga elsewhere was peerless and complicated. Rosecrans had separated his army into three parts over a distance of fifty-seven miles from Ringgold to Alpine. He was obliged to fight in wrong places against heavy odds at times. "The trouble of waging war at Chickamauga for both commanders was that they not only did not know where the enemy stood, they frequently didn't know where their own men were. The mountains and foliage hid troops from view. Communications often broke down."[9] The wide dispersion of the Federal forces seemed to perplex Bragg, resulting in complex sequences of maneuvers in which the failure of Bragg's subordinate officers deprived the Confederates of their opportunity for defeating these isolated Federal units, resulting in flawed piecemeal attacks.[10] On both sides 130,000 men were engaged, with losses in killed, wounded and missing, of 37,000. The battle casualties were exceeded only by Gettysburg and The Wilderness.

Afterwards, Anderson wrote Etta about the situation: "Hindman was ordered by Bragg to attack the enemy in McLemore's Cove at daylight on the morning of the 19th of September. He did not do it. But for some reason he delayed till about 3 P.M., and then it was too late. It now turns out that if he had come up on time and made the attack at daylight as ordered, he would have captured the whole of Negley's Division (6,000 men) with a large train of wagons — there is no telling how much more of Rosecrans's army would have fallen an easy prey to our Army and most likely the whole of it would have been captured, killed, or scattered, saving the bloodshed and battle of Chickamauga, and preventing any possibility of a concentration of the enemy's forces. Bragg has suspended Hindman from his command, and preferred charges against him. Whether or not Hindman will be able to make a good excuse I do not know — and it is not for anyone to determine beforehand. On the morning of the twentieth at Chickamauga, Genl. Polk was ordered to attack at daylight, and did not do it till about 11:00 A.M., losing four or five hours of daylight, which if we had attacked, nothing could have saved Rosecrans's whole army from complete rout and capture. For that failure Polk is also suspended and charges preferred against him. I am inclined to think that Lieutenant General D. H. Hill is the true party to blame for the delay, but as he was under Polk on that occasion, Genl. Bragg could only look to Polk, as he was the man to whom Bragg gave the order."[11]

None of these officers were tried, as President Davis intervened; Polk was exchanged for Hardee, and was sent to Mississippi; D. H. Hill was relieved of his command; and Hindman remained under arrest for several months; consequently Anderson continued to lead Hindman's division.

Realizing his army's peril, Rosecrans made a rapid, disorganized retreat through Rossville Gap back into Chattanooga. The Confederate troops buried their dead, collected arms, artillery, and other military stores the retreating Federals left behind and began trailing the Federals to Chattanooga. "Crossing the Missionary Ridge we could see the blue-coats at work upon their defenses. Our lines were soon extended around Chattanooga, pickets and videttes thrown out, and the investment begun, with forces reaching from the river west of the town to the same stream east and about it, the Yankees having the river at their rear and the country opposite in their possession. We will not attack the enemy in his entrenched position at Chattanooga," said Anderson. "The game is not worth the sacrifice it would cost."[12] General Bragg thought Rosecrans would evacuate the city because it was believed he could not possibly supply and sustain his army. On October 16, General Grant, because of his success at Vicksburg, was given command of the entire western region. Grant's first action as commander was to fire General Rosecrans and replace him with General G. H. Thomas. The promotion was a reward to Thomas for his heroic stand at Chickamauga. He became known as "The Rock of Chickamauga."

President Davis visited General Bragg's headquarters on October 8 to assess Bragg's performance. When he found it to be satisfactory, the officers who petitioned against Bragg were either demoted or reassigned, as noted earlier. At the same meeting, Davis proposed to his old friend Bragg that he send General James Longstreet north to attack a small Federal army under General Ambrose Burnside at Knoxville. This move left Bragg barely 36,000 men to face a hungry Federal force of 60,000 men. Regardless, Bragg was determined to hold his entire line around Chattanooga. But the Confederate army's morale was reaching a new low. It had rained for almost two months, and the men suffered terribly from cold and exposure in the mountains. Most of them had been encamped either in the Chattanooga or Chickamauga creek bottoms. The roads and campgrounds were seas of mud. Thousands of men were ill with fever and chills. Food had been scarce since early October, when the rains impeded wagon traffic.[13]

The Federal forces in Chattanooga were faring no better. The city was under siege. The Rebels controlled the south bank of the Tennessee River from Lookout Mountain to Bridgeport, requiring the Federals to bring their supplies to Stevenson by rail, transfer to army wagons and traverse an old road up the Sequatchie Valley and over the Cumberland Mountains to the north bank of the Tennessee opposite Chattanooga. Although not cutting reinforcements or stopping general supplies, the long, eight-day, sixty-mile distance placed Thomas's men and animals on starvation rations. The boys in blue called this the "cracker line" because that was about all they had to eat.

If a water route was opened, the travel time could be cut in half. To do this, the Confederates would have to be removed from the south bank of the river. Chief engineer General William "Baldy" Smith devised a plan, and during the night of October 16, sent General "Fighting Joe" Hooker with 1,500 men across the river. They were cast loose on boats and drifted downstream past the Confederate sentinels. They landed at Brown's Ferry and secured the heights overlooking the site. A pontoon bridge was put over the river. Hooker's column drove back an outpost commanded by Confederate General E. M. Law at Wauhatchie, and the next day linked up with the Federal bridgehead. Hooker left General J. W. Geary at Wauhatchie to guard the road. The Confederates countered with two night attacks on October 28–29 but failed to wipe out Geary's division. In the fighting at Wauhatchie, General Geary's son was wounded and died in his father's arms. The Federal supply line was open, and on the morning of October 30 the steamboat *Chattanooga* arrived at Kelly's Ford with 40,000 rations and tons of forage. A cry went up from the boys in blue: "The Cracker line is open. Full rations, boys."[14] Crackers were a staple of the bluejackets' ration.

Anderson was unaware that the regular supply line had been re-established. His letter of October 30, written while at Missionary Ridge to Etta at Marietta, Georgia, displays a great deal of affection for her. "I have said that I was willing for you to remain at Marietta a short while longer — to tell you the truth, my dear Et, without knowing how it may occur, yet I have a lingering hope that by some chance or other, I may get to see you again before you go back to Florida. I sometimes, when thinking about you, almost make up my mind to ask General Bragg to let me run down on one train and come back on the next. I would do it for a certainty if it were not that we are in the face of the enemy." Anderson continues: "We shell him occasionally just to annoy him — not with any hope of making him leave Chattanooga by that means. Wheeler has gone to his rear, and we are in hourly expecting of hearing that some of his communications have been cut. In this way, he may be induced to fall back towards Murfreesboro, where forage and provisions are easier of access and his line shorter and more easily defended." The last paragraph of his letter to Et: "Give my love to Mother & all the Monroes, McLearys, etc. Kiss Willie & The & Pat for me. A bushel of kisses for yourself. I believe that every day of my life makes it more essential for me to be with you — I can't stand this thing of being separated from you half as well as I could five years ago. Another Kiss from — Your Patton"[15]

Again the railroads were used extensively by both sides in transporting men and supplies in and out of Chattanooga. The opening of the "cracker line" shaped Grant's strategy. With the corps of G. H. Thomas, Oliver O. Howard and "Fighting Joe" Hooker, Grant waited for Sherman and his corps of 20,000 bluecoats from Vicksburg. Once mustered, the task force would cross the snaking Tennessee River, charge up the high ridges of Lookout Mountain and unseat the Confederates from their fortifications.

Grant would have to spend most of November upgrading the corps with fresh horses and replacement supplies. He ordered occasional night attacks as feelers, giving the appearance that a general engagement was about to begin. The season was getting late. Finally, on November 14, Hooker crossed over the Tennessee River to its south bank while Grant deployed a heavy force in Bragg's immediate front. Hooker's forces began the difficult task of crawling up the mountainside and began skirmishing with General Carter L. Stevenson's division, recently exchanged after being captured at Vicksburg.

Anderson and Walthall were entrenched on Missionary Ridge. In due time Walthalls's brigade was hastened to Lookout Mountain to the support of Stevenson who was occupying the top of the mountain. Here Walthall took position on the west side of Lookout and near the northern slope. Walthall's brigade made a gallant and heroic defense while occupying the mountainside which the enemy's infantry ascended in overwhelming numbers. The Federals were assisted by batteries at Moccasinbend and batteries brought over with them and placed in position on a ridge beyond Lookout Creek.

The northern war poet George H. Boker poetized the "battle above the clouds":

"Give me but two brigades," said Hooker, frowning at fortified Lookout,
"And I'll engage to sweep yond mountain clear of that mocking rebel rou't,"
At early morning came an order that set the general's face aglow:

"Now," said he to his staff, "draw out my soldiers, Grant says that I may go!"
The lower works were carried at one onset, like a vast roaring sea
Of steel and fire, our soldiers from the trenches swept out the enemy:
And we could see the gray-coats swarming up from the mountain's leafy base,
To join their comrades in the higher fastnesses — for life or death the race!

The attacking force under Hooker consisted of Geary's division and
two brigades of another army corps. It was confronted by only a part of
Walthall's brigade until late in the day when Walthall was supported by the
E. W. Pettus and J. C. Moore brigades. General Walthall complained in his
official report, "At no time during this prolonged struggle, whose object was
to prevent the occupation by the enemy, first of the important point near
the Craven house, and afterwards, the only road down the mountain leading from General Stevenson's Division to the main body of the army, did I
have the benefit of my division commander's personal presence."

The division commander referred to by Walthall was "General J.
King Jackson of Georgia, then in temporary command of the division
and dubbed 'Mudwall,' in contradistinction to 'Stonewall' of the Army
of Northern Virginia. It was to 'Mudwall' that Walthall, during the
engagement, vainly sent staff officer after staff officer, as likewise couri-
ers, in search of, and of whom the division commander could not be
found, nor his headquarters located."[16] Hooker battled long and hotly
before Walthall moved under orders to McFarland Springs, where his
brigade bivouacked and moved the next morning and took his position
back on Missionary Ridge.

With Lookout Mountain lost, Bragg's position was now threatened.
Then further bad news as the situation at Knoxville worsened and General Bushrod Johnson and two brigades were dispatched,[17] reducing
Bragg's dwindling army and leaving a gap in the Confederate defensive
line on Missionary Ridge. Rather than retreat, Bragg felt that his position on Missionary Ridge should be held. He moved Jackson, Stevenson
and States Rights Gist from the extreme left of his line to the extreme
right of his line, leaving only A. P. Stewart, Anderson and W. B. Bate
divisions to defend the lion's share of Missionary Ridge, four miles of it
from Rossville Gap to Hardee below Tunnel Hill.[18] Shortly thereafter,
the weakened divisions on Missionary Ridge were ordered into the
trenches and earthworks which had been dug. Bragg's engineers had a
strong natural position; three parallel lines of entrenchments had been
laid out. One line was along the *base* of the ridge, another had been

started about *half way up* the slope and a third was along the *crest*. Anderson's division consisted of his own, Deas's, Manigault's and A. J. Vaughan, Jr.'s brigades of infantry, and A. R. Courtney's battalion of light artillery with eighteen pieces. They were posted at the foot of Missionary Ridge on the west side facing the enemy. A breastwork of logs, rocks and earth had been thrown up along the whole line of defense that covered two miles in length. Although formidable and thought impregnable, the Confederate forces had been split up in order to cover the vast territory of the mountain. Half were at the bottom and the other half on the crest of the mountain.

November 25 — General Grant resorted to psychological warfare when he began massing his corps in front of the Confederates on the ridge. In a bold and imposing demonstration of military power he had his corps stretching for two miles; "While the enemy, like a huge serpent, uncoiled his massive folds into shapely lines in our front,[19] moving forward in solid columns, as compact and orderly as if on parade, finally halting at the base of the ridge." Anderson in his report picks up the action. "During the day, General Deas, commanding at the foot of the Ridge informed me of his belief that his men were inclined to be discouraged at the prospect of having to retire up a steep hill, under the enemy fire, to the top of the ridge." Anderson concurred, "On that morning I protested against the disposition which had been made of the pickets, which was the worst I have ever seen. The line was in two ranks, the front rank at the foot of the hill, and the rear rank on the top. Thus the front rank was not strong enough to hold its position, nor could it retire to the top of the ridge."[20] From the top of the ridge to the entrenchments at the foot was 600 yards; beyond an open field of about 900 yards in width.

At 3 P.M. the immense Union force in the front advanced in three lines, preceded by heavy skirmishes, and then the roar of galling fire of small arms became very heavy as the bluecoats closed in on the Confederate defenders at the base of the ridge. General Joe Hooker and his corps were in front of Anderson's division.[21] General Manigault observed: "I noticed some nervousness amongst my men as they beheld this grand military spectacle, and heard remarks which showed that some uneasiness existed amongst them, and that they magnified the force in their view at least double their actual number."[22] Artillery guns threw shot after shot at them as the Rebels squirmed to get out of their trap. Cannonballs bounced and then spun wildly, bouncing over and into the trenches.

"The consequence was that the troops made no fight at all, but broke and ran as soon as the enemy's overwhelming columns advanced."[23] In General Bragg's letter of 1873 in his discussion of the battle of Missionary Ridge he wrote, "I have always believed our disasters at Missionary Ridge were due immediately to misconduct of a brigade of Buckner's troops from East Tennessee, commanded by General Alex. W. Reynolds, which first gave way and could not be rallied."[24]

General Bragg's official report: "The troops for two days confronted the enemy marshalling his immense forces in plain view, and exhibiting to their sight such a superiority in numbers as may have intimidated weak minds and untried soldiers. A panic which I never before witnessed, seemed to have seized upon officers and men, and each seemed to be struggling for his personal safety."[25]

Realizing the desperate situation, Anderson called on General Bate to hold his position, covering the road for retreat from Missionary Ridge. In this alarming state of affairs, Cheatham ordered the brigade to withdraw to Chickamauga Station and Bragg ordered General Hardee to begin retiring his forces southeast towards Dalton, Georgia. Nevertheless, attacking Union forces' losses were heavy: killed 753; wounded 4,722 and missing 349. Confederate defenders lost 361 killed, 2,160 wounded and 4,146 missing or captured.[26] Anderson's partisan, General Walthall, received a painful wound caused by a minieball passing through his foot; he went to Atlanta for treatment.

At Dalton, Bragg laid some of the blame for the sad situation on Generals Breckinridge and Cheatham who, in Bragg's words, "were totally unfit for any duty from the 23rd to the 27th because of drunkenness."[27] On November 28 Bragg telegraphed President Davis to inform him of the southern loss at Chattanooga and offered his resignation, asking the president for relief from command and an investigation into the causes of the defeat. President Davis accepted Bragg's resignation on November 30 and ordered that General Joseph Johnston would take over the Army of Tennessee. On December 5, General Longstreet and his forces were forced to retreat from Knoxville as General Sherman relieved the besieged city; and *The Richmond Examiner* called it "the gloomiest year of the war."

The campaign, which began August 16, resulted in General Bragg's evacuation of Chattanooga on September 7, only twenty-two days later. The success achieved by the northern troops was one of the most notable of the war, if not the most important. Wilbur Thomas in his biography of General George H. Thomas, *The Indomitable Warrior*, made special reference to this point.

> Confederate General William W. Loring asserted some time before Appomattox that it was apparent that the Chattanooga campaign spelled the end of the Confederacy. He stated that "not a man in the Confederacy felt that the Union had really accomplished anything until Chattanooga fell."
>
> When asked, "You do not mean to say, general, that Vicksburg and Gettysburg were nothing?", he replied, "The loss of Vicksburg weakened our prestige, contracted our territory, and practically expelled us from the Mississippi River, but it left the body of our power unharmed. As to Gettysburg, that was an experiment; if we had won that battle the government at Washington would, perhaps, have tendered peace with a recognition of the Confederacy. Our loss of it, except that we could less easily spare the slaughter of veteran soldiers than you could, left us just where we were."
>
> Continuing the conversation, General Loring was asked, "But in the latter part of 1863 some of your people lost hope?" He replied, "Not exactly that, but they experienced then for the first time a diminution of confidence as to the final result." Further, he stated that it was the fall of Chattanooga, in consequence of the Chickamauga campaign, and the total defeat of General Bragg's efforts to recover it, that caused the loss of confidence in Confederate success.
>
> Regarding the reason Chattanooga was held to be so important, he replied, "As long as we held it, it was the closed doorway to the interior of our country. When it came into your [the Union's] hands the door stood open, and however rough your progress in the interior might be, it still left you free to march inside. I tell you that when your Dutch General Rosecrans commenced his forward movement for the capture of Chattanooga we laughed him to scorn; we

Major General William Wing "Old Blizzards" Loring was a tenacious fighter who had lost his left arm at Chapultepec in the Mexican War.

believed that the black brow of Lookout Mountain would frown him out of existence; that he would dash himself to pieces against the many and vast natural barriers that rise all around Chattanooga; and that then the Northern people and the government at Washington would perceive how hopeless were their efforts when they came to attack the real South."

To another question, "But the capture of Chattanooga convinced you that even the real South was vulnerable, did it?", he commented, "Yes, it was only a question as to whether we could beat back your armies by sheer force of desperate fighting, and as you largely outnumbered us, and our resources were every day diminishing, the prospects to the thinking part of our people looked gloomy indeed." To a final remark, "But, general, there are people in the North who regard the Chickamauga campaign as a failure for the Union cause," he said, "Ah! We would gladly have exchanged a dozen of our previous victories for that one failure."

This judgment finds general support from competent military authorities. Chattanooga was undoubtedly the key to the unlocking of the Confederacy, of which Chickamauga was an extremely important first step. Richmond, on the other hand, was a holding action in effect, perhaps more accurately a stalemate, in proof of which the record of Union battles lost is cited. It was not until after Chickamauga, which prevented General Bragg from retaking Chattanooga, followed by the battles of Orchard Knob, Lookout Mountain and Missionary Ridge in November 1863, and still later the clinching Battle of Nashville in December 1864, that the Confederacy was first cracked, then opened, and finally broken.[28]

IX

Anderson Commands in Florida—The Cow Cavalry

The Confederates began constructing winter quarters at Dalton, surmising that Grant did not intend to carry on any further operations because of the winter. The encampment of each brigade was like a village, and everything went on with a regularity and order that made it an easy task for each general to rule.[1] The lull in the war permitted Anderson to write to Etta more often, and take care of his Florida business. One such letter: "I shall have to have another boy with me. I find that our mess will have to rely upon Peyton (one of Anderson's Negroes) as a permanent cook; I must have a boy to wait on me."[2]

A year earlier President Abraham Lincoln had issued the Emancipation Proclamation on January 1, 1863. By this he declared the slaves in the rebellious states free (but not in the other states) and called upon them to enlist in the service of the U.S. Army. The Confederates rationalized that he took this step as another act of war as commander-in-chief of the Federal army to strike at the cornerstone of the Confederacy, its slaves. The Negroes did not rebel militarily but flocked to the Union forces now occupying so much southern territory. It was a successful plan, so that by the beginning of 1864 there were over 100,000 trained Negroes wearing the Federal blue uniform.

Historians estimate between 60,000 and 93,000 freedmen, Negro slaves, and Indians served the Confederate army in some capacity—nurses, cooks, servants, blacksmiths, musicians, teamsters, ambulance corpsmen, construction workmen for railroads, forts, dykes, trenches, etc.—collectively for four years they were soldiers in the Confederate army even though they did not wear the gray, and 13,000 at one time or another engaged in combat.[3]

With these underlying factors, some general for sure would bring up the opinion of organizing the Negroes for the Confederate army and placing them under command of white officers. Major General Patrick Ronayne Cleburne would broach the subject at a meeting on January 2 at Dalton, Georgia. Patton Anderson set aside this notion in a confidential letter to Lieutenant General L. Polk who had just returned from Mississippi. He dutifully outlines the "cause" to Polk in his letter.

(Confidential)
DALTON, Ga., Jan. 14, 1864.

To LIEUTENANT GENERAL L. POLK,
Enterprise, Miss.

General: After you have read what I am about to disclose to you, I hope you will not think I have assumed any unwarrantable intimacy in marking this communication as "confidential." My thoughts for ten days past have been so oppressed with the weight of the subject as to arouse in my mind the most painful apprehensions of future results, and have caused me to cast about for a friend of clear head, ripe judgment and pure patriotism with whom to confer and take counsel. My choice has fallen upon you, sir, and I proceed at once to lay the matter before you.

On January 2d I received a circular order from the headquarters of Hindman's corps informing me that the commanding general of the army desired division commanders to meet him at his quarters at seven o'clock that evening.

At the hour designated I was at the appointed place. I met in the room General Johnston, Lieutenant General Hardee, Major Generals Walker, Stewart and Stevenson, and in a few moments afterward Major Generals Hindman and Cleburne entered, Brigadier General Bate coming in a few minutes later. The whole, with the general commanding, embracing all the corps and division commanders (infantry) of this army, except Major General Cheatham, who was not present. In a few minutes General Johnston requested Lieutenant General Hardee to explain the object of the meeting, which he did by stating that Major General Cleburne had prepared with great care a paper on an important subject addressed to the officers of this army, and he proposed that it now be read.

General Cleburne proceeded to read an elaborate article on the subject of our past disasters, present condition and inevitable future ruin unless an entire change of policy might avert it.

That change he boldly and proudly proposed to effect by emancipating our slaves and putting muskets in the hands of all of them capable of bearing arms, thus securing them to us as allies and equals, and insuring a superiority of numbers over our enemies, &c.

Yes, sir, this plain, but in my view monstrous, proposition was calmly submitted to the generals of this army for their sanction and adoption, with the avowed purpose of carrying it to the rank and file.

I will not attempt to describe my feelings on being confronted by a project so startling in its character — may I say, so revolting to Southern sentiment, Southern pride and Southern honor?

And not the least painful of the emotions awakened by it was the consciousness which forced itself upon me that it met with favor from others besides the author in high station then present. You have a place, General, in the Southern heart perhaps not less exalted than that you occupy in her army. No one knows better than yourself all the hidden powers and secret springs which move the great moral machinery of the South. You know whence she derived that force which three years ago impelled her to the separation and has since that time to this present hour enabled her to lay all she has, even the blood of her best sons, upon the altar of independence, and do you believe that that South will now listen to the voices of those who would ask her to stultify herself by entertaining a proposition which heretofore our insolent foes themselves have not even dared to make in terms so bold and undisguised?

What are we to do? If this thing is once openly proposed to the army, the total disintegration of that army will follow in a fortnight, and yet to speak and work in opposition to it is an agitation of the question scarcely less to be dreaded at this time and brings down the universal indignation of the Southern people and the Southern soldiers upon the head of at least one of our bravest and most accomplished officers. Then, I repeat, what is to be done?

What relief it would afford me to talk to you about this matter, but as that may not be, do I go too far in asking you to write me?

I start in a few days to go to my home in Monticello, Fla., where I expect to spend twenty days with my family, and I assure you, General, it would add much to the enjoyment of my visit if you would favor me by mail with some of the many thoughts which this subject will arouse in your mind.

> Believe me, General, very truly your friend,
> (Sg) PATTON ANDERSON.[4]

General Cleburne's proposal was kept a secret from the public and was rebuffed by the other generals. Richmond took no steps in approving the plan at this time even though the 1860 census recorded 3,950,000 Negroes in the Confederacy.

Anderson returned to Monticello for a short leave and found his family living in crowded conditions in the house of Etta's brother, Dr. Scott.[5] Anderson was drawing $301 a month, hardly enough to support Etta and the children. The secession had finished its third year and already the individuals who pioneered the cause were experiencing financial difficulties. Business activity was dead or degenerated into unhealthy speculation. Floridians, much the same as others in the lower South, found increased difficulty in making a living while cut off from the outside world and subject to a share in the support of the Confederate armies. "It was the blockade more than battles which steadily exhausted the economic strength of the commonwealth. In a one-staple agricultural society, it is difficult for men to live successfully unto themselves. Exchange is a fundamental law of life and the modern marketplace is the wide world."[6] Patton had one piece of officer's prattle: "General Hardee is to be married soon to Miss Lewis of Demopolis, Alabama. Very rich."[7]

Anderson, returning to Dalton, discovered that since General Bragg was gone, General Hindman had been released from arrest and assumed command of his old corps; Anderson remained in command of his own division. In addition Bragg, almost immediately following the rout at Chattanooga, was appointed chief of staff and advisor to his staunch supporter, Jefferson Davis, with his office now in Richmond.[8]

Anderson Commands in Florida

The year began with Abraham Lincoln, under the auspices of his Amnesty and Reconstruction Proclamation, implementing a plan of the Federal administration to separate Confederate states. He requested the citizens of Florida and Louisiana to form loyal state governments and vote to return to the Union. A convoy of twenty armed transports and eight supply ships with 5,500 Union forces sailed from Hilton Head, South Carolina, on their way to occupy Jacksonville, Florida (for the fourth time), arriving on February 7, 1864. Their mission was multifaceted: to induce Unionists in east Florida to organize a loyal state government; to procure for northern consumption Florida cotton, turpentine and timber; to disrupt the supply of beef being shipped north to Confederate forces; and to clear the state of Confederate resistance. Naturally, any success of these plans could upset the tranquility of the state's 50,000 or more Negroes.

Learning of the Federal advance, General Beauregard at Charleston, who was in charge of the east and west Florida districts, ordered reinforcements by rail from Confederate forces stationed around Charleston and Savannah, to bolster General J. Finegan's Florida troops, with instruction for the Florida cavalry and infantry to check the enemy in any movement toward the interior of the state. The shortage of rolling stock on the Georgia and Florida railroads, and the existence of a gap of twenty-six miles between the two roads subjected the concentration of Rebel reinforcements to a delay of several days as they marched to join Finegan. The Federals having landed, advanced upon Jacksonville on the eighth with three heavy columns of infantry and artillery under the command of two veteran generals, Q. A. Gillmore and T. Seymour. Their

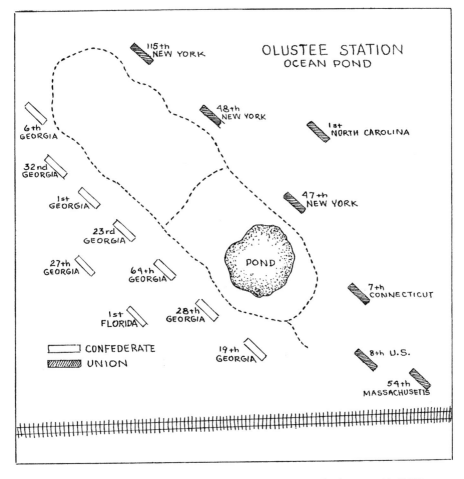

Olustee Battlefield State Historic Site commemorates the largest Civil War battle in Florida, February 20, 1864.[10]

superior numbers forced the limited Confederate defenders to withdraw. In a classic cavalry raid, Colonel Guy V. Henry's mounted brigade dashed on the railroad junction at Baldwin on the ninth; on the tenth they reached Sanderson, a Confederate supply depot which had been fired by the retreating Confederates. On the eleventh they approached Lake City but here the Florida forces skirmished heavily with Henry's cavalry who, assuming the Rebel force was larger, returned to Barbers Station to await the Union infantry force before making a movement on Lake City.[9]

Awaiting his reinforcements, Finegan selected a new position of defense at Olustee Station, thirteen miles east of Lake City. It extended from a lake named Ocean Pond to an impassable swamp south of the Florida, Atlantic & Gulf Central Railroad. The battlefield would straddle the railroad tracks.[11] In several days, reinforcements marching from Georgia joined Finegan's forces, increasing them to an effective assemblage of 5,200 men, plus twelve field pieces. It was decided that the field command would be divided between Finegan and Georgia General A. H. Colquitt.

On February 20 General Gillmore returned to Hilton Head, leaving General Seymour with instructions not to pursue the Rebels. But Seymour thought otherwise and began an advance from Barbers with twelve regiments of infantry (nine of white troops and three of Negroes), estimated at 8,000 men. After a fatiguing sixteen-mile march through the Florida terrain, the Yankees made contact with the Florida cavalry and then as they rushed forward, were met with a storm of minie balls and bullets from the waiting Confederate infantry. The sight of black-faced Yankees unleashed an explosion of hate for the invaders. Bordering on murderous rage, Finegan's forces outfought the unwanted raiders, soundly defeating them in the piney woods of Florida at Olustee (Ocean Pond) Station, and sent the bluecoats reeling in flight for their lives back toward Sanderson, leaving the woods strewn with their dead and wounded, while abandoning ammunition, guns, blankets and knapsacks.

With a disaster on his hands, Seymour evacuated in quick succession the villages of Barbers and Baldwin, and fell back to Jacksonville and St. Augustine. The battle lasted over four hours. Union casualties numbered 400 killed, 418 wounded and nearly 200 prisoners. Confederates lost 93 killed and 841 wounded. The next day the butternuts pushed to within twelve miles of Jacksonville; the cavalry was posted at Camp Finegan on the west side of McGirt's Creek, and the infantry at a new post near the creek, Camp Milton.

While this major Confederate victory was occurring in Florida, Anderson was at Dalton. Here on February 17, Anderson received his well-earned promotion when he was notified that President Davis and the Senate confirmed his being promoted to major general in the Army of Tennessee. With the renewed Union activity in Florida, President Davis decided Anderson's local knowledge and influence was essential and detached him to take command of the Districts of East and West Florida.[12] These two districts were combined into one — the District of Florida.[13] Anderson arrived on March 3, fourteen days after the battle of Olustee. Here he joined his confidant General Beauregard, who had arrived the day before.[14] A few days later, on March 18, while the generals were busy reorganizing the forces at Camp Milton and preparing the defensive line, Beauregard received orders from Richmond withdrawing most of the cavalry from his department; he returned at once to Savannah and Charleston.[15] He left Anderson definite instructions about meeting impending events in his District of Florida:

(a) Your present available forces are not sufficient to enable you to drive the enemy out of Jacksonville, fortified and supported by four or five gunboats.

(b) Palatka would be less difficult in an expedition of sufficient forces from the troops at McGirt's Creek.

(c) Should the enemy advance upon you from Jacksonville, you should retire on Baldwin works slowly, drawing him after you.

(d) Colonel D. B. Harris, Chief Engineer, will remain with instructions for constructing a battery at Fleming's Island on the St. Johns and one near the mouth of Trout Creek, a few miles below Jacksonville.

(e) Captain Pliny Bryan, signal officer, is in charge of the torpedoes to be put in the St. Johns River.

You will please keep me well advised, at Charleston, of all movements of the enemy in your district.[16]

The Lincoln government had been beaten vigorously in the attempt to regain Florida back into the Union, much to the chagrin of the Unionists scattered throughout the state, especially in Jacksonville and St. Augustine.

Anderson temporarily inherited approximately 6,000 infantry, 1,500 cavalry, and 497 artillerymen, *listed* at note 17. They encamped at Camp

Milton and Camp Finegan, eight miles west of Jacksonville. The entrenchments were located three hundred yards from McGirt's Creek, a tortu-
ous and deep moat, three miles in length, built of huge logs firmly
fastened and covered with earth. The flanks of the line were protected
by swamps. Eight miles in the rear at the railroad junction at Baldwin,
powerful stockades and entrenchments stretched about the east, north
and south of the community. These were formidable barriers erected to
guard the railroad and old Federal highway leading west to Lake City
and the state capital at Tallahassee.

The St. Johns River had become the boundary line for East Florida.
General Robert E. Lee, while commanding the coastal defenses of South
Carolina, Georgia and Florida in early 1862, ordered the Florida coastal
area east of the St. Johns River to be evacuated: "The only troops to be
retained in Florida are such as may be necessary to defend Apalachicola
River, by which the enemy's gunboats may penetrate far into the state of
Georgia."[18] Thereafter the U.S. Navy South Atlantic Blockading Squadron
began invading Florida's coastal fortifications, harbors and towns.

The Federals gained all of the populated area without a shot being
fired. Governor Milton protested to the Richmond authorities but was
declined any amends.

Fort Clinch at Fernandina and Amelia Island were seized as the Confederate troops skedaddled to the mainland. The towns of Jacksonville,
St. Augustine, Smyrna and Key West were surrendered to the U.S. Navy
and later occupied by Union forces. Inland along the St. Johns River, the
fortifications built at Fort Steele near Mayport Mills and the impregnable St. Johns Bluff were abandoned, allowing the Union navy freedom
to harass the farms and homes southward to Mandarin Point, then upriver
to Fort Picolata, Orange Mills, Palatka, Welaka, into Lake George to
Volusia, a distance of a hundred miles.

River Warfare

Aside from his duty to prevent any inroads into the middle of Florida
by the Federals, Anderson was cognizant of the U.S. Navy's control of
the St. Johns River and their scatteration policy of seeding the riverbanks
with Federal forces and garrisons. Ever since the invasion in February,
four gunboats were patrolling between the mouth of the river and Picolata,
a distance of sixty miles.[19] They were disruptive in nature, as they shelled

the farm buildings along the riverbanks, destroyed hundreds of small boats (target practice) used for crossing the river, and worst of all for the southerners, offered a "helping hand" to any slave who wished to bolt his home and family to join the Union's cause.[20] Then word reached Anderson that the enemy had moved further south to Palatka and were busy enlarging and supplying their troops. To put a halt to this, Anderson called upon Captain Bryan, a specialist in torpedo warfare whom General Beauregard had left behind to seed the St. Johns River with torpedoes. On March 30 near Mandarin Point,

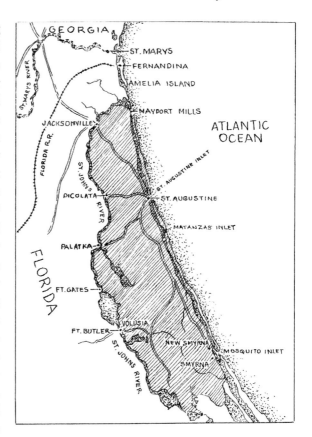

St. Johns River becomes boundary line for east Florida.

Captain Bryan placed twelve torpedoes, containing seventy pounds of small-grain cannon powder, designed to explode when triggered by the bow of a passing ship. The next morning one of the Union's biggest transports, *Maple Leaf*, a double-stacked, side-wheel steamer loaded with camp and garrison equipment for three regiments on a return trip from Palatka, exploded one of the torpedoes off Mandarin Point, opposite the mouth of Doctor's Lake, and sank in three fathoms of water.[21] On April 16 the U.S. Army transport *General Hunter*, on a return trip from the fort at Picolata, hit a mine in the same locale and sank.[22] On May 10 the *Harriet Weed* steamer was blown into fragments by a torpedo a short distance south of Jacksonville. She had two guns aboard and was towing a schooner.[23] The transport *Alice Price* was sunk on July 19 after it struck a torpedo about eight miles south of Jacksonville. *The New York Times* on June 3 had declared, "It is about time that the Florida business should be attended to. It may be all very fine to lose on an average two steamers a month and have nothing to show for it, but it is anything but a paying operation to the Government."[24] Soon after, the Federals began equipping their ships with primitive torpedo catchers — sweeps which cut the torpedoes from their moorings, sending them to the surface where they could be harmlessly exploded. River warfare was a double-edged sword. "[Anderson] saw more than a dozen major vessels of both flags sunk, captured or destroyed as countless Confederate smaller craft were lost."[25]

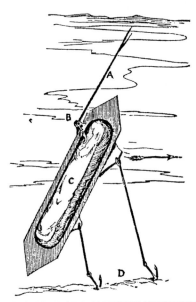

CROSS-SECTION OF A CONFEDERATE TORPEDO

A, iron rod armed with prongs to fasten upon the bottom of boats going up-stream and act upon B, a lever connecting with trigger to explode a cap and ignite the powder. C, canvas bag containing 70 lbs. of powder. D, anchors to hold torpedo in place. This torpedo consisted of a stout sheet-iron cylinder, pointed at both ends, about 5½ feet long and 1 foot in diameter. The iron lever was 3½ feet long, and armed with prongs to catch in the bottom of a boat. This lever was constructed to move the iron rod on the inside of the cylinder, thus acting upon the trigger of the lock to explode the cap and fire the powder. The machine was anchored, presenting the prongs in such a way that boats going down-stream should slide over them, but those coming up should catch.

Earlier in an effort to break the developing stalemate, Anderson issued orders for an advance. "Finegan was directed to take 2,500 men by rail from Baldwin to Waldo, then march to Palatka on the St. Johns in an attempt to capture the Federal garrison there. The movement bogged down because the condition of the railroad from Baldwin to Waldo was so bad that the trip had consumed more hours than miles traveled. At the same time, Federal activity at Jacksonville increased and the expedition was recalled."[27]

Brigadier General Joseph Finegan was an Irish-born Florida planter and mill operator. He spent most of the war commanding the small and widely scattered forces in the state. The high point of his Florida service came in February when he defeated a Union expedition at

---

HDQRS. DEPT. OF S. CAROLINA, GEORGIA, AND FLORIDA,
Charleston, S. C., April 7, 1864.
Maj. Gen. PATTON ANDERSON,
Baldwin, Fla. :
GENERAL: I inclose you herewith the following simple cipher for future use in important telegrams to these headquarters. For very important telegrams the diplomatic cipher should be used. Please inform me of its reception.
Respectfully, your obedient servant,
G. T. BEAUREGARD,
General, Commanding.

[Inclosure.]

A by M	H by R	O by U	U •by F
B K	I S	P I	V Q
C O	J V	Q G	W D
D A	K H	R Y	X T
E N	L X	S E	Y B
F C	M P	T Z	Z J
G W	N L		

Example : Charleston—Ormyxnezul.

Confederate cipher for important diplomatic messages.[26]

Olustee. Sent with Florida reinforcements to the Army of Northern Virginia in May, he was given charge of the Florida Brigade under General Lee. He fought at Cold Harbor and in the trenches at Petersburg, later returning to Florida.[28]

Soon after the abortive raid on Palatka the Federals commenced sending some of their forces away from Jacksonville. Confederate informants reported that twenty-one transports, loaded with 10,000 bluecoats, horses, wagons and artillery returned north to their home base at Hilton Head Island. Accordingly, General Beauregard in May ordered most of the Confederate forces to be removed from Florida. South Carolina, Virginia and Georgia regiments and some cavalry exited Florida to return to Savannah and Charleston, leaving Finegan's brigade (comprised of the 1st, 2nd and 6th Florida Battalions) as the primary infantry force in east Florida.[29] Anderson was left with only 1,700 infantry, 1,200 cavalry and 244 light artillery for the entire District of Florida.

On April 21, Anderson penned a long letter to Etta about their problems and lifestyle:

In Camp
April 21st, 1864

Dear Et,

Your letter of the 18th and 19th by the hands of Dr. Gamble was received last night. Also the money.

I am sorry to hear that you are all still on the sick list. I have lectured you so often of late about taking care of yourself, that I refrain *for once,* saying anything about it.

I think you might ask Aunt for the forks, explaining to her what you want with them. I will also write to her. The gloves fit very well, but as she wishes to be exact, I can only give the following directions etc. The pair just sent are a little too large around the hand just behind the thumb, and the *little* finger is about ¼ of an inch too long. Otherwise, they fit *first rate.*

I am proud that the boys are learning so well. You write me that Pat says he can spell – among other words "Yancy" but *you* don't spell it properly. You have it "Yantsy"!! By the way I think you are becoming a little careless about spelling. I suppose it is because you are always hurried and tired when you write. But I won't "lecture" you on *that* just now.

As to the establishment of the hospital at Monticello, I know nothing about it and have nothing in the world to do with it. It is a matter purely belonging to the Medical Department over which I have no control except those *in the field.* Those connected with Hospitals are entirely independent of me, and are not only jealous of their rights but sometimes become very *defiant.* I have as little to do with the surgeons as possible.

I hear that Mr. Tucker has not moved to Casa Bianca. I wonder if I couldn't rent it from him. I would like very much to do so, and would write to him on the subject but do not know where to address him. Please ask Dr. Scott to write to him, or find out in some way whether I could not occupy it. The house will fall down if someone is not in it! I am rejoiced on Mother's account that Caro has returned. But I confess I have little hope that Mother will not soon find some new trouble, for it seems to be the study of Caro's life to keep Mother constantly under some high state of mental anxiety or trouble. A new sensation will very soon appear, in all probability.

I took up the notion that Dr. Scott thought I was "Interfering too much" with his management of the place, from what you wrote me. You said that Lewis had several times of late received orders which the Dr. knew nothing about/among these he had been hauling bark to somebody in town, and then you went on to say that I ought not to allow it, etc. I merely wrote to you explaining how I came to order him to take the buggy to Station 17, and denied any knowledge of the bark, hauling business &c. By the way I have never had that matter explained yet.

You have written so positively before that he had hauled it and that too without authority that I am puzzled to understand. Certainly Lewis can tell whether he hauled it or not and settle the question. If he were to deny it, and there should be no proof that he *did,* I would believe him.

I see that you don't take to the "Suwannee Spring" project very readily. Well, if we can get the Casa House I would prefer the latter, but I do think you ought to quit Dr. Scott's little crowded establishment. I can readily see why you should wish to be with Mollie, but I don't think you ought to wish to do so at the sacrifice of your own health and that of all your children. Do you remember how you used to abuse the Monticello people about always wanting to live with their Kin? Particularly the Scotts who insisted on Mollie's living in the house with old Mrs. Scott. I fear you have imbibed the same spirit. You ought to reflect about this. I know when you do, you will come to a correct conclusion, and whatever you may determine on, I will abide by it. You have my ideas about it. I wish I could *see* you and *talk* to you about our affairs. If we go on in the way we are now doing, next year will be a sad one, I fear. We will have nothing to live on and nothing to buy it with!! But above all, I think we should look to the *health* of ourselves and children. I want to see you worse than ever. Here's a bushel of kisses for yourself and a peck apiece for Willie, The, Pat and "Crom." Love to Mollie and kisses for her girls.[30]

The withdrawal of such a large number of Confederate forces from Camp Milton left south Florida — a huge unpopulated land mass of pine forests, flatlands, rivers, lakes, swamps, insects, sand and poor roads — to the support of a few scattered Confederate companies who were called upon to defend the wide extent of country along the gulf coast against destructive Union raiding parties who were plundering the plantations, destroying salt works, stealing cattle and carrying off runaway slaves. Federal commanders saw to it that they were in touch with the fugitive class hiding all over Florida. Anderson was aware of this: "The enemy is known to be inciting bands of deserters and fugitives to bloodshed and plunder, and at the same time supply them arms, clothing, food, to win them over to prefer the United States Government."[31]

Anderson decided the St. Johns River was the proper point from which to defend south Florida. "To give up this position South Florida will be practically cut off from the Confederacy. While we hold the river we can extend our forces whenever troops can be detached for this purpose. You will perceive that though South Florida is important, Baldwin is still more so (railroad connection) as the possession of Baldwin determines our ability to communicate with and hold South Florida."[32] Nevertheless, places such as Tampa Bay and Apalachicola were pretty well left to fend for themselves.

Major Buist, commanding heavy artillery, was directed by Anderson to Madison to be given small arms and posted at the Aucilla Bridge as a guard. Colonel Martin was directed to proceed to the point nearest Orange Springs for intercepting Union boat expeditions now operating on the Ocklawaha River.

> In Camp
> May 3rd 1864
>
> Dear Et,
>   Yours of the 29th only reached me last night. I think you wrote on the 30th, the anniversary of marriage, and that I will get it tonight, but not in time to reply by return train.
>   I am truly rejoiced to hear that you are all up once more. I devoutly pray that you may continue so. I have nothing to write, more than what I said in my letter of yesterday. If I were to write every day and a _____ at a time, I would fail to tell you how much I love you.
>   Col. Beard was very unpleasantly situated in the Army of Tenn. Genl. Bragg had placed his *junior* over him and Genl. Johnston merely continued him in position because he did not know what else to do with him. He is a true patriot and a man of excellent qualities in many respects, with some foibles. Under these circumstances I wrote to him and told him if he would apply for and obtain a transfer to my command it would be agreeable to me. He has applied and writes to me that it will be granted, so I look for him soon. I have never applied to be sent away from Florida. I am surprised that you would believe such a story. You know my doctrine is *not* to *apply* for *anything*.
>   Many kisses for the boys, Willie, The, and Pat and also for Bessie. I am glad to hear that they are well and hope they will not be sick again. Love to Mollie and her sweet girls. Also to Aunt. Remembrances to the servants.
>   A bushel of kisses and worlds of love for yourself from
>
> > Your
> > Patton[33]

On May 16, Anderson received orders from the War Department to send a good brigade from Florida to Virginia. He responded immediately by ordering the 1st, 2nd, 4th and 6th Florida Battalions and Bonaud's Georgia Battalion to proceed by railroad without delay, with General J. Finegan in command. Finegan remarked, "I greatly doubt if one-half of the men ordered will leave Florida, and my orders will cause desertions." As the train headed west toward Madison it stopped at Lake City, where "sixty to seventy jumped off and took to the woods." Despite this on May 22, 600 Florida patriots reached Petersburg, Virginia, to join Lee.[34a]

Another love letter to Etta:

Camp Milton, May 19th 1864

> I write a short note to inform you that I go up to Lake City today, where we will make Hd. qtrs. for a short time, and will then go to Middle Fla. unless something happens to prevent it.
> Everything in the way of troops has been sent off except the Cavalry. I feel utterly powerless but I think it is right. The great struggle is to be in Va. We should have every man capable of bearing arms in the Confederacy at that place. If we succeed there, Florida is safe; if not, then it will hardly be worse off than it is now. I have every confidence in the result. God will give us the victory.
> Now that I feel powerless to accomplish anything here, the separation from my dear Et seems more insupportable than ever. As long as I could feel that my presence in the army was of any use at all to the cause, it was consoling to reflect that duty was being performed — but when I feel that I am of no use whatever where I am, I feel like it was *impossible* for me to stay away from you any longer.
> I shall remain in Lake City but a short time and will then proceed to Middle Florida where my Headquarters will have to be established for the purpose of organizing the *Reserves*— for they are our dependence now.
> I am so much disappointed about not getting to see you *tomorrow* that I am almost in the *blues*. But I hope to see you soon *any how*. In the meantime you must be cheerful. Do not repine. The very *anticipation* of the pleasure it will afford me to be with you is *some* comfort — the reality will be earthly happiness in perfection.
> Kiss Willie & The & Pat & Lily for me. Bless their hearts! How I do want to see *them* too! Remember me to the servants.
> Love to Aunt & Mol and Lizzie, Annetta, and Adair.
> A bushel of kisses for yourself from
>
> > Your
> > Patton[34b]

Although Anderson had been in command of the district for less than three months, he began to feel his presence was mundane. It became obvious when he had to transfer General Finegan's battalion to Petersburg. In his correspondence to General S. Cooper, inspector general at

Richmond, on May 17, he remarked, "This will leave my District with one regiment and two battalions of cavalry, three companies of artillery, the sum total of effective forces comprised on my command. Under these circumstances I respectfully submit the question whether I might not be more serviceable elsewhere? Believing that I would be, and having no other desire than that of advancing the interests of the cause, I would earnestly request that I be ordered to some other field if not deemed with those interests."[34c]

Despite the removal of Finegan's forces from Florida to Virginia, Anderson retained the services of Captain J. J. Dickison and his militia cavalry. Dickison, born March 27, 1816, in Virginia, grew up in Georgetown, South Carolina, and later moved to Marion County, Florida, near Ocala where he became a planter. At the start of the war he was elected first lieutenant of the Marion Light Artillery, which did garrison duty in the state. After the Union forces seized the eastern seaboard of Florida, extending south from Fernandina Beach to St. Augustine and Smyrna, and west to the St. Johns River, Dickison organized Company H, 2nd Florida Cavalry in August 1862. Rarely serving with other Florida units, he operated independently in Palatka and the St. Johns River region, proving to be a bane to Federal detachments and supply trains. "Once you crossed the St. Johns River, you were in Dickison's land. The coastal citizens and the army of occupation came to call Dickison, 'Dixie'; the territory he controlled was known as 'Dixieland.'"[35] He had other marks of notoriety, such as "Swamp Fox" and as the "Forest of Florida."[36]

Anderson sent word to him: "Be on your guard and ready for any emergency. I approve your suggestions and direct that you strike the enemy whenever you have an opportunity of doing so to advantage." Utilizing the swampy environment, his forces staged amphibious assaults, sweeping the Federal pickets, scattering Federal raiding parties and returning runaway slaves.[37] Dickison chose to fight rather than retreat. His cavalry unit numbered from 100 to 300 men. the uniform of the day was pretty much that of a white shirt and a straw hat. These guerillas were ceaseless in their attacks and ultimately discouraged the Federals from extending their control beyond the St. Johns. Although Anderson's military operations in Florida lacked the size and casualties of an organized battle, he did get satisfactory results. An example:

"The major-general commanding has great pleasure in announcing to the troops under his command the result of a gallant expedition against the enemy's detached posts, undertaken on the 19th inst. By Capt. J. J. Dickison, Second Florida cavalry. Crossing the St. Johns River in small boats, Captain Dickison surprised and captured the enemy's garrisons at Welaka and Fort Butler, taking 88 infantry and 6 cavalry, with the arms and equipments, and returning with his brave command safely to their camp, bringing in the whole capture, after an absence of forty-four hours, during which time they traveled 85 miles and effected the results herein detailed without the loss of a man. Such an exploit attests more emphatically the soldierly qualities of the gallant men and their skillful leader who achieved it than any commendation it would be possible to give. The major-

John Jackson Dickison, CSA (from Florida State Archives).

general commanding feels, however, that his thanks are due them, and, while thus publicly rendering the tribute so justly due, indulges in the confident hope that every officer and soldier in his district will emulate the patriotic endurance and daring displayed by Captain Dickison and his command." J. Patton Anderson[38]

Several nights later at Horse Landing near Palatka, Dickison and his force ambushed the Union gunboat *Columbine*, a new and superior Federal vessel whose 148 gallant men defended their boat until over half had been killed and the boat sunk by Dickison's artillery piece.

While at McGirt's Creek fortification, a Federal expedition 2,500 strong moved in two columns by night from Jacksonville toward Anderson's Confederates. Three of the eight regiments were black. Anderson retired his small Confederate force without resistance, and then making a detour, attacked the Federal force in the rear, causing them to retreat back to Jacksonville.

Another point of special importance was the calling into the field the *reserve forces* of Florida. The active Confederate force within Anderson's military district was ample for its protecting the district against anything which threatened it in May. However, in June when the whole infantry force was withdrawn for service in Virginia, Anderson was left with an effective Confederate strength of the whole not reaching 1,000 men to protect the district (not including Dickison's cavalry). In early June the Federals, with a superior force from Jacksonville, threatened Baldwin, a rail center and supply depot defended by one company of infantry and 350 cavalry. Since Baldwin was a key link to east Florida and the peninsula, Anderson immediately urged the commandant of conscripts, J. J. Daniels, to hasten the calling up of the reserves to defend the town.

Four companies of reserves who rushed to Baldwin as fast as they were armed. They were barely in time to be ready to meet the advance of the Union men, whose forces numbered eight regiments of infantry, a battalion of cavalry and six pieces of artillery. When the Federal commander learned of the arrival of reinforcements he halted, reconsidered his position, and, recalling the battle of Olustee, retraced his steps back to Jacksonville and St. Augustine.

The wisdom and necessity of calling the reserves into active service, was questioned by many Floridians who felt Anderson was interfering with their subsistence. He replied, "I have given directions for most of the reserves to return to their homes, only retaining such as are absolutely required to guard bridges and stores. I am fully impressed with the importance of husbanding all our agricultural resources and defending the farms, crops and homes of our citizens."

To be sure, Anderson had to scratch to field any type of provost guards for his department. By 1864, Florida had become a haven for thousands of deserters, stragglers from both sides, runaway slaves and felons who were hiding in the swamps and forests. It was a difficult and thankless job to try to maintain civilian control of law and order with the vast waterways and unsettled frontier. There were just too many places to hide. The judicial system cooperated as best it could with the help of county sheriffs who employed disabled soldiers, over- and underage males and reserves to reduce the lawlessness. Anderson, with the help of local cavalry posse, did the best he could on short notice.

The Cow Cavalry

An issue that came to Anderson's attention was the state's commissary department. At the beginning of the war the Confederate Commissary Department was centralized and employed agents to sweep the land in procuring its foodstuffs and animals. By the spring of 1863, the Richmond government decided that each state was to have its own commissary officer. In Florida, Major P. W. White, a lawyer from Quincy, was charged with procuring foodstuffs, especially cattle, for the Confederacy. A shortage of beef to feed these massive armies had resulted from the depletion of state herds, and sources elsewhere were needed. As a result the Confederate commissary forces were required to look to Florida to supply them with beef.

Florida had plenty of open-range beef cattle at the beginning of the war, estimates being about 650,000 head: east Florida (380,000); central Florida (175,000); and west Florida (95,000). The law of supply and demand prevailed for the first two years. East Florida had readily available herds but they were rapidly sold off or were rustled to other states. But when the Unionists took over the eastern part, the efforts to gather beef in this corner of the state were hindered and stopped. Furthermore, during the summer of 1862, commissary agents from the Army of Tennessee began looking to the pastures of Alabama, Georgia and Florida as possible sources of fresh meat. Added to this was the Federal blockade of Texas, cutting off that beef supply, resulting in a shortage. The open-market contract system fell under the pressure of wartime demand. Florida moved into the forefront in plans to keep the Confederate armies fed and fighting.

Floridians boasted that their state became the birthplace of the American beef cattle industry when Ponce de Leon introduced a few cows during his expedition of 1520. Later, Franciscan missionaries and early rancheros maintained small cattle herds, and many of these animals fell into the Indians' hands. The Miccosukees, and later the Seminoles, were the first truly successful herders on the Florida peninsula. The number of cattle in Florida showed a marked rise after the end of the Second Seminole War in 1842, as hardy cattlemen from the Carolinas and Georgia began herding deep inside the Florida Territory, grazing their animals as far south as Kissimmee Valley.[39]

Cattle grazing centered in the lower portion of the peninsula where thousands of square miles of unimproved pine flatlands and innumerable lakes readily served as open range. These cattle were later on referred to as the "Pine Woods" or native Florida cattle. They were the equivalent to the Texas Longhorn and shared the same lineage, but "Pine Woods" cattle had to make do with whatever grew in the thick, desolate pine barrens, thus they were smaller than their Texas Longhorn cousins. Their horns were shorter so they could maneuver in the tree-filled wilderness of Florida. They withstood the Florida heat and insects.

These open-range, semi-wild cattle never received high praise. They weighed about eight hundred pounds on the hoof, and each yielded about three hundred pounds of meat that closely resembled venison in flavor.

With the cattle range in north Florida exhausted, Major White knew that because there were no rail lines to the lower portion of the Florida peninsula he would have to send drovers south to find suitable Pine Wood cattle that had to be extracted from the swamps and driven north several hundred miles to a rail center. This was no-man's-land, infested with bands of deserters, disloyal persons and bandits; there were so many that the Union forces formed two companies of cavalry (Second Florida) from these bands.[40] With this knowledge White proposed to the Richmond government the formation of a special Cow Cavalry battalion of at least three hundred men to protect the drovers and the cattle on the trail. His idea was received favorably and President Davis appointed C. J. Munnerlyn to command the 1st Battalion, Florida Special Cavalry.[41]

Although the state had been swept clean of military-age males early on, Major Munnerlyn got busy recruiting farmers, drifters, cowboys and Negroes to fill the ranks. Once organized, waves of cattle herds of three hundred head or more began traveling up the peninsula. With cries of encouragement from the herdsmen's cracking whips (thus known as "crackers" to this day), the cattle began showing up at railroad terminals such as at Live Oak, where they were sent to the Army of Tennessee. Slaughterhouses and canning factories were located at Madison and Tallahassee to process the beef into a pickled form, sometimes called "salt horse" by the soldiers. The slaughtered animals' hides supplemented the Madison shoe factory that used slaves to manufacture shoes, wagons and buggy harnesses for the Confederate Army. Munnerlyn's Cow Cavalry gave both Confederate armies a large portion of their beef supplies throughout the autumn of 1863. Early in 1864 elements of the Federal 2nd Florida Cavalry, operating out of the Fort Myers area, began to disrupt the drovers, whereupon Munnerlyn had to suspend the drives.[42]

With the arrival of General Beauregard at Camp Milton after the battle of Olustee in February, White of the Florida commissary wired General Beauregard: "We are unable at present to supply the army with beef, and you need expect none until we are given protection to our operations in the peninsula."[43] Beauregard, aware of the need for beef for the armies, also knew the 1862 Conscription Act had put many able-bodied men in hiding so they would not be sent out of state to fight the war. Wisely, he issued a proclamation "promising amnesty and employment in a non-military capacity to all conscripts, absentees, deserters, who would come into the Confederate Subsistence Department in that region." All who joined the Cow Cavalry did receive exemption from regular military service out of state.[44] This proclamation opened the floodgates as an adequate supply of men came forth to fill the ranks with no questions asked. "The cattle battalion resembled a cavalry unit in name only; less-than-perfect military appearance and discipline, it was in actuality a quasi-military detachment raised for a specific mission, the duration of which no one could guess."[45]

The Cow Cavalry took to the field as rapidly as it was formed. By April 1864, it was stationed in the state to protect the cattle drivers and their animals as they moved northward. Captain John T. Leslie established a base at Plant City; Captain Francis A. Hendry established his base at Fort Meade with an area of operations which included the wilderness tract of southwest Florida from the Peace River to Lake Okeechobee. The Rev. Leroy G. Leslie, father of John Leslie, formed a third company in the Tampa Bay area. Many of his 112 militia were members of his congregation. His force fanned out to the north of Tampa and established a base camp at Brookville. Captain W. B. Watson enlisted 98 soldiers in a company at Sanford on the St. Johns River. Lieutenant W. B. Allen covered the village of Orlando, an important watering stop for the herds and men. Captain James Faulkner raised a company of west Florida men for service in Taylor and Lafayette counties. Madison County provided the seventh Cow Cavalry company commanded by Captain J. C. Wilcox, which guarded vital rail terminals in that county and provided protection for Georgia-bound cattle. An additional west Florida unit was raised in Jefferson and Leon counties by William J. Bailey. The ninth company was at Gainesville, under the command of Captain E. J. Lutterloh, which was to defend the rail lines that ran from Gainesville to Cedar Key.[46]

There were nine companies of Cow Cavalry with over a thousand men, scattered over a three-hundred-mile trail, guarding the herds from a country infested with rustlers, bands of traitors and Federal cavalry attacks. During the driving months of 1864 they were bringing out five hundred to 1,000 beef cattle a week despite losses along the trail from lack of rest, water and grazing time.

In the summer of 1864 the plight of Union prisoners at Andersonville, Georgia, continued to escalate. Faced with a daily battle to remain alive, thousands of Union prisoners were starving because the South did not have enough food to feed the ever-increasing numbers of prisoners, which by the middle of August reached more than 30,000 captives behind the stockade's barbed wire. Captain H. M. Allen, at Andersonville, was forced to detach prison guards to look for beef and drive them back to the prison camp for slaughter. Major White in Florida cooperated by ordering all cattle at Madison and Tallahassee to be turned over to the Andersonville party. The depot at Madison supplied 1,170 head for the prisoners. Other than this token gesture, little food of any nature could be supplied them since Confederate combat troops in the field were on short rations, fortunate to be issued any type of meat or corn two days out of seven.[47]

Anderson's limited Confederate forces cooperated with the Cow Cavalry but he himself, being a field commander of combat troops, had reservations about the Cow Cavalry arrangement (amnesty), contending that far too many men remained in the state herding cattle at a time when soldiers were desperately needed in the ranks of fighting regiments.

In a July letter written to White, he explained: "I lay claim to some knowledge of the importance of supplying our armies in the field with beef. Years of service with one of these armies fully enlightened me on that subject. I hope those armies never again suffer the wants and privations in the way of supply ... unfortunately I have seen the want too, of more men in the ranks, to stand up in the hour of trial, to be shot at."[48] Feeling certain that no specific skill was required to work the cattle ranges, he pressed White to comb out the underutilized extra duty men at his supply depots and from the Cow Cavalry. Nevertheless the cliché, "An army moves on its stomach," applied to Florida beef as it continued to sustain the Confederate armies in the field for another year of war.

For a year, southern cowboys operating as the Cow Cavalry struggled to gather the wild scrub cattle into herds and drive them north to a railhead, and the Federals with equal determination captured or scattered the livestock. The services rendered by these patriots undoubtedly saved southern Florida and the cattle in it. In November and December 1864, Florida was cut off from the rest of the Confederacy by Sherman's destructive march through Georgia, and the Cow Cavalry was reorganized and became a part of the Florida state troops under General William Miller in 1865.[49]

X

The Atlanta
Campaign — Jonesboro

The general was well informed of the war's progress during the spring
and summer of 1864. In Georgia, General Grant's orders to General Sherman were simple and clear: get into the interior of Georgia, inflict as much
damage on the state's resources as possible and seize the prize city of the
South, Atlanta. It was up to the Army of Tennessee under the command
of General Joe Johnston to prevent this Yankee strategy. The campaign
began in May at Dalton, Georgia, and thereafter the towns began to fall
victim to General Sherman's juggernaut: Resca, May 15; Cassville, May
18; the battle for Kenesaw Mountain, June 27; and the battles to and into
Atlanta during July. Numbering around 62,000 effectives, the Confederates had been in the immediate presence of Sherman's corps that numbered 100,000 men for seventy-four days and nights of fighting and
retreating. They now encamped in fortress Atlanta at the beginning of
July. An apprehensive President Davis decided to send General Braxton
Bragg to Atlanta to review the situation. Here Davis's military advisor
had extensive conversations with General J. Bell Hood, a more combat-
ive general than Johnston, and on July 17, Hood took over the command
of the Army of Tennessee.

A bitter Joe Johnston remarked, "I know Mr. Davis thinks he can
do a great many things, i.e., to do what God failed to do. He tried to
make a soldier of Bragg but it couldn't be done."[1]

Bragg informed President Davis that Hood's appointment would
give unlimited satisfaction to the president, who believed that military
miracles were brought about by assuming and sustaining the offense; he
wanted a visionary to turn the tide for the Confederacy.

Atlanta's irregular circle of fortifications made it one of the most
strongly protected cities in the war. The ten-mile circumference of high

breastworks, redoubts, cannon emplacements, and rifle pits had been prepared for over a year. General Sherman's plan was to invest Atlanta as quickly as possible. He sent Generals J. M. Schofield and J. B. McPherson toward Decatur, east of Atlanta, while General George H. Thomas, with the bulk of the Union forces, moved toward Peachtree Creek from the north of the city. On the night of July 17, Fightin' Joe Wheeler's cavalry reported the bluejackets were crossing the Chattahoochee River and were moving southward toward Peachtree Creek.

During the 18th of July, Wheeler's cavalry resisted the Union thrust but finally gave way to the wave of blue. They burned the bridges over Peachtree Creek, and then withdrew to the east to oppose McPherson's forces. The Army of the Cumberland spent the next day, July 19, in gaining a foothold on the south side of the creek. All of these crossings by the Union forces were met with fierce resistance of A. P. Stewart's corps. The fighting was severe, resulting in heavy casualties on both sides. By evening half of Thomas's divisions were across the Peachtree Creek while the other half of the army was on the opposite side of the creek. This is what the Confederates had been hoping for — one of Sherman's armies to be divided. Hood embraced the opportunity to strike the divided Federal army.

At 1 P.M. Hardee's forces opened the attack by searching out the left and rear of the enemy that had crossed the creek. As Hardee advanced, Stewart's corps would advance from the right to left hoping to crush Thomas's left flank, and throw the bluejackets back across Peachtree Creek. While Stewart and Hardee were conducting the attack, General Cheatham would maintain his position on the right, facing Schofield and McPherson who were quickly approaching Atlanta from the east. Their movement toward Atlanta necessitated moving Cheatham further to the east, opening a gap in Hood's lines. Hardee tried to fill the gap but discovered Cheatham had moved two miles out of the line. The plan to execute the attack was becoming a failure. As Hardee moved to close the wide gap between his corps and Cheatham, so did Stewart as he ordered Loring and Anderson's old friend, Walthall, to the right. Each change of position to the right cost the Confederates time and allowed Thomas to move more of his troops across Peachtree Creek.

Around 4 P.M. the Confederates began their attack. The Yankees were in plain view about seven hundred yards distant on the opposite side of the field, occupying a ridge running east and west. Finally, after another delay the stiff-jointed Confederate command system was ready for battle even though General Hood was not on the field. Old Blizzard Loring's division moved forward toward the enemy works where it received a terrible fire from the Yankee batteries and repeating rifles. Regardless, with a deafening Rebel yell, the command moved forward and drove the bluejackets from their positions and did not stop until the colors were planted on different points of the breastworks from right to left for a distance of a half-mile. As the Yanks fled in confusion from their works, the steady aim of the Mississippi, Alabama and Louisiana marksmen produced great slaughter on the enemy's ranks.

Loring's victory was short lived when he realized the cooperating Confederate forces had not yet engaged the Yanks and he was stuck between Wm. T. Ward's and Geary's Union divisions which quickly took to enfilading fire on Loring's men from both directions, compelling him to fall back under the cover of a ridge, where the fight continued. Loring's brigades had been hammering at Colonel Benjamin Harrison's (23rd president of the United States) Union forces. Without aid from Stewart or Hardee, Loring held his position till dark. Hood's Confederates had given Thomas a few bad hours but in the end suffered 5,000 casualties without making a dent in the Union lines. Hood would write that the defeat was attributed to Hardee, who failed to carry out Hood's orders. General A. M. Manigault wrote that the battle was a complete failure; it did not delay Thomas twelve hours.

East of Atlanta, Federal General James B. McPherson's Army of the Tennessee was advancing on Atlanta from the vicinity of Decatur. (Union armies were named after rivers whereas Confederate armies were named after states — thus it seems there are two Tennessee armies — "the" is used in front of Tennessee for Federal armies.)

General Wheeler, the old cavalry warhorse for the Confederates, had moved quickly from Peachtree Creek to the vicinity of Decatur where he made a heroic resistance against Blair's advancing XVII Corps at Bald Hill. The pressure on Wheeler's dismounted cavalry soon became too great and at midnight on the 20th he was relieved by Patrick Cleburne's division of infantry which had just completed a forced march from the Peachtree Creek battlefield. From a tree-cleared summit, the well-entrenched Confederates raked the Yanks for a short period with a heavy fire. Union General M. D. Leggett then brought up his crack artillery and from the rear swept the whole Confederate line with a torrent of artillery. With accurate and destructive cannonading, the bluecoats drove out Cleburne's veteran division. Sherman was now knocking at the door east of Atlanta. General McPherson, from the position he had gained on top of Bald Hill, was about two and a half miles from the city. This top became known as Leggett's Hill and became another "Gibraltar" overnight as the Federal artillerymen began to line the hill with cannon that could fire into Atlanta and enfilade a large section of the town. The 20,000 inhabitants began to take flight.

General Hood observed that McPherson's left flank was exposed and decided on another bold move — having Hardee's division attack at daylight and initiate an offensive move on the camped Yankees. Hardee's weary companies, led by Wheeler's scouts, began a fifteen-mile march through Atlanta on the night of July 21. In the city they were joined by Cleburne's division which had just pulled back into the city after its fight at Bald Hill. Completely fatigued, they were forced to march toward Bald Hill without proper rest. But this was Hood's army and he would attack repeatedly, as he felt partial success was productive and of much benefit to the men, improving their morale, infusing new life and fresh hopes and arresting desertion.

The battle of July 22 is usually referred to as the battle for Atlanta. It extended about a mile beyond the Augusta railroad and then back toward Decatur, the whole extent of ground being fully seven miles. Again, with tired men, Hood badly miscalculated his disjointed attack. The bitter battle of Atlanta is too long to be repeated here. So much occurred, such as Generals McPherson (Union) and William H. Walker (Confederate) being killed ... Hardee's tired forces arriving at noon instead of daybreak ... by happenstance the Federal XVI Corps, on its way to reinforce McPherson's left flank, found itself precisely in the spot where it could fall on Hardee's exposed right flank.... In the bloody battle, both sides sustained severe casualties and by nightfall on July 22, the Confederates retired from the battlefield and the Federal line was restored to essentially the same position which it had twenty-four hours earlier. Confederate casualties were about 8,000 to Federal casualties of 3,722. Surgeon Dr. P. F. Whitehead wrote home with the remark, "General Hood will please the administration in Richmond as he is drawing blood." Hood's second sortie was no better than the first one.

General Bragg, at Columbus, sent a telegram to General S. Cooper, adjutant in Richmond on July 23: "After learning the results of yesterday's operation at Atlanta, I have ordered Major General Patton Anderson to report to General Hood. It is important that he should go immediately."[2]

Although Anderson was not a West Point graduate, he was a stern disciplinarian in every sense; General Bragg held him in high esteem, probably because he was as quick to execute a deserter as was Bragg.[3]

Promptly, Special Field Order No. 61 was issued on July 27: "Maj. Gen. Patton Anderson is assigned to command of Hindman's Division, Lee's corps."[4]

> Headquarters Military District of Florida,
> Lake City, July 27, 1864.
> General Orders, No. 32.
> Ordered from this command as unexpectedly as he was ordered to it, the undersigned leaves this for a more active field of duty, and trusts that the recollections entertained of him by the troops of his late command may be as pleasant as those he entertains of them. Fellow-citizens of bygone days, fellow-soldiers of the present, I bid you farewell.
> PATTON ANDERSON, Major-General.

"I received a telegram from Gen. Bragg directing me to report to Gen. Hood at Atlanta without delay for duty in the field. I issued General Orders No. 32 from Lake City on the 27 of July, placing Gen. (J. K.) Jackson in command of the District and (Wm.) Miller of the reserve forces."[5] Bidding Etta and the children goodbye, Anderson started to Atlanta on the morning of July 26, and reached there on the 28th.

Simultaneously, General Hood's third sortie in July was to try to crush Sherman's flank on the west side of Atlanta. He quickly designed another combined assault to forestall Howard's probe around his left. General Stephen D. Lee, who had been just promoted to lieutenant general, was brought from Alabama to take over Hood's corps. He arrived on the 26th and on the 28th he was ordered westward through Atlanta out the Lickskillet Road, to occupy a position from which he could block Howard's extension of the Union right and set him up for a flank attack by Stewart, who would bring his corps out the Sandtown Road that evening. Stewart would be following Lee's advance and then circle the head of the bluecoats and strike from the southwest of Howard's unguarded flank the next morning.

General Hood's orders to Lee were simple: hold the enemy in check on a line nearly parallel with the Lickskillet Road, running through to Ezra Church. Finding the Federal army in its assigned position, General

Lee neither informed Hood nor waited for Stewart's flanking force to get into position. Instead, without pausing even to arrange a coordinated attack with the whole corps, he immediately threw forward whatever unit came first to hand. The result was a piecemeal attack.

The Federal force being engaged was at least 10,000 men with repeating rifles. They were on the crest of a continuous ridge with three sets of battle lines. In terrible July heat, the Rebels rushed on the bluecoats behind their piles of rails, logs and rocks and within thirty minutes, two spirited attacks had been repulsed by the Union men, inflicting tragic losses on Lee's foolish attack. Artillery was finally brought up, which opened heavily upon the Federals for fifteen minutes. Again, Lee ordered another attack.

Meanwhile, the divisions of Loring and Walthall, marching from Atlanta, soon heard the noise of the battle and hastened towards Lee's position, thus abandoning any battle plans to flank Logan. Finding Lee in dire need of assistance, E. C. Walthall's division moved forward into the battle left of Lee's shattered men. Walthall advanced first with Reynold's, and then with J. Cantey and Wm. A. Quarles's brigades, over the same ground and went stumbling over General John C. Brown's dead and wounded and achieving no more success than had Brown. Walthall was then directed to withdraw to the rear of Loring's division, which had been hastily drawn up adjacent to the Lickskillet Road.

The slaughter of Walthall's division in a short period of time indicates the intensity of the firepower of the Union army. Walthall, with the divisions of Reynolds and Cantey, lost 152 officers and nearly 1,000 men — considerably more than a third of his strength! Quarles's brigade, his reserve sent in next to Lee, lost 514 men and all the regimental commanders but one were lost. Madness.

General Walthall, now greatly reduced by losses sustained in assaulting the superior force, was given instructions to hold the position on the Lickskillet Road until Loring's line was complete. *It now became necessary for the general officers to expose themselves to the enemy to encourage their troops to move forward, since portions of the command were refusing to advance.* Line officers with their drawn swords were seen to march to the front of troops that had hesitated.

Loring's veteran division was exposed to heavy incoming fire from the Federals as they formed for their attack. Well-calculated Union volleys and sharpshooters were intense and took their toll. Men fell by the score without ever being within range to deliver an effective volley against the Yankees.

General Loring came up in a hurry and ordered Lee's corps to the left to try to drive the enemy off a hill that they had dug into. The division spread into battle rapidly. The Yankees had them like sitting ducks on a pond, in the open, and the Confederates could see only the smoke from their guns and muskets. They poured shot down on the Rebels, who were moving into regimental battle lines. General Loring was shot from his horse. At the same time Stewart came galloping onto the field, waving Loring's men forward when he was struck in the forehead by a spent bullet. The ricocheting bullet rendered Stewart unconscious as it knocked him from his horse. Some of the troops, thinking Stewart badly hurt, carried him down the road to some shade to make him comfortable. After a short time, Stewart came to and brushed his forehead as if to wipe something away. It was soon discovered that he was not badly hurt. Loring and Stewart were quickly moved to the field hospital. The lieutenant general commanding having been wounded, the command evolved to General Walthall. He directed General W. A. Quarles, to whom his command had passed, to complete the execution of the order to withdraw, but to form on the left of Loring's division instead of going to the rear.

The battle of Ezra Church, Lickskillet Road, Poor House or whichever name you prefer, was an unsettling, bloody, desperate three-hour affair that brought no benefit to Hood's army and cost him some 5,000 more casualties versus only 700 Union casualties. No action of Hood's early campaign did so much as to demoralize and dishearten the troops as this battle of Ezra Church. Among the Confederate generals wounded were Generals Loring, Stewart, S. D. Lee, Brown, and Gibson. General M. D. Ector had been wounded the day earlier and his left leg was amputated. Again Hood was not present on the battlefield at Ezra Church, and the fickle finger of fate points at "Old Temporary Lee," as his troops called him. Union General J. D. Cox remarked in his report of the battle: "The argument which Hood used that Johnston's policy of retrograde had made the troops timid, was not supported by the fact of this day."[6]

Anderson was assigned to take command after the battle of Ezra Church, succeeding the wounded General Brown. On the twenty-ninth he was assigned to, and on the thirtieth of July assumed, command of the division containing Jacob H. Sharp's and Wm. F. Brantly's brigades of Mississippians, Deas's brigade of Alabamans and Manigault's brigade of Alabama and South Carolina troops.[7] General Anderson was back among the troopers he loved.

General Hood ordered a new line of entrenchments prepared to protect the railroad. It began at the existing Confederate defense line west of Atlanta and ran westward for some one and a quarter miles parallel with the Sandtown Road, overlooking the north branch of Utoy Creek.[8] The work of entrenching was pushed with vigor night and day till in the course of ten days the pits were gradually connected and the whole became almost one continuous line of entrenchments, with head-logs and loopholes to protect the sharpshooters. The Union forces had established their main line parallel to and about 800 yards in front of the Confederates, with their skirmishers not much over 100 yards from the Rebels.[10] Anderson's division was resting on the Lickskillet Road and his left on Utoy Creek, with 2,800 bayonets.[11]

Early August found Union General J. M. Schofield's corps along the Sandtown Road, toward the railroad near East Point, Georgia. He moved into the tangled country along Utoy Creek, opposite Anderson, skirmishing at Sunshine Church, Frogtown, Jug Tavern and Mulberry Creek, in the slow extension of the siege line. At one point along their line the Federals erected an earthwork with embrasures for six guns. Anderson recollected, "We had no guns on our main line to deter them from attempting to put more than one piece in position. The embrasure from which this one piece was fired was so mantled, and the cannoneers so well protected, that it was almost impossible for the sharpshooters to do more than confine them to their works." Day after day the bluecoats used it with damaging effect upon Anderson's men.

After several days spent in this mode of annoying warfare, several generals went forward to apprise the Utoy Creek entrenchment. General Manigault would write: "Off we started and soon reached the spot, Generals Lee and Anderson using their glasses to observe with great accuracy the enemy's position. I knowing full well what to expect, did not view the scene with much complacency, expecting every moment that one or more of us would be struck down. Shortly, several rifle balls hummed ominously by us, and we had not been stationary more than fifteen seconds, where a severe concussion in our midst, accompanied by a cloud of dust and smoke, and the smart in several parts of the body of each of us, from small fragments of rock or loose pebbles, gave notice that a shell had burst amongst us. The report of the gun, the bursting of the shell, and the horrid screech which accompanied it, were simultaneous. Fortunately, we had separated from each other a few feet. I turned to see who had fallen, but all were standing. The aide was rubbing his leg where a stone had struck him. General Anderson was picking up his hat, and General Lee brushing from his face and neck the sand and dirt which had been deluged. The shell, a percussion one, had struck and exploded within six or eight feet of us."[12]

In another instance, Brantly's men, by rolling logs ahead of them and digging zigzag trenches, approached so near the Union rifle pits as to be able to throw hand grenades over the breastworks. Sometimes they were so close to the enemy that they could hear every word of command as distinctly as those of his own troopers.

Firing between the parties on the two picket lines was constant during the day and during the night, as scouts penetrated the Union line and kept Anderson well advised of all important movements. "The skirmishing along Patton Anderson's and H. D. Clayton's divisions amounted to almost an engagement for a week."[13] On August 24 Anderson told his troops "that if they could hold our ground a few days longer at

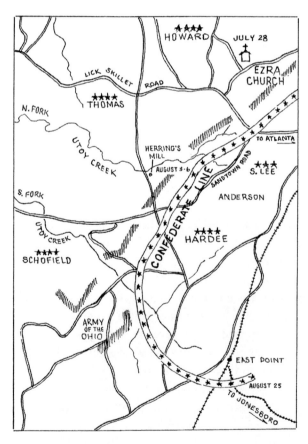

Confederate entrenchments on Sandtown Road[9]

this place, that the victory was assuredly ours, for General Wheeler has gone around Sherman's rear and torn up the railroad, and if they cannot flank us and cause us to retreat, that they will necessarily be compelled to retreat to Chattanooga, or be compelled to starve to death."[14] Obviously enthused by Anderson's speech, Private Vann of the 19th Alabama on the following day describes it to: "Dear Lizzie, There are not many of us dirty Rebs here but what few of us are here are in fine spirits and can whip many a Yank yet."[15] A frequently repeated tale that reflected General Hood's impetuous tactics of always attacking: After the fighting, one of the Federal pickets called out across the lines at twilight, "Well, Johnny, how many of yours are left?" A fatigued butternut replied, still maintaining a semblance of the sense of humor so essential a part of the Confederate soldier, "Oh, about enough for another killing."[16]

On the night of August 25, the scouts reported a movement on the part of the Federal forces which was evident by the rumbling of artillery wagons. On the twenty-ninth, General Sherman, tired of the cat-and-mouse game with no success along the Utoy Creek, commenced moving the army against the Macon Railroad at East Point, Georgia, where he spent the next day wrecking and destroying the railroad thoroughly.

At this stage of the war, General Sherman had special battalions of railroad men for constructing railroads. For the Atlanta campaign they laid the entire line of the Western and Atlantic lines with new rails, and had two hundred engines and three thousand cars on hand to move the estimated thirteen hundred tons per day that would have to be forwarded to keep Sherman's corps supplied. The line traversed from Louisville to Nashville to Chattanooga and then south to Atlanta. The butternuts used to joke that they were sure Sherman carried one or two extra tunnels with him because he could build the lines so quickly. The Construction Corps, composed of 2,000 men, was made of master bridge builders and proficient at tearing up tracks.

These men also decapitated Southern lines as Sherman advanced.

Here the track was heaved up in sections the length of a regiment, then separated rail by rail; bonfires were made of the ties and of fence-rails on which the metal rails were heated, carried to close-by trees or telegraph poles, wrapped around them and left to cool. Included with this efficiency was the trickery of a booby-trap. The deep cuts were filled up with trees, brush and earth, and commingled with loaded shells, so arranged that they would explode on an attempt to rebuild the tracks by the Confederates. The exploding of one such shell could demoralize a gang of Negroes trying to rebuild the railroad for the Rebels.

On August 31, Sherman's advancing Yankees seized Rough and Ready, a village on the railroad halfway between Atlanta and Jonesboro. The Union army in great strength crossed the Flint River and the Federals began maneuvering Hood's splintered forces out of Atlanta, thus splitting up his weakened army into three distinct bodies.

August 29: "I received orders from corps headquarters to hold the division in readiness to move to the left at 4:00 A.M. the following morning. At the appointed hour on August 30 the command started from its position in the line and marched south about two miles in the direction of East Point, where it halted at the Campbellton Road. We rested here till 4:00 P.M., when I was directed to proceed to East Point and relieve Cheatham's division, then in temporary trenches in front of that place. The head of the column reached this position shortly and commenced relieving Cheatham's division. At 9:00 P.M. I received orders to withdraw and follow Cheatham's division in the direction of Jonesboro to protect the Macon & Western Railroad. It was about 11:00 P.M. when my column got in motion, much delay experienced for want of competent guides and the want of roads."[17]

After marching all night, Anderson halted on the 31st when he was informed that General Cleburne was in advance and had sent back information that the enemy had taken possession of a bridge in Cleburne's front. "Very soon Cheatham's division began to move forward, and I followed with the commands well closed up. The all-night march had been toilsome to the extreme for troops who had not been out of the trenches for thirty days. Daylight revealed a wearied and jaded column with ranks considerably diminished by straggling as some butternuts tried to catch a few moments of sleep. The dense woods, without roads, the want of shoes by so many, and the lack of recent exercise contributed to induce a degree of straggling which I did not remember to have seen in any former march of the kind."[18] Anderson reached Jonesboro at 11 A.M. on the thirty-first and halted near the railroad. The Union men were plainly visible in force.

The Battle of Jonesboro, Georgia

(then spelled "Jonesborough")
August 31–September 1, 1864 — On Wednesday morning the weary Confederates, without time for food or drink, advanced to a position

parallel with and about 200 yards west of the railroad. Sharp's gallant Mississippians could be seen pushing their way in small parties up to the very slope of the Union breastworks.[19] They immediately began strengthening the line with logs, rails and such other material that could be found. Union General Howard's corps was posted on the crest of an irregular ridge, and his position rendered stronger by a line of breastworks which he had thrown up earlier.

Anderson recalled: "Our order of battle was in two lines. The first was a continuous line, and was composed of three brigades from each division; the second line was composed of one brigade for each division, posted about 200 yards in rear of the first. I was directed to relinquish the command of my supporting line to General Clayton and to devote myself exclusively to the three brigades in the first line. These were Sharp's, Deas's, and Brantly's. I was not to attack until Gen. Cleburne had hotly engaged the enemy at close range in his front."[20]

At about 2:20 P.M. the quick and heavy rattle of musketry began on Cleburne's line, mingled with the rapid discharge of artillery. The butternuts moved forward deliberately and with resolution. The bluecoats' skirmishers were pushed back up to the main line at the top of the ridge before the Confederate first line was under heavy fire from the enemy's breastworks. Sharpshooters along the line were going "crack, crack, crack" in a lively manner. "My troops moved forward with a spirit and determination that threatened, in spite of the odds, to crown the hill and drive the enemy from his place; but under a heavy deadly fire the men wavered and the rest lay down. For many it would be their last battle. The line was unbroken, and every inch of ground gained was resolutely maintained. Every moment brought death and wounds to the ranks. Officers were constantly falling while engaged in encouraging and urging the men to remain firm. My second line came up in rear of Deas and Brantly, but the ranks were so thinned by the fire to which they had been exposed that the two lines combined were unable to make any farther advance as their firing sputtered out." The ever-lengthening list of casualties blunted the edge of the Confederate forces' offensive power. "Regarding the extreme right of my line as in great danger, I proceeded along the line from Brantly's right toward Sharp's position. Stragglers were pushed up to the firing line and the slightly wounded were encouraged to remain there."[21]

General Manigault observed: "Gen. Anderson, commanding the

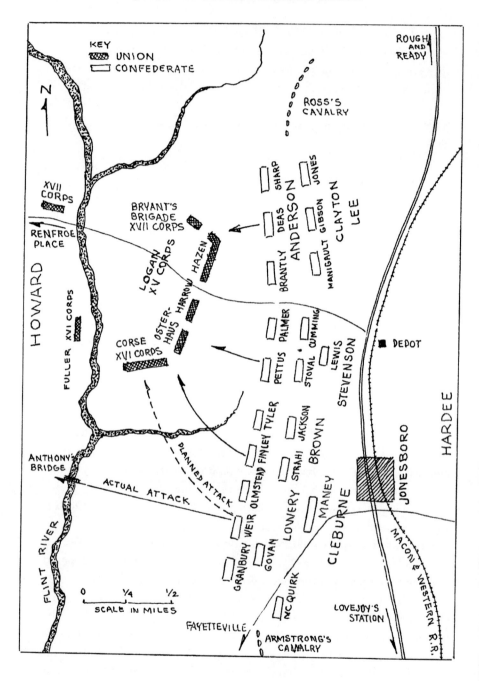

Battle of Jonesboro

division, rode up with an aide, apparently much excited, and ordered me to advance and attack again. As he rode along the line, he addressed the tired troopers and urged them on. It certainly was a act of consummate generalship to put forward 700 or 800, just defeated, and scattered commands, with no other troops to support them within 500 yards, against I do not know how many thousands. The folly of the order was so evident to all that nothing but the habit of obedience to the orders of their superior officers, carried the men forward for a space."[22] Anderson, astride Yancy, had led part of his command within pistol range of the enemy.[23] After having ridden along the line from Brantly's right, urging the men and officers to stand a little longer until reserves could be brought forward, he reached a point near Sharp's left. A bullet slammed into Anderson, knocking him off Yancy. The bullet passed through his mouth, breaking his jaw, nearly severing his tongue.[24] He was carried to the rear in dangerous condition; he lost a great deal of blood and the surgeon thought he had received his death wound.[25] The hemorrhage nearly proved fatal, but was finally arrested near daylight the next day. General S. D. Lee later wrote: "Gen. Anderson was terribly wounded in the face and passed immediately by me, being borne from the field. A more painful sight was seldom seen."[20] The wounding of General Anderson saw General Edward Johnson succeed to the command of the Mississippians.

XI

To the End of the War — Bentonville

By telegram Etta received the news of her husband's being wounded, and immediately made arrangements to travel to Atlanta. She was in luck with her travel plans when General Sherman terminated the Jonesboro engagement and decided to let the shattered but lethal Confederate army veterans go unmolested as he returned his own weary and exhausted army back into Atlanta to claim the spoils of his victory. An armistice between both sides was declared for ten days, which permitted both armies to rest, reorganize, recruit and exchange prisoners. Since Anderson's wound was no longer life threatening, the united couple was able to travel around the Union's position and return safely to Monticello. At the time, the Confederacy maintained six hospitals in Florida with a total of 515 beds. They were located at Lake City, 150; Madison, 75; Tallahassee, 100; Quincy, 126; Marianna, 50; and Camp Lay near Madison, 14.[1] Anderson elected to stay at home for convalescence. It was his pleasure to be home with his Etta and the children. He took advantage of his spare time to write his autobiography in a plantation ledger book for his children. In addition he completed his battle reports.[2]

While recuperating he kept apprised of the war and movement of the Army of Tennessee. On September 25, President Davis arrived from Richmond at Palmetto Station, Georgia, for a review of the condition of the Army of Tennessee. He was upset by the fall of Atlanta, denouncing General Joe Johnston and Georgia governor Joseph E. Brown as little better than traitors who had befallen the cause. He aroused the men and officers, pronouncing that the tables were to be turned; Forrest's and P. D. Roddey's cavalry were already in central Tennessee, and this army was to follow along. The strategy was to checkmate Sherman and isolate him by attacking the isolated rear of his communications and railroad supply line, requiring him to turn out of Atlanta and chase them. By the 1st of October, Hood's army was on the move into the mountains of northern Georgia, attacking Big Shanty, a depot of Sherman's on the Western & Atlantic Railroad. Then Ackworth, Allatoona and Resca. Sherman could not catch the will-o'-the-wisp butternuts who, by snaking in and out of the mountains of Georgia, were laying waste to his railroad. Enough! Sherman resolved to leave General Thomas, "The Rock of Chickamauga," at Nashville to handle Hood. The game was over.

Anderson, recovering in Florida, began focusing on the future and its expectations of him and the cause. With resolution and devotion, he followed the unconquerable Army of Tennessee as it moved into Alabama and Tennessee. But Anderson's army was moving away from him. Of a more immediate interest were Sherman and his 65,000 troopers marking time in Atlanta. Would he move to free the 30,000 suffering and starving Union prisoners at Andersonville prison, ninety miles south of Atlanta? Or would he invade Florida for its beef, corn and horses to supply his army for its next move?

The answer came from Washington on October 16, when Sherman received permission to undertake a march across Georgia to the ocean without the benefit of his railroad supply line or orders to free the Andersonville souls. Sherman chose the most immediate route via Macon and then to Savannah, Georgia, a seaport to the Atlantic Ocean where he could link up with the Federal navy for his supplies and reinforcements. Sherman and Hood were moving in opposite directions, freeing both commanders to seek new adventure and adversaries.

It was getting late in the season, but that was of no concern to General Hood as he moved his army freely into Alabama. On October 19, he encamped at Gadsden. In pouring rain his fatigued army crawled and staggered toward Decatur, Alabama, with a severe fight to obtain the Tennessee River crossing; he had to withdraw and move to Leighton on the 30th to wait for supplies and improved weather. He resumed moving westward, crossing the Tennessee River at Florence on November 13. Here he met General Beauregard, who brought free advice and the change of strategy from President Davis, who now disapproved of the invasion. It was too late. Hood's army was three hundred miles to the west of Sherman, offering little relief for the Georgia farms and their inhabitants.

By this time, Sherman had evacuated and burned out Atlanta and was marching his three corps southeast toward Macon. He learned that earlier, back in Atlanta, when Hood assumed command and after several major defeats and heavy loss of life, Hardee became disenchanted with Hood's leadership and accepted a transfer to the command of the Atlantic coast. With Sherman's serious movement into Georgia, a quick fix was on Richmond's mind, as Braxton Bragg was ordered to halt Sherman's march! Crafty Bragg replied, "that no practicable combination of my available men can avert disaster."[3] Hardee was placed at Savannah with an independent command as Bragg took over his district.

A general such as Anderson, in repose, was always privy to what was going down from the returning soldiers, deserters and the self-discharged who entered Florida on their way home or seeking refuge. They found many listeners to the latest news and rumors from their theater of war. Anderson took special interest in hearing about his comrades, especially Bragg and Hardee, now at Savannah.

"At Savannah, Hardee had to scrape together adequate forces to defend the seaport. The tactician spent time locating and training artillerists, building wharves, and placing obstructions on all roads into the small city. Since Sherman's objective or even his whereabouts were unknown to Hardee, he spent the month of November arming the area to block the Federal advance wherever it may come from, and at the same time receiving inactive forces from Augusta, Charleston, and Bragg at Wilmington, North Carolina."[4]

General Sherman was a staunch advocate of the potency of economic compression as a military policy.[5] He contended that the invading army was entitled to all it could get from the people of the territory. His general order of November 9, 1864, provided that the army would forage liberally upon the country during the march.

Sherman's corps departed Atlanta beginning November 16; while his bands played *The Battle Hymn of the Republic* his army of 62,000 teenaged adventurers marched across the state in twenty-seven days, covering 222 miles, destroying as they went, pilfering farm animals, burning plantations and inflicting dastardly deeds on defenseless citizens. Ripping the heartland of Georgia were the corps of H. W. Slocum and Oliver O. Howard and Judson Kilpatrick's cavalry. By the middle of December the "bummers" approached Savannah, ready to take on 10,000 butternuts with limited combat experience who were divided among makeshift divisions of Generals G. W. Smith, Lafayette McLaws, and A. R. Wright.

"Beauregard arrived from Charleston on December 9, and spent the day conferring with Hardee, setting forth the guiding principles for the defense of Savannah: 'Having no army of relief to look to, and your forces being essential to the defense of Georgia and South Carolina, whenever you shall have to select between their safety and that of Savannah, sacrifice the latter, and form a junction with General Sam Jones, holding the left bank of the Savannah and the railroad to this place as long as possible.'[6] Beauregard asked Hardee about his plans for evacuation. Hardee told him that none had been made, as he was relying on the gunboats in Savannah Harbor to ferry his troops to South Carolina. Beauregard thereupon directed Hardee to begin at once the construction of pontoon bridges across the Savannah River."[7]

December 10 and December 11 saw heavy skirmishing as both wings of Sherman's army closed in on Hardee's defenses. Slocum broke the Savannah and Charleston rail communications, and halted traffic on the Savannah River. Howard penetrated south to Flemingo, breaking the Gulf Railroad, and Fort McAllister, the isolated bastion controlling the Great Ogeechee River, fell to General W. B. Hazen's bluecoats. Beyond Fort McAllister were the Union fleet and great quantities of supplies and heavy siege guns, which were Sherman's destination. On December 16, Hardee and his generals agreed that Savannah should be evacuated. On December 17 Sherman demanded Hardee's surrender. The next day, Hardee, "in frozen language that he could command so well, wrote Sherman, refusing to surrender."[8]

Hardee was stalling for time for the pontoon bridges to be completed, which they were on December 19. "About thirty rice flats seventy to eighty feet long were fastened end to end, and joined with a floating dock from the north side of Hutchinson's Island, completing the evacuation route over the Savannah River. During the morning of December 20, General Ezra Carman's Union brigade, now on the South Carolina side of the river, witnessed a scene that they never forgot as, over the pontoons, it seemed, came the entire civilian population of Savannah, wagons, family carriages, men and women on foot. To discourage Carman's bluecoats from molesting this procession, Hardee strongly reinforced Wheeler's line to the west of the line of retreat. Wheeler's men fired lavishly, using the surplus ammunition they knew would have to be destroyed. Then Hardee's infantry (three divisions), preceded by forty-nine pieces of artillery, crossed over without incident."[9]

Hardeeville, South Carolina, became an assemblage point for not only Hardee's forces, but also those of General W. B. Taliaferro, who was sent from Charleston with what men he had to join Wright's, McLaws's, and Smith's divisions.[10]

Sherman's primary objective was a base on the Atlantic Ocean for his corps, as his men already felt the need for supplies; in the Union camps hard crackers were selling for a dollar. Sherman enjoyed the comforts of Savannah; he stayed almost a month before his next advance into South Carolina.

Anderson's holidays would become even more glum as the worst of news came by telegraph. First, the tragic five-hour battle at Franklin, Tennessee, on November 30. The charge and battle had all the elements of mass grandeur. In the forests of the southern states it was a rare thing to have a battlefield on which the contending armies could be seen. Usually they fought in tangled woods, thickets and mountains where the extent of the engagement was by the sound of the distant artillery, the crash of musketry or the Rebel yell. Here at Franklin, both sides could see the field and follow the movements of the Confederates. It was now 3 P.M. and Hood must attack soon, as the sun would set at 5 P.M.

The field and staff were all mounted, and they could be seen riding their lines and dressing them up just as though they were on brigade drill. The Confederates were marching in a straight line, parade fashion, across the Franklin plain, in full view of the whole Union army. It was documented in many Union officers' reports that for a moment their men were spellbound with admiration in seeing this tidal wave marching at them. Many had read and heard the saga of Gettysburg but never had any of them seen it firsthand. Now for a minute, 20,000 bluecoats peered down their gun barrels to behold 18,000 gallant Confederates with flags flying, moving proudly over the open plain to the attack.

Each division was marching to one common center, the breastworks and Franklin; thus the field of battle began to converge to a narrower front. Generals and staff officers leading them on horses or walking in ranks — eighteen brigades of infantry with cavalry support, their gray uniforms soiled and worn with hard service — were indistinguishable in the ranks. Beneath the slouched hats were sunken eyes, empty bellies longing for a biscuit and thousands without shoes in the cold mud. This was the Army of Tennessee, the ghost army — but not obvious to the Yankees was that this army was still flushed with hope, pride and ambition, and this chivalry, after four years of fighting, would lead the charge to victory. They marched over the plains of Franklin until within three hundred yards of the Yanks' breastworks, when a cannon boomed from Fort Granger across the river. This was the signal — and then the Rebel yell and musketry from the charging butternuts. Suddenly a sheet of flame and smoke burst forth from the entire crescent Union breastworks, filling the air with grape, shell, and rifle bullets that soon ended with a thump as it crashed into the onrushing Rebels. "On, forward, forward" was the cry, as it was death to stop. The whole Confederate front was being decimated by a crossfire of repeating and revolving rifles. And now they were in front of well-grown and almost impenetrable thorny hedges of Osage orange. It was strongly supported by sharpened branches made into an abatis and deeply imbedded in the earth and immovable. Over this plain no organized force could go — General Walthall had two horses shot from under him. It was growing dark but still the Confederates charged.

Colonel W. D. Gale, Stewart's adjutant, said it was not a battle. The fight was furious and the carnage beyond anything he had ever observed. It was murder. Broken brigades were quickly reformed. Volleys of fire staggered the Confederate lines and men went down like leaves in the fall of the year. The fight lasted until about 9 P.M. There was much hand-to-hand combat in the dark. Nighttime and physical exhaustion brought an end to the battle. It was truly five hours of tragic fighting as it became the grave for the Army of Tennessee. Hood's losses were 1,750 killed and 3,800 men wounded and left in Franklin hospitals; 702 were captured. With the walking wounded, Hood's total casualties were probably over 7,000 men. Franklin was another of Hood's outrageous failures.

Union Colonel Opdycke said he never saw the dead lie so thickly. "I saw them upon each other, dead and ghastly in the powder-dimmed star-light." Second bishop of Tennessee, the Rev. Charles Todd Quintard and chaplain to the Army of Tennessee, wrote up a very descriptive picture of the dead Confederate generals.

> After the battle General Strahl's horse lay by the road-side and the General by his side – both dead. All his staff were killed. This varies from the story of him handing up ammunition when he got killed (?)
>
> General Gist, of South Carolina, was lying dead with his sword still grasped in his hand and reaching across the fatal breastworks.
>
> General Granberry of Texas, and his horse were seen on the top of the breastworks, — horse and rider, — dead!

Major-General John C. Brown, General George Gordon and General Carter were seriously wounded — the last named, mortally.

Major-General Cleburne's mare was dead on the works and the General himself was pierced with no less than forty-nine bullets.

Brig.-General Adams was killed leaping his horse, "Old Charlie," over the outer works. Both horse and General Adams was [sic] instantly killed.

I found General Manigault wounded in the head and Major Prince, of Mobile, wounded in the foot.

General Quarles had his left arm shattered ... I found General Cockrill of Missouri, wounded in the legs and in the right arm.

This roster of dead and wounded contemporaries shocked Anderson: *What would have happened if he were with the ranks at Franklin?*

When the battle was over, the city of Franklin was evacuated by the Union command, which retreated hastily toward Nashville, still fearful of Hood's hornets. Who would lead a crushed army with five general officers killed, six general officers wounded, six colonels killed and nine wounded? Hood continued to be the villain as he chased those damned bluebellies.

Then the frightful setback at Nashville in December in freezing rain, ice and snow, found Hood's broken army in flight out of Tennessee, recrossing the Tennessee River on a pontoon bridge at Florence on New Year's Day 1865, and retreating to the safety of Tupelo and Corinth, Mississippi, having sustained 23,000 casualties out of a total strength of 38,000 Confederates.

The Confederacy that had been so confidently launched in Montgomery nearly four years previous was rapidly on the decline and unraveling. Every day added to the paralysis steadily creeping over the southern cause. There was little room left for belief of any sort in the ultimate success of the Confederacy by the beginning of the new year unless you were still one of the hard-core patriots. Even General Sherman's march to the sea in November, and General Hardee abandoning the strategic city of Savannah at the last minute on December 21, failed to shake Anderson's loyalty for the Confederacy.

1865

In Richmond, the Confederate Congress expressed increasing dissatisfaction with the Davis administration and talked of restoring Joseph

E. Johnston to command and making Robert E. Lee general-in-chief. On January 13, General Hood requested to be relieved from his command, which took effect ten days later. While Sherman spent about a month in Savannah feeding and clothing his troops, and filling the wagon trains with ammunition and rations, his plans shifted toward South Carolina, the traitor state. By the middle of January Sherman, with 60,000 bluejackets, began moving north with two columns; one threatening Charleston, South Carolina, and the other Columbia, South Carolina, the capital. Hardee had moved his Rebel force north to Charleston.

General Joseph E. Johnston

At General Lee's request, Joe Johnston was called up out of retirement in hopes he could unite the scattered and fragmented Rebel armies so they could halt Sherman's advancing corps. Out of necessity there was then a great consolidation of the depleted Confederate regiments, battalions, batteries and ranks, resulting in many brigades having two or more units combined under a single commander.

At Charleston, General Hardee had a makeshift force of: Wheeler's cavalry (5,000); A. R. Wright (2,000); Taliaferro (4,600); McLaws (7,000) infantry; and five hundred Georgia militia under G. W. Smith. "Hardee arranged his men at Charleston into what he hoped would be a deadly defensive coil. Wheeler stayed along the New River and the Savannah River. McLaws's division would constitute Hardee's main line of resistance along the Salkehatchie River with Wright's division supporting McLaws to the ocean. Taliaferro remained in Charleston and G. W. Smith concentrated his reserves at Branchville, a critical South Carolina railroad junction."[11]

"Realizing the calamity at hand, President Davis had transferred Beauregard to the West. Before he departed he left instructions with Hardee that preparations must be made for the evacuation of Charleston, and he urged the War Department to extend Hardee's control to include Augusta, Georgia, which was done."[12] "General Beauregard knew of the impending advance of Sherman's forces into South Carolina and ordered everything left of the Army of Tennessee in Mississippi to be moved east towards Augusta, Georgia. Remnants of the Army of Tennessee from as far as five hundred miles at Tupelo, Mississippi, began moving eastward by boat, train, and walking towards Augusta, Georgia. Piecemeal parts of the Army of Tennessee began arriving at Augusta on February 11, but were too late to save on fire Columbia, the capital. Sherman's rapid advance was already heading north towards Fayetteville, North Carolina. The second week in February saw the continuing deterioration of the military situation as the Confederate array of arms became so stretched that it could not seriously impede Sherman. Finally, Beauregard and Hardee recognized the hopelessness of the situation and decided on February 14 to abandon Charleston."[13]

February — Hardee's forces evacuated Charleston, South Carolina, on the seventeenth, while news came of the fall of Columbia, South Carolina. With this news, Anderson wrote: "This is a dark day in the history of the present war, but I believe a brighter day will soon dawn upon us. If dissention and faction do not distract us, we will certainly achieve our independence. The course of some prominent men in Georgia just at this time is much calculated to grieve the spirit of all true Southerners. It is to be hoped that they will desist from their factious teachings and practices (peace) and soon unite with the patriots of the land to prosecute with unanimity and vigor the war which our enemies are determined to wage against us."[14]

The last of Hardee's forces crossed the Santee River on February 25, and McLaws's division reached Cheraw, South Carolina. Anderson, unsettled with current events and out of a sense of duty, and in the vain hope of being able to effect some last-minute benefit to the faltering cause, decided to return to active duty against the advice of his physician. Etta recorded Anderson's movements: "My husband returned to the army in North Carolina in March. He was assigned to a new command from Charleston and assigned a South Carolina division, composed of Col. George P. Harrison, Jr.'s brigade, Colonel A. M. Rhett's brigade, and

Maj. A. B. Rhett's battalion of artillery."[15] "This was in General Hardee's army which contained McLaws's division, which mustered Col. G. P. Harrison, and General Taliaferro's division containing Rhett's brigade and Rhett's artillery."[16]

March 3 — Hardee, receiving orders to move to Fayetteville, evacuated Cheraw, closely followed by Sherman's right wing. At Fayetteville on the ninth, he found General Johnston waiting for him with instructions: "If Sherman does not move toward Raleigh, Hardee should proceed to Smithfield and unite with Bragg's forces moving up from Wilmington, and with the Army of Tennessee moving from Augusta, Georgia."[17]

After crossing the Cape Fear River, Hardee turned his forces toward his supply depot at Averasboro, North Carolina, arriving through the 13th of March. Heavy Carolina rains were falling all day on the 15th, with rivers flooding and mud everywhere. "Old Reliable" Hardee, as his men called him, chose his ground well as skirmishing began in late afternoon as Slocum's advance guard fell upon Hardee's pickets. Hardee had about 8,000 effectives[18] assembled, now without the services of Colonel Rhett, who was captured before Averasboro, and General Elliott, who had been wounded.[19] In the absence of official records of when and where Anderson joined Hardee, there is an eyewitness account of his presence at Averasboro. A midnight strategy meeting had been called, and a sixteen-year-old aide to the inspector general on Taliaferro's staff would write: "There were thirteen generals in the room — Hardee, Hampton, Wheeler, Taliaferro, McLaws, Haygood, Elliott, Kennedy, Kerhaw, Connor, *Anderson*, Jackson of Georgia, and Pemberton or Longstreet."[20] There is every likelihood that Patton was present for the battles of Averasboro and Bentonville, as in the Carolinas, he commanded Taliaferro's division.[21]

Averasboro, North Carolina

March 16, 1865 — Slocum's trailing column overtook Hardee's corps, defending itself on a narrow ridge with the Black River on one side and a swamp on the other. Two divisions of the XX Corps moved against Hardee's front while a brigade of Union men was sent to try to envelop the butternuts' right. Here Case's brigade drove back Taliaferro's division to a second line where McLaws's division was entrenched. Darkness ended the Federal attack on this line.[22] This was a delaying action by Hardee; Anderson was present for the skirmish. Johnston ordered Hardee to march at once for Bentonville, where other Confederate units were uniting to present a solid front against Sherman. Tired, hungry and wet, Hardee's patriots moved out that night toward Elevation, North Carolina. Time was of the essence.

General Sherman's two separated corps, creating a "Y" formation, began drifting apart, which Johnston knew. Still the tactician, his purpose now was to destroy the exposed forces one at a time before they could be reunited. Johnston approved Bentonville, some twenty miles west of Goldsboro, for the surprise confirmation. By marching all that day, the forces of Stewart from the Army of Tennessee and Bragg arrived soon after nightfall at Bentonville, while Hardee's tired columns had to camp on the road six miles from the village.

Bentonville, North Carolina

"There was never a battle line where so much of 'rank' commanded so little of 'file.' Johnston, a full General, was in command, with Beauregard, of the same rank, as second in command. Bragg, another General, commanded one wing, and Lieutenant-Generals Hardee and Steward, the others. Lieutenant-General D. H. Hill ... commanded a corps; Lieutenant General Hampton, the cavalry, with Major-General Wheeler as his second in command. There were the Major-Generals also: Hoke, Taliaferro, Stevenson, Cheatham, Bate, Brown, McLaws, 'Old Blizzards' Loring with one arm gone, Patton Anderson, Walthall, Butler — and all of them together commanding but twenty thousand men, the faithful remnants of divisions and corps which had fought all over the South for four years."[23]

March 19 — Union General W. P. Carlin, while attempting to flank the entrenched Rebels, ran into Loring's and Hill's forces, who received them with a sheet of fire. The bluecoats reeled under the volley with great gaps in their line, and halted their advance. Hardee's legions, because of inaccurate state maps, were late in arriving at Bentonville. McLaws was the first to reach the area and was sent to the far left to join General Hoke. Taliaferro with Stephen Elliot, Jr. and Rhett's brigades began arriving around 2:00 P.M. and were dispatched to the far right to join General Stewart's forces and the Army of Tennessee. With everything in place, the shrieking Rebel yell echoed the opening of the battle as the Confederate right wing swept forward. Ragged gray- and butternut-clad patriots charged one more time through woods and across fields in perfect order with colors flying. Before long G. P. Buell's brigade, seeing the Confederates advancing on its unprotected left flank, broke, panic stricken, throwing away guns and knapsacks and running like a flock of sheep. It was followed moments later by Hobart's brigade and then Robinson's. While the fugitives fled westward through the fields and woods, demonstrating to the Rebs as well as the outside, in the words of one of them, "some of the best running I ever did." "Hardee paused briefly to reform and sent Taliaferro's division and the corps of (W. B.) Bate in pursuit."[24]

At about 5:30 P.M., troops spearheaded by troops from Taliaferro's division and Cheatham's corps, Army of Tennessee, assaulted the Union 20th Corps. Every available Federal was placed in the line. "The onset (attack) was the most desperate of the war," one Federal wrote. "Column followed column in succession to carry the Confederate advance at any cost. Heavy and confused fighting continued well after dark."[25] The Confederates chased the Union command westward through the fields and swamps until the bluecoats ended up safely behind the lines of the XX Corps. The Federals were driven nearly a mile and routed from their two lines of breastworks. Captured were 417 prisoners and eight pieces of artillery. For a brief moment on this Sunday afternoon, the old spirit of the Army of Tennessee and others was revived. Unfortunately, it was only the afterglow[26] and the Union line at Bentonville had held.

While Johnston repositioned his lines during the early morning hours of Monday, March 20, fresh units from Howard's column continued to arrive. Sherman's instructions for Slocum were to fight a defensive action until the remainder of the Union army arrived. On the morning of the 21st, Sherman's army was reunited and in position on three sides of the Confederate works. Rain fell on the night of March 21, turning the heavily wooded banks of Mill Creek and much of the battlefield into a quagmire. General Johnston, learning that Schofield had reached Goldsboro with 23,000 men — a force alone larger than Johnston's — ordered his army to cross Mill Creek by the bridge at Bentonville and retreat toward Smithfield, which stood midway between Raleigh and Goldsboro. Losses at Bentonville were: Federals, 194 killed, 1,112 wounded and 221 missing; Confederates: 239 killed, 1,694 wounded and 673 missing.[27]

As Johnston's army completed its retrograde to Smithfield, Sherman moved his forces on to Goldsboro, arriving on the 23rd of March. Sherman's combined command equaled 90,000 bluejackets in comparison to a grand total of 13,363 effective butternuts.[28] With these figures at hand, Johnston sent a telegram to Robert E. Lee that he must move his force in front of Richmond. "Sherman's course cannot be hindered by the small force I have. I can do no more than annoy him. I respectfully suggest that it is no longer a question whether you leave present position; you have only to decide where to meet Sherman. I will be near him."[29] General Lee replied the same day: "Where, in your opinion, can we best meet Sherman?"

General Johnston, uncertain whether Sherman's march on Richmond would be through Raleigh or by the most direct route through Weldon, North Carolina, bivouacked his army around Smithfield. By doing this he made possible a junction with the Army of Northern Virginia, should Lee abandon his entrenchments around Richmond in order to fall on Sherman's rear with a combined Confederate army.[30] A journal dated April 1, in Smithfield, North Carolina, mentions Senator Louis Wigfall of Texas arriving at Johnston's headquarters as well as Major Generals John C. Brown of Tennessee and Patton Anderson of Florida, with a portion of their commands.[31] No official records or sightings report the exact position of Anderson and Yancy at Bentonville.

"March 28 brought a crisis to General Lee at Petersburg as he saw by the morning's light what he had long feared: massive blue columns crawling to the southwest to assail his flank. Lee sent a warning to Richmond that it must be abandoned, and President Davis sent his family southward by train to Charlotte, North Carolina. By April 1, General 'Little Phil' Sheridan, with a large force of combined cavalry and infantry, smashed Lee's thinly spread forces at a rural settlement called Five Forks, inflicting heavy casualties and turning Lee's flank. By Sunday, April 2, Lee's situation at Petersburg was hopeless as he had to abandon his entrenchments known as 'Ace of Spades.' Retreating along both sides of the James River, a general movement which was to lead westward up the valley of the Appomattox River, his retrograde became a rout as his hungry and starved army fled in the wildest confusion under Federal withering fire."[32]

The Confederate government had no apparent plans for such a catastrophic ending, as it was forced to take flight in one day. President Davis quickly outlined the evacuation and ordered several ten-car trains to be brought up for removing the government to Danville, Virginia, a hundred and forty miles south of Richmond. The presidential train packed with the president, his Cabinet members and department heads left Richmond late that evening followed by a second train containing the Confederate treasury and the Virginia banks' specie. They journeyed to Danville and there awaited news from General Lee. In the interim, Johnston in North Carolina reorganized his army one more time. J. Patton Anderson was positioned as commanding Taliaferro's division, Stewart's corps, Army of Tennessee, April 9 to April 26, 1865.

"After an eighteen-hour journey the presidential train reached Danville, carrying such notables as Attorney-General George Davis; Postmaster General John Reagan; Secretary of the Navy Stephen R. Mallory; Secretary of the Treasury George A. Trenholm; Secretary of State Judah P. Benjamin; and late arrival, Secretary of War John C. Breckinridge, former Vice President of the United States. Both packed trains were greeted by cheering crowds as the expectation was that Danville would be the next capital of the Confederacy."[33]

General Lee was trapped and with escape impossible, he was forced to meet with General Grant and surrender his Army of Northern Virginia. "On Palm Sunday, April 9, Robert E. Lee rode out from his army to meet General Grant at McLean House at Appomattox Courthouse. Grant's terms of surrender were generous, even magnanimous, but Confederate troops received the news as the end of their world."[34] "On the afternoon of April 10, Davis and his Cabinet received the news of the surrender. Secretary of the Navy Mallory said, 'The news fell upon ears of all like a fire bell in the night.' Shortly the group received word that General George Stoneman, driving in from East Tennessee, was looting, burning and cutting communications and that the President's party must flee or be captured. Davis telegraphed General Johnston about the emergency and asked him to meet the Cabinet in Greensboro. The official party left for the fifty-mile journey, and reached that city on April 11."[35]

XII

The End of the Confederacy

When Sherman learned of the surrender he began ordering his forces towards Johnston's small army. "Reveille sounded in the Army of Tennessee's camps on April 10 and the three corps commanders prepared to move out toward Raleigh. After the long rest at Smithfield there would be much straggling on the march. Crossing over the Neuse River at Battle's Bridge, they marched to Raleigh which they found to be a beautiful town. Women lined both sides of Fayetteville Street and handed out meat, bread, and tobacco to the passing soldiers. Anderson said most of the stragglers reached camp during the night."[1]

Joe Johnston realized that to negotiate an advantageous peace settlement with Sherman he would have to keep his scattered army intact and prevent it from being surrounded as Lee's had been at Appomattox Court House a week earlier. "The infantry camped on a line stretching from Page's Station, eight miles west of Raleigh, to Durham's Station, twenty-six miles west of Raleigh. Anderson reported that the wholesale straggling of the eleventh had been virtually eliminated due to slow marching of his troops."[2] Rumors of Lee's surrender were aplenty and soon confirmed as ragged Confederate soldiers from Lee's army began passing through on their way home.

With Lee's army out of the way and Johnston resting his small force at Raleigh, the Union cavalry was free to pursue the Davis government. Since Lee's surrender made no provisions for dissolving the Confederacy, the president ordered the cause moved further south by railroad to Greensboro, North Carolina, now headquarters of General Beauregard's remaining forces. Here the last remnants of the Confederate government were parked at the railroad station awaiting the arrival of Generals Beauregard and Johnston.

"Greensboro was now in an uproar, thronged by straggling soldiers from the armies of Lee and Johnston. Houses were closed. The people were afraid to take anyone in. The city did not want to harbor Davis and the Cabinet because of the ominous approach of Sherman, the collapse of the Confederate government, and the threat of anarchy posed by rioting, pillaging Confederate troops in the streets. John Breckinridge arrived in Greensboro late on April 12, bringing more details of Lee's surrender. He conferred with Johnston and Beauregard during the night, and agreed with them that further resistance would be useless. There was still the matter of convincing Jefferson Davis. President Davis protested that Lee's surrender was not the end; the remaining Confederate armies could carry on the war until the people of the North wearied of it, and acceptable peace terms might be won."[3]

Despite Davis's plea to continue the war, both generals agreed there was no choice but for Johnston to ask Sherman for an armistice. The meeting was arranged. The morale of the troops hit rock bottom as they awaited the outcome of this meeting. "Johnston said he would accept the best terms he could get but, to the dismay of Davis, he surrendered not only his own army but most Confederate troops still in uniform throughout the eastern theatre, including remnants of the Army of Tennessee under his command in North Carolina and scattered forces in South Carolina, Georgia, and Patton's own State, Florida. The army of General Richard Taylor in Alabama, Mississippi and Louisiana were excluded."[4]

"Though Johnston secured fair terms of peace, they fell far short of the goal for which the Confederate commander had fought for — Southern independence."[5] "An odd omission, in the eyes of later generations of Americans, was the lack of emphasis, or even comment, on the future status of the Negro slave. Though this issue was to become the flashpoint in Washington's formulation of Reconstruction policies, neither Federal nor Confederate field commanders raised the question in surrender negotiations, which angered Abolitionists and others in the North."[6] It was arranged that the Confederate soldiers should not be mortified at this time by surrendering in the presence of enemy troops such as was done at Vicksburg and Appomattox. The paroles were sent to the different regiments, signed by the officers, and distributed among the men. The severance pay, which the Army of Northern Virginia did not participate in — they received nothing with their paroles — was an insult. The Confederate Cabinet at Greensboro, carrying the residue of gold and silver coins of the Confederacy, which exceeded at least $500,000, gave Joe

Johnston $39,000 in Mexican silver coins to pay the men and officers. Each man received $1.15 pay: four quarters, one dime, and a five-cent piece in Mexican coinage. Some of these men had not been paid for over a year. Did the Confederate Cabinet still have hopes of continuing the government elsewhere?

On April 20 the officers were told the basis of the negotiations, and the generals explained the substance of the negotiations to the assembled brigades. Final discussions were held on April 26 and in accordance with the terms of this military convention, Johnston's army was to be paroled and not surrendered. The parole roster issued on May 2, 1865 read:

A. P. STEWART'S CORPS
Anderson's (late Taliaferro's) Division
Major. General J. Patton Anderson
Elliott's Brigade
Rhett's Brigade

The division totaled 2,626[7]

Sherman gave General Schofield the responsibility of carrying out the parole terms. Officers were allowed to retain their side arms, and their private horses and baggage. The men in the ranks were permitted to keep their horses and private property and have the use of army wagons and mules for their march home. For protection and hunting on the way, each returning body of soldiers was permitted to take a number of rifles, equal to one-seventh of their numerical strength.[8] "It took until May 1 to get the parole forms printed and the apparatus set up for handling the process. The parole forms themselves were simple and to the point.

> (*Name of soldier*) has given his solemn obligation not to take up arms against the Government of the United States until properly released from this obligation; and is permitted to return to his home, not to be disturbed by the United States authorities so long as he observes this obligation and obeys the laws in force where he may reside."[9]

"Johnston and Beauregard devised a plan whereby only the officers would actually receive their signed paroles on the spot where they signed them. The enlisted men's documents were kept by their unit commanders and were not handed out until the units were formally disbanded. Those soldiers who had stayed with Johnston until the end could perhaps take some pride from the fact that Johnston never actually 'surrendered' his men — he merely ended hostilities and 'dispersed' his men."[10] The Army of Tennessee would be dismantled and paroled. Before a small audience of officers whose divisions had shrunk to the size of companies, "Old Joe" Johnston spoke his farewell words:

> Comrades: In terminating our official relations, I earnestly exhort you to observe faithfully the terms of pacifications agreed upon; and to discharge the obligations of good and peaceful citizens, as well as you have performed the duties of thorough soldiers in the field. By such a course, you will best secure the comfort of your families and kindred, and restore tranquility to our country.
>
> You will return to your homes with the admiration of our people, won by the courage and noble devotion you have displayed in this long war. I shall always remember with pride the loyal support and generous confidence you have given me.
>
> I now part with you with deep regret — and bid you farewell with feelings of cordial friendship; and with earnest wishes that you may have hereafter all the prosperity and happiness to be found in the world.

Characteristically for many, the end of the war never came. Ironwilled General Anderson refused to accept or sign the parole! He said "to sign it implied a regret for what he had done, and he had none." Later on, Etta reiterated that Anderson did not believe the time had come to give up. "His noble men, though having been under him so short a time, told him they would follow him anywhere, and to submit to no terms he thought dishonorable." Etta continued: "Those above him knew his sentiments and signed the terms of surrender before he reached the place, though his rank gave him the right to be present in the caucus."[11] There were other generals who shared similar beliefs; Walthall, Featherston, Rhett, Wade Hampton and Joe Wheeler were still unwilling to accept the surrender and the end of the war.[12]

With events in a hostile array and the railroad destroyed to the south of Greensboro, escape would become more difficult for the president and his shrinking entourage. Now considered fugitives, the party would have to switch to horses, ambulances and carriages to escape from the Federal cavalry. A few rationalized there was plenty of room left in the Confederacy. Over in Texas were Kirby Smith and his army but that was a thousand miles away. They continued traveling south to Jamestown, High Point, Lexington and Salisbury, finally reaching Charlotte, North Carolina, on April 19.

Here the president learned that John Wilkes Booth had assassinated President Lincoln and Andrew Johnson was sworn in as the new president. Now, the Davis party hesitated because the northern press the blamed the assassination on Confederate operatives. Some of the Cabinet members were ill and tired of running and just wanted out to go to their homes. At this late date, could his handful of men surrender or dissolve the Confederate States of America? No, they did not have the authority. Jefferson Davis was president only in name of a nation that no longer existed. The dwindling entourage of patriots continued south to South Carolina — York, Chester and Newberry. One by one, they departed for whatever reason and in whatever direction they chose. Davis, after joining his wife, was apprehended at Irvinsville, Georgia, on May 10, and would spend the next two years in prison at Fort Monroe, Virginia, before being released.[13]

"The image of Davis in flight with vast sums of money appealed to such newspapers as *The Boston Transcript*, which called him a haughty, insolent and malignant traitor ... a swindling bankrupt and fugitive thief, running away from justice and his creditors, with the assets of the Confederacy."[14]

The Virginia banks' money that had been secreted at Washington, Georgia, was returned to Virginia minus a substantial amount of gold confiscated by Federal soldiers and robbers. The Confederate treasure train of $500,000 or more in gold and silver coins, after having been distributed for this and that to many parties along the way, was now reduced to $35,000 and arrived in Florida aboard two wooden wagons. This was distributed to the driver and guards, and the defunct Confederacy had a zero balance here in America. There was no accounting for funds left in England, France or Canada.

Of course Braxton Bragg made it back to Texas with $2,000 in gold coins to be taken to the Trans-Mississippi Department. By the time he got home, the department had been surrendered. His luck had changed.

The war was over and the Army of Tennessee paroled and dispersed. There were now tens of thousands of Confederate veterans in a hurry to get back home. The rail system — what was left of it — was ravaged and useless, so they would have to walk home or hitch a ride on a wagon. The dirt roads, paths and trails were unmarked, since milestone markers and wooden signposts had long disappeared. If you journeyed by yourself, the danger of ambush from the highwaymen and bushwhackers was ever present, including the new fear of being stopped and intimidated by a black Union soldier. For weeks the ranks had been dwindling by desertion, and now that the war was over many small groups of men just took off, which was dangerous. The generals quickly came to the rescue; they led their units back to the various state capitals, since many had retained their maps and could find the way.

A disenchanted Anderson borrowed a wagon and four mules from General Schofield for his four-hundred-mile trek back to Monticello. Anderson did not keep any records of the trip. To the best of one's belief he most likely returned to Florida with his corps commander, A. P. Stewart, who was returning troops to Mississippi. Since he was lucky enough to keep his loyal mount, Yancy, the unridden horse for the return trip trotted alongside the wagon. Furthermore, the makeshift convoy was supplied with wagons for carrying provisions. Schofield had given them ten days of rations and a "spun truck" of thread (spin cards) which they were to trade off for provisions on the march. The women in the country would exchange food for desperately needed thread for making and mending clothes. "From various sources General Stewart and Patton made it to Spartanburg, South Carolina, on May 9; Cowpens, May 10; the east bank of the Tiger River — road jammed with soldiers — moving towards Cross anchor, May 11; Laurens Court House, May 12; the south bank of the Saluda River, at Puckett's Ferry; passed through Cokesburg and Abbeville, the town full of soldiers. In order to avoid the crowd en route for Washington, Georgia, we have taken a road leading across the Savannah River at Barksdale's Ferry, May 13th; the Yankees occupy Washington, hence to avoid them, we will go directly after crossing the river to Warrenton, then to Sparta, May 14th & 15th. About ready to leave South Carolina and strike for the Georgia shore, May 16th. Greensboro, Georgia, May 17th; starting for Griffin and Monticello, Georgia." (Journal of B. L. Ridley records.) Also, Mary Martha Reid of St. Augustine, Florida, who established the Florida Hospital at Richmond, records she traveled along with Davis's train as far as Abbeville where she says she was taken in charge by Generals Featherston and Loring, (A. P. Stewart's corps) and she came home via Chattahoochee and Quincy, Florida. For certain there was no straggling of the homebound veterans. Anderson was ill conditioned for the final chapter of the Confederacy, returning home haggard and sickly to his Etta.

Any thoughts Anderson may have had on his way back to Florida to obtain another command in the Confederacy evaporated rapidly. Florida surrendered on May 10 as black Union troopers occupied Tallahassee without opposition. States' rights governor John Milton, believing that death would be preferable to reunion and emancipation, committed suicide. General Richard Taylor of the Department of East Louisiana, Mississippi and Alabama surrendered his forces on May 8. On June 2 General E. Kirby Smith in the Trans-Mississippi Department at Galveston, Texas, surrendered.

Locked out of finding any more military commands, Anderson had to face up to the fact he had linked his fate and career with that of the Confederacy. After spending four years on the battlefields for the cause, he would be forced to accept that his military career was gone, and that he must embark on some totally new endeavor if he had the strength to do so. His prewar personality would have to be recast and he would join thousands of others who were suddenly without professions and would have to re-establish themselves in new vocations.

The patriots of the South fought over almost every foot of their home state territory for four long years, in more than 2,000 battles and skirmishes with unfavorable odds. Their coasts and rivers were blockaded and filled with over 600 gunboats and vessels manned by 35,000 sailors. The new Confederacy protested the struggle until over one-half of their men and boys were dead or wounded, the casualties of war and disease. They fought for their belief in the great principle of local self-government, the privilege of managing their own affairs and for the protection of their homes and farms. The South would detract not an iota from the patriotic motive and endeavor of those opposing them. But now their experiment in independence had been brought to a conclusion by force. The War Between the States petered out and then vanished.

"Florida, a great state conceived in the excitement of revolution and secession, had crumbled in disaster. The terms of capitulation extended to all Confederate troops in the state were essentially the same as those of Sherman and Johnston. The pockets of resistance were paroled at different points within the state during May: at Baldwin, Waldo, Lake City, and Tampa. The Federal army of occupation arrived in time to prevent much of the Confederate government's property of food and cotton being seized by the public."[15]

"The Confederate Florida government had an empty treasury, with $600,000 of acknowledged debt, and a much larger amount repudiated.

Their bonds dishonored by years of neglected interest payments; a school fund robbed of its last dollar to aid in the war; the railroad system half completed, bankrupted; there were no schools or school system any longer; no benevolent institutions as they were all broke; no alms houses for the poor; no penitentiary and scarcely a jail — such was the inheritance bequest to the State by the fortunes of war."[16]

"Martial law was declared by military proclamation to be the only law existing in Florida. All proceedings at law, or acts of the Confederate government were declared null and void, thus the commonwealth government as organized under the Confederacy passed away."[17] "However, local officials throughout the state, judges, clerks, justices of the peace, and various county and town officers were advised to continue for the present in office."[18]

Naturally, Anderson's arrival home from the war was a source of elation for Etta and the children. After three and a half years of separation, it was a relief to get back to everyday affairs. Unfortunately, the Andersons' well-being was jeopardized almost immediately. Union greenbacks and gold and silver specie had become the medium of exchange for business and banks. Those without — the poor returning veterans, poor whites and freed Negroes — had to resort to the old-fashioned barter system for their existence. Anderson's dilemma stemmed from the collapse of the Confederate government. All paper money and bonds had become worthless in the marketplace.

When Casa Bianca was sold in 1860, the Andersons were paid in new Confederate dollars. Thereafter, busy with the war and her husband's military absences, Etta neglected to invest the bills or exchange them for gold or silver coins as Confederate money began losing its value. What a bitter pill; Anderson discovered the money was still in the new packages as it had been paid to him. Of course it was now worthless. Once a man of means, a member of the aristocracy, he had traded in his plantation to become a patriot of the new Confederacy. The government was bankrupt and so was he. Once wealthy, he now had few assets — not even his health.

The restocking of the southern plantations and farms would be a slow process. The livestock had been seriously depleted; havoc had been brought upon farm implements and machinery; financial and business institutions suffered almost complete collapse. The banks of the South could not be restored immediately, so there was an absence of assistance in any adequate quantity. Channels of trade had been dislocated by the war. The whole South would have to face economic reconstruction.

Even before Anderson returned home, Union General Q. A. Gillmore, commanding the Department of the South, which included Florida, issued on May 14 an emancipation order for the slaves.* Accordingly, the plantation owners had to call together their slaves and tell them they were free. As they abandoned their shackles to enjoy their new liberty, thousands deserted their plantation shacks to flock into the Federal military camps and into the local towns, "to seek knowledge of this 'freedom' which kind Fortune had finally granted them."[19] Freedom came without instructions. Many of the slaves were slow in comprehending the extent of this social revolution; they were free but a long way from being equal. Induced by the security of food and shelter, many of the Negroes returned home to the plantations where they had been slaves. Nearly all of the planters made satisfactory arrangements with their Negroes to remain on the plantation and cultivate the crops, being compensated for their labor, either in money or a share of the crop.

Thus began sharecropping, crop liens and tenant farming which would affect both black and white farmers for the next hundred years. Still, the whites were unwilling to accept blacks as fellow citizens, adopting segregation and other discriminatory practices.

In June, the new president, Andrew Johnson, set out to restore the southern states' legal status without recrimination, and with the least possible disruption in the lives of his fellow southerners. Anderson received a U.S. government document pardoning him for taking part in the late rebellion. Accompanying the paper was a form addressed to the Honorable William Seward, secretary of state, to be signed by Anderson in acknowledgement and to signify his acceptance of the terms of the pardon and to sign an Ironclad Oath form. The Ironclad Oath of Loyalty Act had been passed by the Federal Congress in July 1862. It was so named because it required an oath taker to swear that the signee never would voluntarily bear arms against the United States, would swear to support and defend the Constitution of the United States and forsake allegiance to state authority. This oath was administered generously throughout the war to persons doing business with the Federal government;

*Lincoln's Emancipation Proclamation issued 22 September, 1862 freed all slaves in those parts of the nation in rebellion; slaves east of the St. Johns River had been freed for three years.

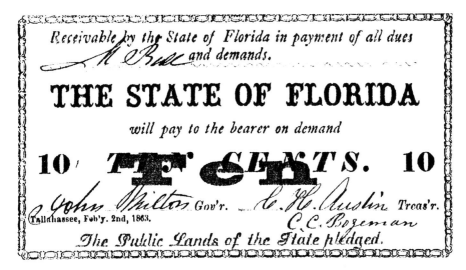

A worthless "shin plaster"

administered to Confederate prisoners of war who wanted to be paroled; required of southerners who wanted reimbursement for damages by foraging Federal troops; and Union sympathizers who wanted to return their states to the Union. These ironclad provisions remained in effect at the close of the war in April 1865. Consequently, soldiers such as Anderson who had participated in the South's war effort and who refused to sign this oath were barred from voting and holding political office. The oath effectively wrenched state government from the white man's control.

"Federal efforts to force ex–Confederates to take an oath of allegiance even though the oath was neither restrictive or punitive, men like Patton felt that they were being treated as aliens in their home country; they hotly denied that they had been treasonable — or done anything other than resist what their leaders depicted as oppression. The Jefferson Davis doctrine that the Confederacy had merely defended the Constitution against its despoilers was widespread in the South. Friction and occasional violence spread through the region as Federal authorities sought to force the oath upon former soldiers and officials, even those who had surrendered and been properly paroled with guarantees that they would not be disturbed further if they ceased resistance to the Federal government."[20] Although Robert E. Lee signed the oath of allegiance[21], Patton Anderson refused to sign it.

Subsequent Reconstruction enforcement acts complicated the oath by giving administering officers discretionary power to decide whether a resident of a former Confederate state, based on his past activities, was eligible to swear loyalty. The result was many oaths of allegiance in various forms. In 1884 Congress removed all the iron from the oath when it passed into law a new oath of allegiance, removing all portions of the older restrictive oaths.

A further annoyance to the defeated southerners was the unpalatable, distasteful, newly created Freedman's Bureau in 1865. It was organized for the relief of the newly freed slaves and included thousands of southern white refugees who were given food and clothing provided by the Federal government. Government employees and volunteers from northern relief societies and churches helped the newly freed slaves to find jobs, set wages and terms of contracts with planters, settled blacks on public lands and established a system of schools. For blacks, the agency represented a step toward independence and civil rights.

During its existence, the Federal bureau was severely criticized for inefficiency and corruption, and was finally discontinued. The most uplifting and equalizing piece of legislation of 1865 was the U.S. Congress chartering the Freedman's Savings and Trust Company to encourage liberated slaves to save money to buy homes and land. Only blacks

---

I, _____, of _____ County, State of _____ do solemnly swear or affirm, in presence of Almighty God, that I will henceforth faithfully support, protect and defend the Constitution of the United States and the Union of the States thereunder; and that I will, in like manner, abide by and faithfully support all laws and proclamations which have been made during the existing rebellion with reference to the emancipation of slaves. So help me God.
. . . .

Sworn and subscribed to this the . . . . . day of . . . . A.D., 1865, before . . . .
. . . . J. P.
It is hereby certified that the above is a true copy of the original oath taken and subscribed by . . . .
. . . . J. P.
[Facsimile]

Example of one of many oaths of allegiance used after the war (Civil War Library and Museum, Philadelphia, Pennsylvania).

were permitted to become depositors and most of those who did invested their dreams as well as their hard-earned money in the institution. By 1872, thirty-seven branches in seventeen states had been opened.[22] Operated by blacks, the Freedman's Bank charter required at least two-thirds of all deposits to be invested in U.S. securities; this stipulation was later amended to include real estate. But poor management, an incompetent staff and erratic bookkeeping undermined the bank's stability. Bad loans were made to speculators, often as a result of political influence. When the Panic of 1873 hit the nation, many loans defaulted and the Freedman's Bank failed.[23] There was no government bailout in those days. What was depressing about the affair was that over 480,000 Negro families had saved over $57 million by their hard work within less than eight years, and now it was gone. This was a fine start for African-Americans but a poor ending. What did survive are the bank records recording the names and family relationships of account holders.

"Rather than stay behind and debate the meaning of treason, or humbly await the return of their rights as citizens of the newly reunited United States, many of the elite and professional Southerners who could afford to, 'closed the gate behind them,' so to speak, and headed out of the country."[24] The Southern Colonization Society was organized to find locations for settlements of these exiles. A colony was created in Brazil and became successful for growing cotton and raising cattle as well as and saving the southerners' honor. This brain drain continued as returning officers and volunteers, in order to avoid the uncertainties of defeat, removed themselves to Mexico, Cuba, England and France; others went north to work in the western states, Canada and even in New York. Leaving was their remaining gesture of defiance to the new Freedman's Bureau. When it became perfectly clear the Rebels would not be held accountable (treason) for their service with the Confederate forces, many did return to their home states. The adventurous Andersons stayed home in Florida. He was not in any condition to take to a new world.

Regardless of the outcome of the conflict, wealthy planters seemed to weather the storm very well in the cotton belt of Florida. Anderson was the exception because he had sold the plantation. Otherwise, "Business began to pick up during the late summer of 1865 even with the uncertain condition of labor. Much cotton had been hidden away during the war. This, with the confiscated cotton of the late Confederate government, served as a substantial initial basis for trade."[25] "Shortly after the close of the war in April, there was tremendous activity in the cotton business along the Chattahoochee, stated a one-time cotton clerk in Apalachicola. Probably as many as 200,000 bales were shipped out of Apalachicola in the summer, once the blockade of Southern ports was removed by President Johnson, effective July 1, 1865."[26]

With this backdrop the summer of 1865 found Anderson's health and spirit so broken from his wounds and efforts to cling to their privileged status that the family traveled to Memphis, Tennessee, to spend some months with his mother, Mrs. Margaret L. Bybee, and visit with his brother who had left Washington state and was practicing law in Memphis. By Christmas a *New York Times* reporter wrote: "Florida has passed through the fiery ordeal. She has experienced a dark night and tempestuous weather, but the day has dawned, the storm has ceased."[27]

XIII

The Bittersweet End

1866

The Andersons returned to Monticello. Indubitably, the couple's profound love for one another overcame the ravages of war and the collapse of their affluence because on May 17, 1866, their fifth child was born. They were blessed with Margaret Bybee Anderson, so named for Anderson's mother and stepfather, Dr. Joseph N. Bybee, of whom Anderson was very fond. Still, he continued to be defiant and would not sign the oath, making it impossible for him to resume legal practice, engage in politics or even procure food assistance for his family.[1]

With all of "these goings-on," dear Aunt Ellen seemed to fare well. Having lived with and off of the Anderson's during the war, she gained access to the money she had deposited in the New York bank. Although it was all that remained of a once-impressive estate, the money withdrawn was in greenbacks. How much she shared with the Andersons is not recorded, but for the Anderson family to survive those days, there must have been outside help.

Ellen's favorite slave, her maid Rebecca, after her freedom purchased a small home with her own money. Rebecca paid her former mistress a heart-warming tribute in a letter addressed: "My Dear Mistress. We hear you now have no home, and we write to beg you to come and live in ours. We will move into the kitchen. It is plenty good and you can have the house, and we will wait on you and be so glad to do something to show you how we remember your goodness to us. Dem old days at Casa Bianca was the happiest we have ever seen."[2] Ellen spent her final years paying visits to different relatives. While visiting Oxford, Mississippi, Ellen died and was buried there. At the end there was nothing for Etta to inherit. Anderson did sell his last plat of land in Olympia, Washington, that he had been holding and received $300.

It was becoming clear to him that a sharp political conflict was shaping up when the first Reconstruction Act (Military Bill) became law. A virtual military dictatorship, it carved the South into five military districts. This was followed in 1866 with the Fourteenth Amendment, which enfranchised the Negro and in effect disenfranchised nearly all southern white men.[3] "The Army of Occupation presided over voter registration, barring many Loyal Confederates and registering more than 100 percent of the blacks in some localities. Northern Carpetbaggers, Southern Scalawags, and their gullible black followers conspired to get themselves elected to public office at all levels."[4] "This sudden implementation of black suffrage had a revolutionary impact on Southern racial relations and political power. In response to these developments, in every Southern state a powerful white supremacist opposition developed that refused to accept its legitimacy."[5] These people became the conservatives of the South, which fitted J. Patton Anderson. "Those Southern whites who laid claim to it during Reconstruction were intent upon conserving their wealth, property, privileges, and ruling position. To say that they were conservative was to put it politely; they were in fact reactionary to the point of hoping to restore the status quo antebellum, including some form of slavery if at all possible."[6]

Because Congress had as yet no southern members, in 1867 it replaced the pro–South form of Reconstruction as conducted by President Johnson with a congressional Reconstruction designed by radical Republicans to discipline recalcitrant southern states. "Radical representatives came to Florida to form secret black societies to organize black voters, who now had suffrage by Congressional mandate. The success of the 'black' Republicans was manifest in the result of the 1868 elections, when sixteen Republicans but only eight Democrats [the party of white Southern conservatives which Anderson favored] were elected to the state senate and thirty-seven Republicans but only fifteen Democrats to the lower house. Of the fifty-three Republicans, thirteen were 'carpetbagger' Northerners who had come South to take advantage of Florida's new opportunities, twenty-one were 'scalawag' Southerners who had supported the Union, and nineteen were blacks."[7]

"For the whites, Reconstruction would be recalled for several generations as a source of shame and bitterness. Most scorned 'Negro rule' and resented it as the apparent Northern desire for revenge, while others lamented the political wrangling, the exploitation, and the corruption that abounded,"[8] resulting in much lawlessness in central Florida among the plantation owners and the small white farmers.

In order to retain and protect their families, whites in the rural South began to organize secret societies. They were not interested in confronting the U.S. Army of Occupation; instead they were intent upon restoring their white supremacist attitude that had prevailed for the past hundred years. Passwords, secret handshakes and other secret signs were common among the members who congregated in secrecy. Their modus operandi developed into riding at night with torches, wearing flowing white robes and white face masks, carrying bullwhips, lynch ropes and threats of harm to bring the newly freed and unarmed blacks and those newcomers from the Yankee North to "toe the Southern line of accepting the white man's politics and supremacy or else!" These Klansman ideals swept the defeated nation as nightriders recruited thousands of members. Known as Knights of the White Camellia, Knights of the Golden Circle and, more recently, the Ku Klux Klan, these societies dealt and measured out justice as they saw fit. These klaverns continued to flourish and exist well into the 1900s as the Ku Kluxers introduced a practice that dated back to medieval Europe when the Scottish clans set hillside crosses ablaze as symbols of defiance to the enemy. First shown on the silver screen in movie houses across the country, the twentieth-century Klansman began burning wooden crosses around 1915 to intimidate the blacks, minorities, immigrants and anyone suspected of betraying their shadowy ideals. For over a hundred years the newly freed African-Americans slowly, when possible, removed themselves from the rural South, exchanging their peonage for civil rights in the industrial cities north of the Mason-Dixon line.

Anderson apparently felt that rather than live under the radical Reconstruction Acts as inaugurated and enforced by U.S. military authorities in Florida and a newly elected Reconstruction governor, he would prefer to leave his home state, like thousands of others were doing at the time, and try a new life in Memphis, Tennessee, where he might find more friends sympathetic to the lost cause. "In Memphis, more than 1,900 new dwellings were underway before the year 1865 came to an end. Under the stimulus of a booming cotton market (prices reached fifty cents per pound), the city's wharves were crowded night and day with stevedores and huge drays. Hundreds of portable sawmills, brought down from the North, began cutting in the vast forests of the region, and Memphis became a leading lumber center."[9]

In addition to the prosperity, Memphis was becoming a gathering center for many conservatives and Confederate acquaintances; Anderson's mother and brother lived there. His health was a concern to the family. The jaw wound caused him to lisp slightly, but this did not affect his ability to speak.[10] More serious were his recurrent bouts with malaria he had contracted during the Mexican War. The long hot Florida summers intensified the fever in his worn-down physical and mental condition. Maybe a move out of Florida would be beneficial to both Anderson and the family.

Unfortunately, the family lived in genteel poverty in Memphis. Anderson became a member of The Confederate Historical Association of Memphis, which began in 1866 and now had over 225 members, with names of such notables as Nathan B. Forrest on its roster. Also arriving after being imprisoned for several years was former President Jefferson Davis, now employed as president of the Carolina Insurance Company.[11] When friends attempted to have Anderson's legal disabilities removed so that he might run for the office of mayor of Memphis, he adamantly refused. Signing the pardon (oath), he felt, would have been dishonorable.[12]

Entrance to Elmwood Cemetery, Memphis, Tennessee. Twelve Confederate generals are buried here.

Over the next few years he would edit an agriculture magazine, which he enjoyed doing, and later become a collector of delinquent taxes in Shelby County.

In April of 1872 the Andersons sold their last plat of land in Olympia for $200.[13] Unfortunately the general continued to suffer from his Mexican War affliction, resulting in broken health to the extent that by September 20, he lay on his deathbed. This date was the ninth anniversary of the battle of Chickamauga, a day he always remembered with pride. When this date was pointed out to him, he weakly called out, "How we whipped them that day!"[14] In response to a question asked by his aged mother who was deeply interested in his spiritual happiness, then "Patton replied he had no fears as to himself; his only anxiety was in regard to his poor, helpless family, and fixing his eyes upon his wife Etta and children he so fondly loved, his great soul gently passed away. The nerve of steel and the stoic bravery which Anderson exhibited in battle did not desert him in death, and he died with all the calmness and serenity of a true philosopher."[15]

Major General J. Patton Anderson was interred in Elmwood Cemetery, Memphis, Tennessee. Here the southern patriots began to gather again, as a total of twelve Confederate generals would eventually find their way home to this Confederate conservatory.[16]

The Memphis newspaper continued: "The wealth of the Indies could not have corrupted him; nor the wheel and the rack move him to the betrayal of a cause he had once espoused. He remained unreconstructed to the end."[17]

No fancy monuments were erected for this patriot (courtesy White Mane Publishing Co.—*Generals at Rest*).

Many comrades, learning of Anderson's death, sent expressions of sympathy to Etta. Old Braxton Bragg, who always held Anderson's military leadership in high esteem, wrote to Etta: "Your fine boys need no richer inheritance than to bear their father's name."

1873 and Afterwards

Without Anderson's meager income and with no means of supporting the five children, Etta was offered a home by her brother, Cromwell Adair, in Morganfield, Kentucky. She accepted the offer and lived there for the next ten years. Etta Adair Anderson was fashioned very much like her aunt Ellen "Florida" White. Even though she had little personal wealth, she managed to have a wide circle of acquaintances and traveled whenever possible.

After her husband's death, Etta, while absent on a visit to Florida, left his horse, Yancy, in charge of a former soldier of Anderson's, who was sexton of Elmwood Cemetery in Memphis. While there, Colonel Pinson, formerly of the C.S.A., died and was being buried with military honors. At the occasion, Yancy was tied at the cemetery gate by the sexton. As the procession passed in with music, old Yancy became restive, broke his bridle and immediately took position near the hearse, and marched with it, keeping correct time to the music. He was not contained, and stood still at the grave until the service was concluded, and then returned by himself to his stable.[18] Old Yancy was game for the move to Kentucky and was full of spirit as he was returned to pasture in the Bluegrass State, and led a life of quiet ease on Mr. Adair's farm. He survived his master about nine years and lived to be 25 years old.[19]

In the same year, 1873, "Old Reliable" William J. Hardee passed over, having settled on his Alabama plantation after the war.

On a trip to Monticello in 1876 to see her sister, Etta sent an interesting letter to former President Jefferson Davis, still living in Memphis. It pertained to her oldest son, Preston Anderson, who at age eighteen, had designs of applying for admission to West Point. A proud Etta wrote to the president: "Do you think he can go without sacrificing his own principles (he hated the Yankees) as a Southern boy?" Her request follows:

Monticello, Florida, March 25th 1876

My dear Mr. Davis,

Can you spare a few moments of your valuable time, and will you do me the great favor and advise me on a subject that has greatly troubled me of late and on which I feel utterly incapable of judging. So many have such different views in regard to our cause from what my husband had that I begin to doubt almost and did not know to whom else I could go. My eldest son has been for the past Winter at Oxfor Miss[?] with Genl. Stuart. He finished his first year at college in June. His Uncle who has been paying his expenses has written him that he cannot keep him at school any longer than that time _____ he is very anxious to go on with his education and to make an engineer of himself. He seems to have a good mind and is fond of study. He will be twenty in July – is obedient and steady, will be controled [sic] entirely by my wishes. He has written, adding my consent to his applying for a position at West Point. Would prefer Annapolis, but thinks he is too old to enter. In writing he says: "Not, Mother, that I wish to make a soldier of myself or that I have any love for the Yankees but I think they have stolen enough from the South to entitle each southern boy to an education without feeling any obligations to them." He may take the proper view of it but do you think he can go to either without not only sacrificing his own principles as a southern boy-but his father's? Now, Mr. Davis if you think so, as great as the trial would be, I would rather he would do without an education than to get it at such a sacrifice. While I am writing I will make another request but for another. There is a promising young lawyer here who served through the war as a private in Genl Bragg's Army. Was nineteen months in one of the worst of Northern prisons, and I should have said he is still true to his principles. He has asked me several times the past winter to write and request your Autograph for him. So if you will endeavor to write me, enclose it in the letter. Direct to this place. The children join me in kind regards to Mrs. Davis and the children. It would be difficult to send all the messages that have been give me, for you. The people here *all* love you, and feel that you have suffered for them. One lady sends love and says it has always been her greatest desire to meet you here. She says she has little hope of doing so, but hopes to greet you in that happy home above where there is no more suffering.

Believe me always your friend
Etta A. Anderson

Please direct to Mrs. *Patton* Anderson (from the files of PUTNAM COUNTY ARCHIVES & HISTORY[20].

Jefferson Davis in his reply was profound in his interpretations of the rights of a former enemy.

17th April 1876

My dear Mrs. Anderson

On my recent return from New Orleans, your letter of the 27th _____ was received.

Under the circumstances stated, there can be no valid objection to sending your son to the U. S. Military Academy.

That institution is supported by the people, the cadets apportioned among the states; except ten who are appointed by the President, and they were provided especially for the Sons of Soldiers, who not having residence, as citizenship in any state, were not in the line of salvation (?) to represent any district of a State.

If then every true Son of the South is to be excluded from the U.S. Military and Naval academies, it would follow that the people of each Southern State must be misrepresented in those institutions, and the people must furnish the means to support and educate their enemies (only).

The objections to sending your son to West Point, are not, I think, referable to the principles his honored Father gallantly maintained, both in the council and the field; but to other considerations, which you and he can better decide than I. Questions of sentiment, or of future career, are not subject to political laws, or logical deductions; and no one is capable of giving advice worthy of being put in the balance against your own knowledge and judgment in regards to them.

Mrs. Davis had a fall some weeks since, and is yet suffering from the effects of it.

She and Winnie and I will probably sail in the early part of May, from New Orleans for England. Where they will remain probably until next winter, possibly longer; but any stay will only be for the time necessary to transact the business on which I am going over.

Mrs. Davis, like myself, was very glad to hear from you, and she unites with me in cordial good wishes for you and yours.

I am ever faithfully your friend,
JEFFERSON DAVIS (SS)

From the files of PUTNAM COUNTY ARCHIVES & HISTORY

In October 1876, Etta received news that their friend Braxton Bragg dropped dead on September 27. Bragg was once again denounced as about the worst general in the Confederacy. Anderson, if alive, would have defended Bragg against this opinion. Etta continued visiting Florida, with particular entries made about visits to Palatka, Florida. Reconstruction leaders achieved notable gains in state services, public schools, criminal code, etc. Apart from the decisive social issue of racial equality, the populace shared the goals of Democratic economic growth and development. Once the backwater of the rural South, postwar Florida promised to become a boom state, and every white man with or without means, Republican or Democrat, wanted a part of it. Between 1860 and 1880 the population swelled to 269,493, an increase of 90 percent.[21]

Reconstruction "came to a dramatic end with the Compromise of 1877, when the Republican presidential candidate Rutherford B. Hayes bargained his way to the White House by promising to withdraw the last Federal troops of occupation from the South. After twelve years of often corrupt and oppressive rule since the death of Lincoln, the white South was free. Its people had endured the 'long night.'"[22]

Since Florida was prospering, Etta and her grown children — William Preston, Theophilus Beatty, James Patton Jr. and Margaret Bybee — all returned to the state for good in 1883 and settled in Palatka along the St. Johns River. Riding with the family was Anderson's spirit. He, like so many other veterans, never gave up on the cause; ironically the Ku Klux Klan regained its power when the 1887 legislature authorized a poll tax, and by 1890 most blacks were excluded from the voting booth as well as from the legislature. "Reconstruction was over, and so were the chances of freedmen to establish a secure place in Florida government and society. No black would serve again in the legislature until 1968."[23] "Now under a peonage system or forced labor, non-convict black and poor white workers were compelled to labor until certain 'debts' were satisfied, which they never or rarely were."[24] Jim Crow legislation was in place for separation of the races once again.

On December 5, 1889, Jefferson Davis died at the age of eighty years old at New Orleans. "The comments of newspapers made it obvious that Davis had outlived many of the animosities he had generated. In Atlanta, *The Constitution* announcement read: 'This morning is another page in the history of the world. Jefferson Davis is dead! ... he will be mourned in millions of hearts today.' *The World* said: 'The death of Jefferson Davis ends a most remarkable chapter in history,' etc."[25] Newspapers in the North were hardly less laudatory in their comments.

Retiring in 1884, after replacing Grant as commander-in-chief of the United States Army, William Tecumseh Sherman died in New York City in 1891.

While attending the funeral of his arch-opponent, Joseph Eggleston Johnston caught a cold and died shortly afterwards.

Edward Cary Walthall died in office as United States senator.

Casa Bianca Plantation in Jefferson County lay abandoned until it was bought and restored at the turn of the century. The plantation house was struck by lightning and burned to the ground in 1910.

Etta remained active as she organized the Patton Anderson Chapter of the United Daughters of the Confederacy in July 1896. One of their first projects was to erect marble headstones on the graves of former Confederate servicemen, eventually placing sixty-two markers throughout Putman County and several outside the area. Etta lived to be eighty-three years old, dying on February 23, 1917. She never remarried.

The only surviving members of the Anderson family at that time were Mr. J. Patton Anderson Jr. of Morganfield, Kentucky, and Miss Margaret Anderson, living in Palatka. Miss Maggie, as she was known, delved in local and family history and was responsible for much of the reference material used to produce the biography of her father. She was active in local organizations and her church, the First Presbyterian of Palatka. Miss Maggie lived to be ninety-nine years old, dying May 7, 1965.

Finis

The iniquity of oblivion scattereth her poppy and deals with the memory of men without distinction to merit and perpetuity … who know whether the best of men be known, or whether there be not more remarkable men forgot, than any that stand remembered in the known account of time.

Sir Thomas Browne, 1686.

APPENDIX

J. Patton Anderson's Confederate Staff Officers 1861–1865[1]

J. Patton Anderson (1822–72). Colonel, 1st Florida Infantry Regiment. Appointed from Florida, Brigadier General, P. A. C. S., to rank from February 10, 1862. Promoted to Major General, P. A. C. S., to rank from February 17, 1864.

Staff

Anderson, W., Captain, O. O., January 1, 1863.

Barth, William G., Captain, A. A. G., April 1862 to September 1863, and February 9, 1865.

Beall, Thomas B., Major, Q. M., August 27 to September 1863.

Browne, R. H., Lieutenant, A. I. G., January 1, 1863.

Bryan, E. Pliny, Captain, A. A. G., April 1864. Died September 30, 1864.

Bulkley, Henry D., Captain, A. C. S., April 1862.

Cain, J. S., Brigade Surgeon, September 30, 1863.

Carruth, E. B., Major, C. S., September 1863.

Davidson, William M., Lieutenant, A. D. C., May 1862 to September 1863, and February 9, 1865.

Downing, J. B., Captain, V. A. D. C., January 1, 1863.

Eggleston, J. P., Captain, A. C. S.

Gamble, Carey B., Surgeon, April 1862.

Hill, R. J., Major, Q. M.

Huger, Daniel E., Captain, A. A. G., February 18, 1863.

Janes, John W., Lieutenant, 5th Georgia Infantry Regiment; Staff, A. A. D. C., April 6, 7, 1862.

Jordan, William McR., Lieutenant, A. A. D. C., April 1862.

Kinchloe, D. A., Division Surgeon, February 9, 1865.

Lanier, S. M., Captain, C. Q. M., January 13, 1863.

Lundy, W. L., Acting Division Surgeon, February 9, 1865.

Mattison, J. B., Lieutenant, O. O., September 1863.

May, Lambert, Captain, A. A. & I. G., September 1863.

Mayer, Simon, _____, A. A. A. G., February 9, 1865.

Peyton, James T., Major, Q. M., March 15, 1863.

Pinckney, R. Q., Major, C. Q. M., January 13, 1863.

Scanlan, _____, Mr., V. A. D. C., January 1, 1863.

Sibley, John T., Captain, A. Q. M., April 1862.

Sykes, E. T., Captain, acting temporarily on staff, January 1, 1863.

Travis, E. F., Captain, A. I. G., February 9, 1865.

Notes

Chapter I

1. Larry Rayburn, *Wherever the Fight Is Thickest—General James Patton Anderson*, 314.
2. J. Patton Anderson autobiography, 58.
3. *Ibid.*, 59.
4. T. Harry Williams, *Napoleon in Gray P. G. T. Beauregard* (Baton Rouge: Louisiana State University Press, 1955), 13.
5. *Ibid.*, 14, 15.
6. Dunbar Rowland, *Military History of Mississippi, 1803–1898* (Jackson: Mississippi Department of Archives and History, 1908) 31.
7. Anderson autobiography, 59.
8. Nathaniel Cheairs Hughes, *Gen. William J. Hardee—Old Reliable* (Baton Rouge: Louisiana State University Press, 1965), 35.
9. Rowland, *Military History*, 32.
10. Diane Neal and Thomas W. Kremin, *The Lion of the South, General Thomas C. Hindman* (Macon, Ga.: Mercer University Press, 1993), 15.
11. *Ibid.*, 16.
12. Anderson autobiography, 60.
13. *Ibid.*
14. Neal and Kremin, *The Lion of the South*, 17.
15. Patricia L. Faust, *Historical Illustrated Encyclopedia of the Civil War* (New York: Harper & Row Publishers, 1982), 208.
16. Anderson autobiography, 60.
17. Robert F. Hine and Savoie Lottinville, *Soldiers in the West: Letters of Theodore Talbot* (Norman: University of Oklahoma Press, 1972), 122.
18. Anderson autobiography, 61.

Chapter II

1. Anderson autobiography, 61.
2. Margaret B. Anderson Uhler, Civil War letters, footnote, 10.
3. *Ibid.*
4. Uhler, Civil War letters, 20.
5. Uhler, Civil War letters, footnote, 10.
6. Anderson autobiography, 61.
7. *Ibid.*
8. Oliver Nixon, *How Marcus Whitman Saved Oregon*, 6th edition (Chicago: Star Publishing Co., 1895), 264. And J. H. Segars, *In Search of Confederate Ancestors. The Guide Journal of Confederate History Series*, vol. 9 (Murfreesboro, Tenn.; Southern Heritage Press, 1993), 13, 14. "The 1850 census was the seventh of the nation, first being conducted in 1790. It revealed the name and birthplace, age, sex, race, occupation. It had a schedule for listing slaves."
9. John Stoutenburgh Jr., *Dictionary of the American Indian* (New York: Bonanza Books, 1990). Quileutes—the only living representatives of the Chimakum, a linguistic family of the Northwest coast who were whalers and lived in and around La Push, Washington, on the Pacific Coast.
10. Urban E. Hicks, "Reminiscence of a Journey to Shoalwater Bay" (Tacoma: Washington State Historical Society).
11. Clinton A. Snowden, *History of Washington, the Rise and Progress of an American State*, vol. 3 (New York: The Century History Co., 1909), 49.
12. Uhler, "He rarely spoke about this until the time of the fall of Vicksburg." (Anderson was not at this battle.) It became known when some officer writing to another revealed the story.

185

13. Snowden, *History of Washington*, vol. 3, 220. There were small pockets of pioneers in the territory. Clark County, being the ancient seat of the Hudson's Bay Company and nearest the Willamette Valley for which most of the emigrants had set out, had the largest population. Thurston County was next and the Hudson's Bay stations on the Cowlitz and at Nisqually helped to populate Lewis and Pierce counties.

14. Emolument Report, General Accounting Office, Record Group 217, National Archives and Records Administration, December 21, 1854.

15. Snowden, *History of Washington*, vol. 4, 141, 142.

16. *Ibid.*

17. *Ibid.*

18. Anderson autobiography, 63.

19. *Ibid.*

20. *Ibid.*, 64.

21. *Ibid.*

Chapter III

1. Uhler, "Florida's White Southern Belle," 299.

2. *Ibid.*

3. *Ibid.*, 302

4. *Ibid.* In 1834, Col. White was retained by Prince Achille Murat, his neighbor in Jefferson County, to represent him in his claim to money and property that had been confiscated by the French government. Murat's mother, Princess Caroline, was Napoleon's sister. Col. White was not successful in restoring Murat's fortunes, but his endeavor led him to Florence, where he and Ellen were entertained by Princess Caroline.

5. Newspaper, *Monticello Constitution*, not dated.

6. Rayburn, *Wherever the Fight Is Thickest*, 315.

7. William Watson Davis, Ph.D., *The Civil War and Reconstruction in Florida*, vol. 53, no. 131 (New York: Columbia University, 1913), 26.

8. Michael Gannon, *The New History of Florida* (Louisville: University Press of Florida, 1996), 232.

9. Uhler, Civil War letters, footnote, 157.

10. Anderson autobiography, 64.

11. E. T. Sykes, *Walthall's Brigade, Army of Tennessee1862–1865* (self-published, 1905), 503.

12. *Ibid.*

13. The Confederacy, *McMillan Information Now Encyclopedia*: 552, 553, 554.

14. Julia Floyd Smith, *Slavery and Plantation Growth in Antebellum Florida, 1821–1860* (Gainesville: University of Florida Press, 1913) 148–159. "Planters were dependent upon New York, since almost everything connected with the plantation was bought on credit. Often this factor or commission merchant advanced cash payments to overseers, based on the potential value of the unharvested crops on the cotton exchange which traded in cotton futures."

15. Uhler, "Florida's White Southern Belle," 305, 306.

16. *Ibid.*

17. The *Encyclopedia of the Confederacy*, "Religion and Slave family life," 568.

18. Larry Eugene Rivers, *Slavery in Florida, Territorial Days to Emancipation* (Gainesville: University Press of Florida, 2000), 113.

19. Uhler, "Florida's White Southern Belle," 308.

20. Charles W. Ramsdell, *Behind the Lines in the Southern Confederacy* (Baton Rouge: Louisiana State University Press, 1972), 7.

21. Rayburn, *Wherever the Fight Is Thickest*, 315.

22. Uhler, "Florida's White Southern Belle," 305, 306. This information was from a portion of an undated letter from Etta Anderson to an unidentified niece. Why she did not disclose the sale price is unknown. Without the slaves and a coming war, the price may have been a bargain on paper.

Chapter IV

1. John E. Johns, *Florida During the Civil War* (Gainesville: University of Florida Press, 1963), 5.

2. Neal and Kremin, *The Lion of the South*, 82.

3. Archie P. McDonald, *To Live and Die*

in Dixie, How the South Formed a Nation. Journal of Confederate Book Series, vol. 10 (Murfreesboro, Tenn.: Southern Heritage Press, 1999), 29.

4. Johns, *Florida During the Civil War*, 218. *Convention Journal* (1861): 18, 19. The committee consisted of the following men: Sanderson of Duval County; Allison of Gadsden County; McIntosh of Franklin County; Gettis of Hillsborough County; Tift of Monroe County; Owen of Marion County; Dawkins of Alachua County; Wright of Escambia County; Morton of Santa Rosa County; Ward of Leon County; Anderson of Jefferson County; Ladd of Wakulla County; and Boker of Calhoun County.

5. *Ibid.,* 17, 21.

6. *Ibid.*

7. *Ibid.,* 219. Apalachicola Arsenal at Chattahoochee contained a number of small arms, 5,122 pounds of powder, and 173,476 cartridges; Fort Barrancas, 44 cannon with ammunition; Barrancas Barracks, one field battery; Fort Pickens, 201 cannon and ammunition; Fort McRee, 125 sea coast and garrison cannon; Fort Taylor, 60 cannon; Key West Barracks, 4 cannon; Fort Marion, 6 field batteries and some small arms; Fort Jefferson on Tortugas and Fort Clinch on Amelia Island had incomplete fortification.

8. "Pensacola in the Civil War," Pensacola Historical Society, publication, vol. 9, no. 2, Spring 1989, 12.

9. "Civil war and Reconstruction of the Gulf Coast," *Gulf Coast Historical Review*, vol. 4, no. 2, Spring 1989, 9. Two hundred and twenty-five Alabamans, under Col. Tennent C. Lomax, were ordered to Pensacola to implement Governor Perry's recommendations.

10. *Ibid.,* 16.

11. Anderson autobiography, 65.

12. Neal and Kremin, *The Lion of the South*, 83.

13. Richard A. Martin and Daniel L. Schafer, *Jacksonville's Ordeal by Fire* (Jacksonville: Florida Publishing Co., 1984), 35.

14. Confederate and Union pay schedule from *North & South* magazine, no. 6, vol. 1, 13.

15. Pensacola Historical Society, 15.

16. Sykes, *Walthall's Brigade*, 68.

17. Lawrence L. Hewitt, *Braxton Bragg— The Confederate Generals: Volume 1*, edited by William C. Davis (New York: Doubleday, 19991), 113.

18. *Ibid.*

19. *Ibid.*

20. Stewart Sifakis, *Who Was Who in the Civil War* (New York: Facts on File Publication, 1988), 68.

21. Paul Taylor, *Discovering the Civil War in Florida: A Reader and Guide* (Sarasota, Fla.: Pineapple Press, Inc., 2001), 34.

22. *Gulf Coast Historical Review*— These were New York prisoners released on condition they join the army and fight the Confederates. They were made up of thieves, plug-uglies, and other dangerous characters gathered from the slums of New York City, 31.

23. Johns, *Florida During the Civil War*, 51.

24. *Ibid.,* 35.

25. Sykes, *Walthall's Brigade*, 502.

26. Pensacola Historical Society, 18.

27. Uhler "Florida's White Southern Belle," 306.

Chapter V

1. Hewitt, *The Confederate General*, vol. 1, 23.

2. Anderson autobiography, 66.

3. Putman County Archives & History, Palatka, Florida. Years later Etta wrote: "When the war was over, Yancy continued to have a passion for military music and parades, and always participated as far as possible, whenever any parade passed his pasture. He was a great pet with the Anderson family throughout the war and thereafter."

4. Pensacola was surrendered on May 10, 1862, and occupied by the Federal forces until the end of the war.

5. Uhler, Civil War letters, 158, 159.

6. Anderson autobiography, 66.

7. James W. Raab, *A Dual Biography, Tilghman/Shoup*, 159.

8. Sifakis, *Who Was Who in the Civil War*, 43, 44.

9. Raab, *A Dual Biography*, 159, 160.

10. O.R.s, vol. 10, part 1, 494, 495.

11. Thomas Lawrence Connelly, *The Army of the Heartland, the Army of Tennessee, 1861–1762*, (Baton Rouge: Louisiana State University Press, 1967), 160.

12. Rayburn, *Wherever the Fight Is Thickest*, 318–320.

13. Raab, *A Dual Biography*, 162.

14. Frank R. Carvell Jr., *The Kentucky Brave—1861–1862*. Taps-Southern Bivouac (Paducah, Ky.: S.B.C. Publishing Co., 1999) 56, 57.

15. See the roster of Army of the Mississippi.

16. Rayburn, *Wherever the Fight Is Thickest*, 318–320.

17. Mark Mayo Boatner III, *The Civil War Dictionary* (New York: David McKay Company, 1959), 757.

18. Carvell, *The Kentucky Brave*, 86.

19. William C. Davis, *Breckinridge, Statesman, Soldier, Symbol* (Baton Rouge: Louisiana State University Press, 1974), 23.

20. Robert K. Sneden, *Eye of the Storm, A Civil War Odyssey* (New York: The Free Press, 2000). These terrorist acts printed in this book applied to all theaters of the Civil War.

21. Williams, *P. G. T. Beauregard*, 151, 152.

22. O.R.s, Series 1, vol. 52, part 2, 307.

23. Rowland, *Military History of Mississippi*, 321.

24. E. B. Long and Barbara Long, *The Civil War Day by Day, An Almanac 1861–1865* (New York: Da Capo Press, Plenum Publishing Corp., 1971), 214.

25. Thomas L. Connelly, *Army of the Heartland*, 176.

26. *Ibid.*

27. Long, *The Civil War Day by Day*, 218.

Chapter VI

1. Anderson autobiography, 67.

2. Hughes, *General William J. Hardee*, 20, 21.

3. Sifakis, *Who Was Who in the Civil War*, 281.

4. Kenneth Radley, *Rebel Watchdog, The Confederate States' Army Provost Guard* (Baton Rouge: Louisiana State University Press, 1989), 39.

5. *Ibid.*, 92.

6. Robert C. Black, *The Railroads of the Confederacy* (Chapel Hill: The University of North Carolina Press, 1952), 182.

7. *Ibid.*

8. Grady McWhiney, *Braxton Bragg and Confederate Defeat— Volume 1*, Field Command. (New York: Columbia University Press, 1969), 269.

9. Hughes, *General William J. Hardee*, 120.

10. *Ibid.*, 121.

11. Anderson's papers, Special Collection.

12. Hughes, *General William J. Hardee*, 121.

13. Long, *The Civil War Day by Day*, 267.

14. Rayburn, *Wherever the Fight Is Thickest*, 322.

15. Connelly, *The Army of the Heartland*, 250.

16. Anderson autobiography, 67.

17. Faust, *Historical Illustrated Encyclopedia of the Civil War*, 567.

18. Map — Perryville, October 8, 1862.

19. John Bowers, *Chickamauga and Chattanooga, The Battles that Doomed the Confederacy* (New York: Harper Collins Publishers, 1994), 7. "Bragg never learned a new tactic — or forgot an old one. At Shiloh and Perryville he had sent men forward with elbows touching, a maneuver of Napoleonic grandeur, and then had seen their neat lines turn asunder by rifle and artillery fire, he had witnessed rout and confusion and barbaric hell when men strode forward in close marching order and attacked on rough terrain."

20. Robert Hawk, *Florida's Army* (Englewood, Fla.: Pineapple Press, Inc., 1988), 95. "The 1st, 3rd, 4th, 6th, and 7th Regiments of Florida Infantry and the First Florida Cavalry, all went to serve with the Army of Tennessee. The 1st Florida and 3rd Florida infantry regiments suffered terrible casualties at Perryville and thereafter were consolidated into a single unit, 1st–3rd Florida."

21. John B. Jones, *A Rebel War Clerk's Diary*, vol. 1 (Alexandria, Va.: Time-Life Books, Inc., 1981), 176.
22. Anderson autobiography, 67.
23. R. Lockwood Tower, *A Carolinian Goes to War, Arthur Middleton Manigault* (Columbia: University of South Carolina, 1988), 48.
24. Bowers, *Chickamauga and Chattanooga*, 8, 9.
25. Faust, *Historical Illustrated Encyclopedia of the Civil War*, 722.
26. Long, *The Civil War Day by Day*, 722.
27. Alexander F. Stevenson, *Battle of Stones River* (Boston: James R. Osgood and Company, 1884), republished by *Civil War Times*, 1974.
28. Robert O. Neff, *Tennessee's Battered Brigadier, The Life of General Joseph B. Palmer* (Historic Traveler's Rest, 1988), 54.
29. *Ibid.*
30. Sykes, *Walthall's Brigade*, 513.
31. Thomas Lawrence Connelly, *Autumn of Glory, The Army of Tennessee, 1862–1865* (Baton Rouge: Louisiana State University Press, 1971), 56.
32. Neff, *Tennessee's Battered Brigadier*, 57.
33. Stevenson, *Battle of Stones River*, 37.
34. Anderson's papers, Special Collection.
35. Stevenson, *Battle of Stones River*, 44.
36. *Ibid.*, 174, 175.
37. *Ibid.*, 138, 139.
38. Rayburn, *Wherever the Fight Is Thickest*, 324.
39. Anderson autobiography, 67, 68.
40. William C. Davis, *Breckinridge*, 347.
41. Sykes, *Walthall's Brigade*, 503, 505.
42. *Ibid.*
43. *Ibid.*
44. *Ibid.*
45. McWhiney, *Braxton Bragg*, 369.
46. Sykes, *Walthall's Brigade*, 506.
47. Bowers, *Chickamauga and Chattanooga*, 16.
48. Sykes, *Walthall's Brigade*, 497.
49. *Ibid.*, 505.

Chapter VII

1. *Florida Confederate Military History*, vol. 16, 168 — On the morning of the 28th the 1st, 3rd, and 4th Florida Regiments were ordered to move into line of battle on the Lebanon Pike; this brigade and Palmer's were the last of Breckinridge's command transferred to the west side of Stones River on the 31st, and made the final unsuccessful assault upon the Federal center, where hundreds of brave men had already fallen. The 1st and 3rd Florida under Colonel Miller gained the cedar break so prominent in the action in that part of the field, and the 4th advanced as far, but with much heavier loss. Ordered back to the east side of the river, they fought bravely in the attack made by Breckinridge on January 2nd. It was the last regiment to leave the field, and it made a gallant fight to save Major Felix Robertson's brigade battery, sustaining heavy loss in doing so.
2. Anderson's papers, Special Collection.
3. Uhler, Civil War letters, 155.
4. Sykes, *Walthall's Brigade*, 614.
5. Col. Harold B. Simpson, *Simpson Speaks on History: Booze in Battle* (Hillsboro, Texas: Hill College Press, 1986), 66, 69.
6. *Ibid.*, 66, 69.
7. Anderson autobiography, 164.
8. E. T. Sykes, "A Cursory Sketch of General Braggs Campaign, by Major E. T. Sykes, Retreat from Murfreesboro," *Southern Historical Society Papers*, vol. 11, paper number 3, 490.
9. McWhiney, *Braxton Bragg*, 389.
10. *Ibid.*, 392.
11. Burke Davis, *The Long Surrender* (New York: Vintage Books, 1989), 107.
12. Sykes, *Walthall's Brigade*, 548, 549.
13. Alfred Grant, *The American Civil War and the British Press* (Jefferson, N.C.: McFarland, 2000), 55.
14. The transfer of delivery service between the United States Post Office and the Confederate States of America Post Office was completed smoothly; after June 1, 1861, mail delivery within each area was not a problem, but mail service between the two parties was nonexistent.
15. Uhler, Civil War letters, 160.
16. *Ibid.*, 165.
17. Sykes, *Walthall's Brigade*, 591.
18. Rayburn, *Wherever the Fight Is Thickest*, 326.
19. John Fiske, *The Mississippi Valley in*

the Civil War (New York: Houghton, Mifflin, 1900), 253, 257.
20. *Ibid.,* 257.
21. Anderson's papers, Special Collection.
22. Fiske, *The Mississippi Valley in the Civil War,* 258.
23. Sykes, *Walthall's Brigade,* 591.
24. Bowers, *Chickamauga and Chattanooga,* 126.
25. William Haines Lytle, *Poems of William Haines Lytle* (Cincinnati, Ohio: Robert Clark Company, 1894).

Chapter VIII

1. *Southern Historical Society,* vol. 10, 2.
2. Uhler, Civil War letters, 168.
3. Tower, *A Carolinian Goes to War,* 85.
4. *Ibid.,* 84. Map modified by author, and O.R.s, series 1, vol. 31, part 2 — reports, 659 below.
5. J. Patton Anderson's report, courtesy of The Western Reserve Historical Society, Cleveland, Ohio.
6. *Ibid.,* 169.
7. Bowers, *Chickamauga and Chattanooga,* 126, 127.
8. Sykes, *Walthall's Brigade,* 591.
9. Bowers, *Chickamauga and Chattanooga,* 48.
10. Boatner, *Civil War Dictionary,* 150–152.
11. Uhler, Civil War letters, 166.
12. *Ibid.,* 167.
13. Connelly, *The Army of the Heartland,* 274.
14. Boatner, *Civil War Dictionary,* 143.
15. Uhler, Civil War letters, 167.
16. Sykes, *Walthall's Brigade,* 538, 539.
17. Boatner, *Civil War Dictionary,* 144.
18. Davis, *Breckinridge,* 387.
19. Gen. William Bates, O.R.s, series 1, vol. 31, part 2 — reports, 739.
20. J. Patton Anderson's report, courtesy of The Western Reserve Historical Society.
21. *Ibid.*
22. Tower, *A Carolinian Goes to War,* 137.
23. J. Patton Anderson's report, courtesy of The Western Reserve Historical Society.
24. Sykes, *Walthall's Brigade,* 606.
25. Braxton Bragg, "Lookout Mountain and Missionary Ridge, Report of General

Braxton Bragg," *Southern Historical Society Papers,* vol. 11, 208, 209.
26. Boatner, *The Civil War Dictionary,* 147.
27. Tower, *A Carolinian Goes to War,* 154.
28. Wilbur Thomas, *General George H. Thomas, The Indomitable Warrior* (New York: Exposition Press, 1964), 338, 339.

Chapter IX

1. Wilbur Thomas, *General George H. Thomas, The Indomitable Warrior* (New York: Exposition Press, 1964), 338, 339.
2. Uhler, Civil War letters, 169.
3. Nelson W. Winbush, "Ancestor Proud to Fight for Flag," *The Civil War Courier,* vol. 17, issue 2 (2001), 14.
4. Sykes, *Walthall's Brigade,* 552–554.
5. Uhler, Civil War letters, 173.
6. Davis, *The Civil War and Reconstruction in Florida,* 217.
7. Uhler, Civil War letters, 170.
8. Sifakis, *Who Was Who in the Civil War,* 68.
9. *Southern Historical Society Papers,* vol. 9: 16, 17, Reports of General Beauregard, March 25, 1864, and General Joseph Finegan. Also excerpts from *Jacksonville's Ordeal by Fire,* by Martin and Schafer: 192.
10. For more information, consult Olustee Battlefield State Historic Site; write P.O. Box 40, Olustee, FL 32072.
11. *Ibid.*
12. O.R.s, series 1, vol. 52, part 2, 626.
13. O.R.s, series 1, vol. 35, part 1— reports: 639.
14. Alfred Roman, *The Military Operations of General Beauregard,* vol. 2 (New York: Da Capo Press, 1994), 189–191.
15. *Ibid.*
16. *Ibid.*
17. O.R.s, series 1, vol. 35, part 2, 459.

DISTRICT OF FLORIDA.
Maj. Gen. PATTON ANDERSON.
12th Georgia Battalion, Maj. George M. Hanvey.
4th Florida Battalion, Maj. John H. Gee.
Robinson's Independent (Florida) Company, Capt. W. J. Robinson.
28th Georgia Battalion, Maj. A. Bonaud.

1st Florida Battalion, Lt. Col. Charles F. Hopkins.
2d Florida Battalion, Lt. Col. Theodore W. Brevard.
6th Florida Battalion, Lt. Col. John M. Martin.
26th Virginia, Col. Powhatan R. Page.
59th Virginia, Col. William B. Tabb.
6th Georgia, Lt. Col. John T. Lofton.
19th Georgia, Col. James H. Neal.
23rd Georgia, Col. James H. Huggins.
27th Georgia. Col. Charles T. Zachry.
28th Georgia, Col. Tully Graybill.
1st Georgia Regulars, Col. William J. Magill.
32d Georgia, Lt. Col. William H. Pruden.
Reynolds' Independent (Florida) Company, Capt. B. L. Reynolds.
4th Florida Battalion (one company), Capt. G. J. Floyd.
Guerard's (Georgia) battery, Capt. John M. Guerard.
Milton (Florida) Artillery, Company A, Capt. Joseph L. Dunham.
Echols (Georgia) Artillery, Capt. John H. Tiller.
Chatham (Georgia) Artillery, Capt. John F. Wheaton.
Kilcrease (Florida) Artillery, Capt. F. L. Villepigue.
Gamble's (Florida) company heavy artillery, Capt. Robert H. Gamble.
29th Georgia Battalion Cavalry (seven companies).
2d Florida Battalion Cavalry.
5th Georgia Cavalry, Col. Robert H. Anderson.
5th Florida Battalion Cavalry, Maj. G. W. Scott.
2d Florida Cavalry, Col. Caraway Smith.
Cone's (Florida) Independent Company, Capt. W. H. Cone.
Stark's (Florida) Independent Company. Capt. J. D. Stark.

18. O.R.s, series 1, vol. 6: 403, 404.
19. O.R.s, series 1, vol. 35, part 1, 373.
20. Davis, *The Civil War and Reconstruction in Florida*, 224. "The Federal government reports 1,044 Florida Negroes enrolled as soldiers in the Union army during the war. This was about one-tenth of the adult Negro male population of military age. Most of the recruits were from East Florida."
21. O.R.s, series 1, vol. 35, part 1, 381.
22. *Ibid.,* 115.
23. *Ibid.,* 117.
24. Martin and Schafer, *Jacksonville's Ordeal by Fire*, 223.
25. *Ibid.,* 225.
26. O.R.s, series 1, vol. 35, part 2, 406, 407.
27. Don Hillhouse, *Heavy Artillery & Light Infantry*, 74, 75.
28. Sifakis, *Who Was Who in the Civil War*, 218.
29. *Ibid.,* 75.
30. Anderson's papers, Special Collection.
31. Davis, *The Civil War and Reconstruction in Florida*, 264, 265.
32. O.R.s, series 1, vol. 35, part 2, 443.
33. Anderson's papers, Special Collection; Anderson autobiography, 339.
34. Three references combined: (a) Hillhouse: 76, 77. (b) Uhler: 174, 175. (c) O.R.s, series 1, vol. 35, part 2, 488.
35. Robert Hawk, *Florida's Army* (Englewood, Fla.: Pineapple Press, 1986), 103.
36. Bruce S. Allardice, *More Generals in Gray* (Baton Rouge: Louisiana State University Press, 1995), 77.
37. *The Encyclopedia of the Confederacy*, 257.
38. *Florida Confederate Military History, vol. 56*, 89.
39. Robert A. Taylor, *Rebel Storehouse: Florida in the Confederate Economy* (Tuscaloosa: The University of Alabama Press, 1995), 10.
40. Davis, *The Civil War and Reconstruction in Florida*, 260, 265.
41. Robert A. Taylor, "Cow Cavalry, Munnerlyn's Battalion in Florida, 1864–1865," *Florida Historical Quarterly*, vol. 65, 198, 199, and Rivers, *Slavery in Florida*, 237.
42. Gannon, *The New History of Florida*, 241.
43. O.R.s, series 1, vol. 35, part 2, 437, 442.
44. O.R.s, series 1, vol. 35, part 1, 369.
45. Taylor, *Rebel Storehouse*, 120, 223a.
46. Taylor, "Cow Cavalry," 204–210.

47. *Ibid.*
48. Taylor, *Rebel Storehouse*, 120, and "Cow Cavalry," 210.
49. *Ibid.*

Chapter X

1. Stanley F. Horn, *The Army of Tennessee* (Wilmington, N.C.: Broadfoot Publishing Co., 1987), 343.
2. O.R.s, series 1, vol. 38, part 5, 904.
3. Hewitt, *The Confederate General*, vol. 1, 24.
4. *Ibid.,* 930.
5. O.R.s, series 1, vol. 35, part 2, 595.
6. O.R.s, series 1, vol. 53, part 3, 345, 346.
7. O.R.s, series 1, vol. 38, part 3, 769.
8. William R. Scaife, *The Campaign for Atlanta*, chapter 7, Utoy Creek, 124.
9. Boatner, *The Civil War Dictionary*, 863, map modified by author.
10. O.R.s, series 1, vol. 38, part 3, 770.
11. *Ibid.,* 769.
12. Tower, *A Carolinian Goes to War*, 242.
13. O.R.s, series 1, vol. 38, part 3, reports, 763.
14. Albert Castel, *Decision in the West, The Atlanta Campaign of 1864* (Manhattan: University of Kansas Press, 1992), 483, 484.
15. *Ibid.*
16. Jacob D. Cox, *Atlanta, Campaigns of the Civil War*, vol. 9 (Dayton, Ohio: Morningside House, 1987), 186.
17. O.R.s, series 1, vol. 38, part 3, 772.
18. *Ibid.,* 773.
19. Rowland, *Military History of Mississippi*, 359.
20. O.R.s, series 1, vol. 38, part 3, 773.
21. *Ibid.,* 774.
22. Tower, *A Carolinian Goes to War*, 247.
23. Hughes, *General William J. Hardee*, 238.
24. Castel, *Decision in the West*, 503, and Rayburn, *Wherever the Fight Is Thickest*, 335.
25. *Ibid.*
26. *Southern Historical Society Papers*, vol. 5, Report of the battle of Jonesboro, 130.

Chapter XI

1. Johns, *Florida During the Civil War*, 237 (Notes).
2. Uhler, Civil War letters, Florida Historical Society, vol. 65, 339.
3. Hughes, *General William J. Hardee*, 254.
4. *Ibid.,* 254–272.
5. Ralph Andreano, *The Economic Impact of the American Civil War* (Cambridge: Schenkman Publishing Co., 1962), 79.
6. *Ibid.,* 258.
7. *Ibid.*
8. *Ibid.,* 264.
9. *Ibid.*
10. *Ibid.*
11. *Ibid.,* 274.
12. *Ibid.*
13. *Ibid.,* 277.
14. Anderson autobiography and Uhler.
15. *Southern Historical Society Papers*, vol. 24, 71, 72.
16. *Confederate Military History*, vol. 6, South Carolina: 359; O.R.s, series 1, vol. 47, part 2, 1122, and *Dictionary of American Biography*, by Charles Scribner and Sons, 267.
17. Hughes, *General William J. Hardee*, 280.
18. *Ibid.,* 282.
19. *Confederate Military History*, vol. 6, South Carolina, 368, and John Barrett, *The Civil War in North Carolina* (Chapel Hill: The University of North Carolina Press, 1963), 321.
20. *Confederate Veterans Magazine*, vol. 23, 204.
21. Boatner, *The Civil War Dictionary*, 14, 35; Faust, *Historical Illustrated*, 31; and Hughes, *Gen. William J. Hardee*, 286.
22. *Ibid.*
23. Ralph Selph Henry, *The Story of the Confederacy* (Wilmington, N.C.: Broadfoot Publishing Co. 1989), 455.
24. Weymount T. Jordan Jr., *The Battle of Bentonville* (Wilmington, N.C.: Broadfoot Publishing Co.), 19.
25. *Ibid.,* 20.
26. James W. Raab, *W. W. Loring — Florida's Forgotten General*, (Manhattan,

Kans.: Sunflower University Press, 1996), 204.

27. Mark L. Bradley, *The Battle of Bentonville, Last Stand on the Carolinas* (Campbell, Calif.: Savas Woodbury Publishers, 1996), 404.

28. O.R.s, series 1, vol. 47, part 2, Correspondence, 1460.

29. *Ibid.*, 1453, 1454.

30. Barrett, *The Civil War in North Carolina*, 368.

31. Hugh R. Simmons, *The Story of the 12th Louisiana Infantry in the Final Campaign in North Carolina* (Lafayette: The Louisiana Historical Society), 22, 23. Also Mark L. Bradley, *This Astounding Close: The Road to Bennett Place* (Chapel Hill: The University of North Carolina Press, 2000), 64. "Johnston's friend and political ally, Senator Louis T. Wigfall, arrived in Smithfield, en route to his home in Texas, after the Confederate Congress had adjourned."

32. Burke Davis, *The Long Surrender*, 14–17.

33. *Ibid.*, 32.

34. *Ibid.*, 58.

35. *Ibid.*, 60–62.

Chapter XII

1. Bradley, *The Battle of Bentonville*, 88, 91.

2. Bradley, *This Astounding Close*, 116

3. Hughes, *General William J. Hardee*, 63–70.

4. *Ibid.*, 93, 94.

5. Bradley, *This Astounding Close*, 182.

6. Hughes, *General William J. Hardee*, 71, 72.

7. O.R.s, series 1, vol. 47, part 1, 1063.

8. Simmons, *The Story of the 12th Louisiana Infantry*, 23.

9. William R. Trotter, *Silk Flags and Cold Steel, The Civil War in North Carolina: The Piedmont*, vol. 1 (Winston-Salem, N.C.: John F. Blair, Publisher, 1988), 360.

10. *Ibid.*, 361, 362. Bradley in *This Astounding Close*, 294. Roster shows almost a thousand fewer men when they were surrendered, indicating many just walked off and went home.

Anderson's Division (1,722)
Maj. Gen Patton Anderson (41)

Elliott's Brigade (1,132) GRN
Lt. Col. J. Welsman Brown (4)
22nd Georgia Battalion, Maj. Mark J. McMullen (363)
27th Georgia Battalion, Maj. Alfred L. Hartridge (155)
2nd South Carolina Artillery, Maj. F. F. Warley (461)
Manigault's Battalion (South Carolina), Capt. Theodore G. Boag (149)

Rhett's Brigade (549) GRN
Col. William Butler (6)
1st South Carolina (Regulars), Lt. Col. Warren Adams (259)
1st South Carolina Artillery (Regulars), Lt. Col. Joseph A. Yates (230)
15th South Carolina Battalion (Lucas' Battalion), Capt. Theodore B. Hayne (54)

11. Anderson autobiography, 72.

12. Uhler, Civil War letters, 339.

13. James C. Clark's book, *Last Train South*, is the most complete work on the escape of the Confederate government and its Cabinet members, and is recommended by this author for further reading.

14. Burke Davis, *The Long Surrender*, 105.

15. Davis, *The Civil War and Reconstruction in Florida*, 329.

16. *Ibid.*, 684.

17. *Ibid.*, 334.

18. *Ibid.*, 334.

19. *Ibid.*, 341–343.

20. Davis, *The Long Surrender*, 191.

21. *Ibid.*, 285.

22. Faust, *Historical Illustrated*, 290.

23. *Ibid.*, 290.

24. Raab, *W. W. Loring*, 208.

25. *Ibid.*, 373, and footnote #1, 374.

26. *Ibid.*

27. *Ibid.*

Chapter XIII

1. Ramsdell, *Behind the Lines*, 57. People had to abandon their stance on states' rights and slavery by taking the oath of allegiance in order to procure food for their families.

2. Uhler, footnote.

3. T. Frederick Davis, "The Disston Land Purchases," *The Florida Historical Quarterly*, 17, no. 3 (1939).

4. Stetson Kennedy, *After Appomattox — How the South Won the War* (Gainesville: University Press of Florida, 1995), 7.

5. Otto H. Olsen, *Reconstruction and Redemption in the South* (Baton Rouge: Louisiana State University Press, 1982), 4, 5.

6. Kennedy, *After Appomattox*, 14.

7. Michael Gannon, *Florida, A Short History* (Gainesville: University Press of Florida, 1993), 48.

8. *Ibid.*, 50, 51.

9. Davis, *The Long Surrender*, 228.

10. Rayburn, *Wherever the Fight Is Thickest*, 336.

11. Davis, *The Long Surrender*, 238.

12. Uhler, Civil War letters, 152, 153.

13. *Thurston County Property Records Index 1854–1889. Washington Territory.*

14. Uhler, Civil War letters, 153.

15. *Ibid.*, 153.

16. Photograph by Richard Owen. Richard and James Owen, *Generals at Rest* (Shippensburg, Pa.: White Mane Publishing Co., 1952), 212.

17. Obituary, Memphis Tennessee newspaper (unnamed).

18. Putman County Archives and History, Palatka, Florida.

19. *Ibid.*

20. *Ibid.*

21. Gannon, *Florida: A Short History*, 51, 53.

22. Davis, *The Long Surrender*, 257, 258.

23. Gannon, *Florida: A Short History*, 56.

24. *Ibid.*, 73.

25. Davis, *The Long Surrender*, 263.

Appendix

1. Joseph H. Crute, Jr., *Confederate Staff Officers, 1861–1865* (Powhatan, Va.: Derwent Books, 1982); based upon Marcus Wright, *List of Staff Officers of the confederate Army* (Washington, D.C.: Government Printing Office, 1891).

Bibliography

The principal sources for information regarding the Army of Tennessee and Gen. J. Patton Anderson are the Official Records, referred to as O.R.s, published by the War Department. Found in seventy volumes in 128 parts, these are *The Official Records of The Union and Confederate Armies*, as printed in 1891.

Primary Sources

Autobiography of Gen. Patton Anderson. *Southern Historical Society Papers*, vol. 24. Richmond, Va.: Southern Historical Society, 1896.

James Patton Anderson Collection. P.K. Yonge Library of Florida History, University of Florida, Gainesville.

James Patton Anderson Papers. Special Collections, Robert Manning Strozier Library, Florida State University Library, Tallahassee.

Confederate Military History. *Florida*. Vol. 16. Wilmington, N.C.: Broadfoot Publishing Co., 1988.

Rayburn, Larry. "Wherever the Fight Is the Thickest — General James Patton Anderson." *The Florida Historical Quarterly*, vol. 60, no. 3, January 1982.

Uhler, Margaret B. Anderson. "Civil War Letters of Major General James Patton Anderson." *The Florida Historical Quarterly*, vol. 56, no. 1, July 1977.

_____. "Florida's White Southern Belle." *The Florida Historical Quarterly*, vol. 55, January 1977.

Secondary Sources

Allardice, Bruce S. *More Generals in Gray.* Baton Rouge: Louisiana State University Press, 1995.

Andreano, Ralph. *The Economic Impact of the American Civil War.* Cambridge: Schenkman Publishing Co. 1962.

Ashely, Joe and Lavon. *Oh for Dixie! The Civil War Record and Diary of Capt. William V. Davis.* Colorado Springs: Standing Pine Press, 2001.

Barley, Ronald H. *Battle for Atlanta, Sherman Moves East.* Alexandra, Va.: Time-Life Books, 1985.

Barrett, John G. *The Civil War in North Carolina.* Chapel Hill: The University of North Carolina Press, 1963.

Black, Robert C. III. *The Railroads of the Confederacy.* Chapel Hill: The University of North Carolina Press, 1952.

Boatner, Mark Mayo III. *The Civil War Dictionary*. New York: David McKay Company, Inc., 1959.

Bowers, John. *Chickamauga and Chattanooga, The Battles that Doomed the Confederacy*. New York: Harper Collins Publishers, 1994.

Bradley, Mark L. *The Battle of Bentonville, Last Stand in the Carolinas*. Campbell, Calif.: Savas Woodbury Publishers, 1996.

_____. *This Astounding Close, The Road to Bennett Place*. Chapel Hill: The University of North Carolina Press, 2000.

Bradshaw, Charles H. "A history of Washington state court system." In *The Bench and Bar of Washington: The first Fifty Years, 1849–1900,* edited by Arthur Beardsley. Olympia: Washington State Archives, 1950.

Buker, George E. The Inner Blockade at Florida and the Wildest Blockade-Runners." *North & South,* 4, no. 2 (2001).

Burne, Zed H. *Confederate Forts*. Natchez: Miss.: Southern Historical Publications, Inc., 1977.

Burnell, Gene M. *Florida's Past,* vol. 2. *Pensacola's One-Man Economy, Col. William H. Chase*. Sarasota, Fla.: Pineapple Press, 1998.

Carvell, Frank R. Jr. *The Kentucky Brave—1861–1862. Taps-Southern Bivouac*. 1 March 1863 (poem). Paducah, Ky.: S.B.C. Publishing Co., 1999.

Castel, Albert. *Decision in the West, The Atlanta Campaign of 1864*. Manhattan: University of Kansas Press, 1992.

Catton, Bruce. *The American Heritage Picture History of the Civil War*. New York: America Heritage Publishing Co., 1960.

Clark, James C. *Last Train South, The Flight of the Confederate Government from Richmond*. Jefferson, N.C.: McFarland, 1984.

Collins, Alan C. *The Story of America in Pictures — revised*. New York: Doubleday & Company, Inc., 1953.

Connelly, Thomas Lawrence. *Army of the Heartland, The Army of Tennessee, 1861–1862*. Baton Rouge: Louisiana State University Press, 1967.

_____. *Autumn of Glory, The Army of Tennessee, 1862–1865*. Baton Rouge: Louisiana State University Press, 1971.

Cox, Jacob D. *Atlanta, Campaigns of the Civil War,* vol. 9. Dayton, Oh.: Morningside House, 1987.

Crute, Joseph H. Jr. *Confederate Staff Officers, 1861–1865*. Powhatan, Va.: Derwent Books, 1982.

Cullum, G. W. *Biographical Register of the Officers and Graduates of the United States Military Academy*. New York: Houghton, Mifflin & Co, 1891.

Current, Richard N. *The Encyclopedia of the Confederacy*. New York: Simon & Schuster Macmillan, 1993.

Davis, Burke. *Sherman's March,* (1988) and *The Long Surrender,* (1989). New York: Vintage Books, a division of Random House, Inc.

Davis, T. Frederick. "The Disston Land Purchases." *The Florida Historical Quarterly,* 17, no. 3 (1939).

Davis, William C. *Breckinridge, Statesman, Soldier, Symbol*. Baton Rouge: Louisiana State University, 1974.

Davis, William Watson. *The Civil War and Reconstruction in Florida,* vol. 53, no. 131. New York: Columbia University Press, 1913.

Dickison, John J. *Military History of Florida,* vol. 10, *Evans Confederate Military History*. Wilmington, N.C.: Broadfoot Publishing Co., 1987.

Faust, Patricia L. *Historical Illustrated Encyclopedia of the Civil War.* New York: Harper & Row Publishers, 1986.

Fiske, John. *The Mississippi Valley in the Civil War.* New York: Houghton, Mifflin and Co., 1900.

Fleming, Francis P. and Towland H. Rerick. *Memoirs of Florida.* The Southern Historical Society, vol. 1. Atlanta, Georgia.

Fleming, Walter L. *Civil War and Reconstruction.* New York: Columbia University Press, 1905

Gannon, Michael. *Florida, A Short History,* 1993 and *The New History of Florida,* 1996 Gainesville: University Press of Florida.

Grant, Alfred. *The American Civil War and the British Press.* Jefferson, N.C.: McFarland, 2000.

Hanna, A. J. *Flight into Oblivion.* Richmond, Va.: Johnson Publishing Co., 1938.

Hawk, Robert. *Florida's Army.* Englewood, Fla.: Pineapple Press, Inc. 1986.

Henry, Ralph Selph. *The Story of the Confederacy.* Wilmington, N.C.: Broadfoot Publishing Co., 1989.

Hewitt, Lawrence L. "Braxton Bragg." In *The Confederate General, Volume 1,* edited by William C. Davis, New York: Doubleday, 1991.

Hillhouse, Don. *Heavy Artillery & Light Infantry. A History of 1st Florida Special Battalion & 10th Infantry Regiment.* Rome, Ga.: Self-published, 1992.

Hine, Robert F., and Savoie Lottinville. *Soldiers in the West. Letters of Theodore Talbot.* Norman: University of Oklahoma, 1972.

Horn, Stanley F. *The Army of Tennessee.* Wilmington, N.C.: Broadfoot Publishing Co., 1987.

Howell, H. Grady. *To Live and Die in Dixie. A History of the Third Mississippi Infantry, C.S.A.* Jackson, Miss.: Chickasaw Bayou Press., 1991.

Hughes, Nathaniel Cheairs Jr. *Gen. William J. Hardee — Old Reliable.* Baton Rouge: Louisiana State University Press, 1965.

Johns, John E. *Florida During the Civil War.* Gainesville: University of Florida Press, 1963.

Jones, John B. *A Rebel War Clerk's Diary.* Alexandria, Va.: Time-Life Books, Inc, 1981.

Jordan, Weymount T. Jr. *The Battle of Bentonville.* Wilmington, N.C.: Broadfoot Publishing Co.

Kennedy, Stetson. *After Appomattox — How the South Won the War.* Gainesville: University Press of Florida, 1995.

Long, E. B., and Barbara Long. *The Civil War Day by Day. An Almanac, 1861–1865.* New York: Da Capo Press, Inc. Plenum Publishing Corp., 1971.

Lytle, William Haines. *Poems of William Haines Lytle.* Cincinnati, Ohio: Robert Clarke Company, 1894.

Martin, Richard A., and Daniel L. Schafer. *Jacksonville's Ordeal by Fire.* Jacksonville: Florida Publishing Co., 1984.

McDonald, Archie P. *To Live and Die in Dixie. How the South Formed a Nation.* Journal of Confederate Book Series, vol. 10. Murfreesboro, Tenn.: Southern Heritage Press, 1999.

McWhiney, Grady. *Braxton Bragg and Confederate Defeat,* vol. 1. Field Command. New York: Columbia University Press, 1969.

Moore, Jerrold Northrop. *Confederate Commissary General.* Shippensburg, Pa,: White Mane Publishing Co., Inc., 1996.

Neal, Diane, and Thomas W. Kremin. *The Lion of the South, General Thomas C. Hindman*. Macon, Ga.: Mercer University Press, 1993.

Neff, Robert O. *Tennessee's Battered Brigadier, The Life of General Joseph B. Palmer*, published by Historic Traveller's Rest, 1988.

Ness, George T. *The Regular Army on the Eve of the Civil War*. Baltimore: Toomey Press, 1990.

Nixon, Oliver W. *How Marcus Whitman Saved Oregon*. 6th ed. Chicago: Star Publishing Co., 1895.

Nulty, William H. *Confederate Florida. The Road to Olustee*. Tuscaloosa: The University of Alabama Press, 1990.

Olsen, Otto H. *Reconstruction and Redemption in the South*. Baton Rouge: Louisiana State University Press, 1982.

Osborne, Tish. "Shiloh Church, A Project for Generations." *The Civil War Courier*. October 2001.

Owen, Richard and James Owen. *Generals at Rest*. Shippensburg, Pa.: White Mane Publishing Co., Inc., 1952.

Patterson, Gerard A. *Rebels from West Point*. New York: Doubleday, 1987.

Raab, James W. *A Dual Biography: Lloyd Tilghman and Francis Asbury Shoup: Two Forgotten Confederate Generals*. Murfreesboro, Tenn.: Southern Heritage Press, 2001.

_____. *W. W. Loring — Florida's Forgotten General*. Manhattan, Kan.: Sunflower University Press, 1996.

Radley, Kenneth. *Rebel Watchdog, The Confederate States' Army Provost Guard*. Baton Rouge: Louisiana State University Press, 1989.

Ramsdell, Charles W. *Behind the Lines in the Southern Confederacy*. Baton Rouge: Louisiana State University Press, 1972.

Rivers, Larry Eugene. *Slavery in Florida, Territorial Days to Emancipation*. Gainesville: University Press of Florida, 2000.

Robertson, Fred L. *Soldiers of Florida in the Seminole Indian and Spanish-American Wars*. Board of State Institutions, 1903.

Roman, Alfred. *The Military Operations of General Beauregard*, vols. 1 and 2, New York: Da Capo Press, 1994.

Rowland, Dunbar. *Military History of Mississippi, 1803–1898*. Jackson: Mississippi Department of Archives and History, 1908.

Scaife, William R. *The Campaign for Atlanta*. Cartersville, Ga.: Self-published, 1985.

Segars, J. H. *In Search of Confederate Ancestors. The Guide*. Journal of Confederate History Series, vol. 9. Murfreesboro, Tenn.: Southern Heritage Press, 1993.

Shofner, Jerrel H. *Florida, a Failure of Moderate Republicanism. History of Jefferson County*. Tallahassee, Fla.: Self-published, 1976.

Sifakis, Stewart. *Who Was Who in the Civil War*. New York: Facts on File Publication, 1988.

Simmons, Hugh R. *The Story of the 12th Louisiana Infantry in the Final Campaign in North Carolina, January to April, 1865*. Lafayette: The Louisiana Historical Society, 1992.

Simpson, Col. Harold B. *Simpson Speaks on History*. Hillsboro, Tex.: Hill College Press, 1986.

Smith, Julia Floyd. *Slavery and Plantation Growth in Antebellum Florida, 1821–1860*. Gainesville: University of Florida Press, 1914.

Sneden, Robert K. *Eye of the Storm, A Civil War Odyssey*. New York: The Free Press, 2000.

Snowden, Clinton A. *History of Washington, The Rise and Progress of an American State,* vols. 3 and 4. New York: The Century History Co., 1909.

Sobel, Robert. "Machines and Morality: The 1850s, Panic and Politics." *Barron's,* March 17, 1997.

Stevenson. Alexander F. *The Battle of Stones River.* Boston: James R. Osgood and Company, 1884. Republished by *Civil War Times,* 1974.

Stoutenburgh, John Jr. *Dictionary of the American Indian.* New York: Bonanza Books, 1990.

Sykes, E. T. *Walthall's Brigade, Army of Tennessee, 1862–1865.* Self-published, 1905.

Tatum, Georgia Lee. *Disloyalty in the Confederacy.* Chapel Hill: The University of North Carolina, 1934.

Taylor, Paul. *Discovering the Civil War in Florida, A Reader and Guide.* Sarasota, Fla.: Pineapple Press, Inc., 2001.

Taylor, Robert A. "Cow Cavalry, *Munnerlyn's Battalion in Florida, 1864–1865.*" *Florida Historical Quarterly,* vol. 65.

_____. *Rebel Storehouse, Florida in the Confederate Economy.* Tuscaloosa: The University of Alabama Press, 1995.

Thomas, Wilbur. *General George H. Thomas: The Indomitable Warrior.* New York: Exposition Press, 1964.

Tower, R. Lockwood. *A Carolinian Goes to War, Arthur Middleton Manigault.* Columbia: University of South Carolina, 1988.

Trotter, William R. *Silk Flags and Cold Steel, The Civil War in North Carolina: The Piedmont,* vol. 1. Winston-Salem, N.C.: John F. Blair, Publisher, 1988.

Turner, George Edgar. *Victory Rode the Rails.* New York: The Bobbs-Merrill Co., Inc., 1953.

Williams, Harry T. *P. G. T. Beauregard, Napoleon in Gray.* Baton Rouge: Louisiana State University Press, 1955.

Winbush, Nelson W. "Ancestor Proud to Fight for Flag," *The Civil War Courier,* vol. 17, issue 2, March 2001. Buffalo, New York.

Wingfield, Marshall. *General A. P. Stewart, His Life & Letters.* Memphis: The West Tennessee Historical Society, 1954.

Wittenberg, Eric J. *Glory Enough for All, Sheridan's Second Raid and the Battle of Trevilian Station.* Washington, D.C.: Brassey's, 2001.

Newspapers and Periodicals

Bonney, William P. "History of Pierce County." Vol. 1. Tacoma, Wash.: Pioneer Historical publishing and the Washington State Historical Society, 1927.

Bragg, Braxton. "Lookout Mountain and Missionary Ridge. Report of General Braxton Bragg. *Southern Historical Society Papers,* vol. 11, paper 3, 208, 209.

"City of Olympia and Olympia Heritage." Olympia, Wash.: Olympia Heritage Commission, 1992.

"Civil War and Reconstruction on the Gulf Coast." *Gulf Coast historical Review,* vol. 4, no. 2, Spring 1989. Mobile: History Department of the University of South Alabama.

Faulk, Odie B., and J. D. Thompson. "The Atlanta Campaign." Presented at the Confederate history Symposium. Hillsboro, Tex.: Hill College, 1988.

Hicks, Urban E. "Reminiscence of a Journey to Shoalwater Bay." Tacoma, Wash.: Washington State Historical Society, 1892.

"Pensacola in the Civil War." Pensacola Historical Society Publication, vol. 9, no. 2, Spring 1978. Pensacola: Pensacola Historical Society, 1978.

Pictorial History of the United States. Henry Davenport Northrop, by J. R. Jones, 1893.

Sykes, E. T. "A Cursory Sketch of General Bragg's Campaign, by Major E. T. Sykes, Retreat from Murfreesboro." *Southern Historical Society Papers*, vol. 11, paper number 3, 490.

The World Book Encyclopedia, Field Enterprises Educational Corp., vol. 3, p. 240 and vol. 14, p. 566. Chicago, Ill.

Federal, State and County Sources

Department of The Army. Historical Reference Branch. U.S. Army Military History Institute. Carlisle, Pennsylvania.

Florida Department of State. Division of Historical Resources and The Florida Room. Tallahassee, Florida.

The Florida Historical Quarterly, Florida Historical Society, Melbourne, Florida, in cooperation with the Department of History, University of Central Florida, Orlando.

The Museum of The Confederacy. Richmond, Virginia. John M. Coski, Historian.

National Archives and Records Administration. Textual Archives. College Park, Maryland.

Putman County Library System. Palatka, Florida. Mary E. Murphy, Archivist.

St. Johns County Historical Society. St. Augustine, Florida. Charles Tingley, Archivist.

Washington State Archives & Records Management Division. Olympia, Washington.

Washington State Historical Society, Tacoma, Washington.

The Western Reserve Historical Society, Cleveland, Ohio.

Index

Numbers in **boldface** refer to pages with photographs.